The Black Book
of the American Left

The Black Book of the American Left

*The Collected Conservative Writings
of David Horowitz*

Volume IX
Ruling Ideas

Second Thoughts Books
Los Angeles

First American edition published in 2015 by Second Thoughts Books.

Manufactured in the United States and printed on acid-free paper. The paper used in this publication meets the minimum requirements of ANSI/NISO Z39.48 1992 (R 1997) *(Permanence of Paper)*.

Book design and production by Catherine Campaigne; copy-edited by David Landau; research provided by Mike Bauer.

FIRST AMERICAN EDITION

LIBRARY OF CONGRESS CATALOGING-IN-PUBLICATION DATA

Horowitz, David, 1939–
    The black book of the American left : the collected conservative writings of David Horowitz / by David Horowitz.
    volumes   cm.
    Includes bibliographical references and index.
    ISBN 978-1-941262-08-5 # (hardback)
        1. Social movements—United States—History.   2. Radicalism—United States. 3. Anti-Americanism—United States.   4. Horowitz, David, 1939– Political and social views.   I. Title.
HX86.H788 2013
    335.00973   2013000496

10   9   8   7   6   5   4   3   2   1

Contents

Introduction to
Ruling Ideas

This is the ninth and final volume of my writings about progressivism, a movement whose goals are the destruction of America's social contract at home and the defeat of American power abroad.

When I began the project of describing this movement in the 1980s, the emergence of the left as a mainstream force in America's political life was fairly recent and inadequately understood. Conservatives in particular often failed to appreciate the anti-American animus of the left and its apocalyptic goals. At the same time, conservatives imprudently accepted the left's deceptive claims to be "liberal" and "progressive," ascribing to it idealistic intentions that masked its malignant designs. The contents of these volumes were conceived as a corrective to these false and disarming impressions.

The primary source of this confusion is the fact that left-wing politics are based on expectations of an imaginary future rather than assessments of a usable past. The left's primary focus is not on practical improvements based on an analysis of previous practices, or a conception of the limits imposed by human nature, but on changes designed to satisfy the moral prejudices that make up the leftist faith.

Nowhere is this clearer than in the left's quest for "equality," which is the organizing principle of its "transformative" proposals. Equality before the law is a foundational principle of American democracy and its pluralistic community. But this is not the equality proposed by the left, which demands instead an unrealizable and destructive equality of outcomes. In the real world human inequalities of talent, intelligence, physical attributes and application are immutable facts of life, which result in inequalities of wealth and power. The seeds of social inequality are planted in the human genome and are nourished by disparate cultures, which include circumstances of birth and upbringing that governments cannot control. Attempts to establish such control have invariably resulted in the most repressive regimes in human history, and in the end have failed to produce either equality or wealth.

The ideal of an egalitarian future is doomed to failure because it is unanchored in any human reality. It is sustained as an ideal because it allows advocates to regard themselves as revolutionary pioneers of a "better world." It further prompts believers to devalue the present and dismiss the past, which allows them to distance themselves from the destructive results of their social experiments. Thus progressives habitually dismiss the disasters they have engineered, however epic in scope, by attributing the monstrous results to inadvertent "mistakes," when they were in fact the logical consequences of their utopian ideas.

When the Soviet socialist system collapsed, progressives created an artificial distinction between the ideal, which they called "real socialism," and the disaster, which they called "actually existing socialism." This allowed them to avoid any recognition of their role in the human catastrophe they had supported and served for generations. Consequently, the experience had no lessons for progressives because in their self-absolving view it wasn't "real socialism." This delusion has now been passed to the next generations as a result of the left's infiltration of America's educational system and its transformation into a training and recruitment center for collectivist causes and ideas.[1]

The current term leftists use to describe their utopian vision of the future is "social justice" rather than communism or socialism.

---

[1] See Volume 8 in this series, *The Left In The University*. Cf. alsohttps://www.nas.org/projects/making_citizens_report/the_report

The new name is part of a familiar process by which the left attempts to shed the disasters of its past. One would be hard-put to distinguish the goals encapsulated by "social justice" from the communist attitudes of previous generations. Like communism, "social justice" is a promise of harmony and redemption. Like communism it describes a future in which inequality, poverty, bigotry and the timeless corruptions of the human spirit are miraculously rectified by political parties and the state. Like communism, "social justice" requires for its realization a remake of humanity. Like communism, therefore, it can only be achieved through the destruction of individual freedom, and the thwarting of normal human desires and interests in order to achieve an allegedly greater social good.

The bloody history of progressive experiments during the 20th century should have buried the illusion that human beings can be transformed into creatures radically different from what they have been for the five thousand years in which their actions have been recorded. Human societies are reflections of the human beings who create them, not the other way around. Inequality, bigotry, hypocrisy and greed are elements of a genome that thousands of years of evolution have failed to alter or repair. As a result, progressive states dedicated to "social justice" have flooded the earth with the corpses of innocents who stood in their way, and created poverty and misery on an unprecedented scale. Yet the religious fantasy of a liberated future persists to this day among an alarming array of constituencies, and the left's assault on individual freedom proceeds as though these historical tragedies had never taken place.

The tenacity of the progressive illusion and its imperviousness to experience are natural effects of its religious nature. The solace provided to believers through hope in a redeemed future is as existentially crucial as a belief in God or in life after death. It makes relinquishing the illusion as devastating as a loss of religious faith. How else explain the persistence of a fantasy that has proven so destructive?

Since the industrial revolution, the progressive illusion has been encouraged by advances in technology that might seem to augur human possibility without limit. Yet to date these advances, however impressive, have not led to dramatic improvements in human behavior—specifically its moral dimensions—let alone the degree of improvement that utopian visions require. Meanwhile, the same advances have produced new technologies of totalitarian control along with vastly amplified means of destruction that serve to magnify human barbarism and put into question the very survival of civilization.

Half a century ago Friedrich Hayek described "social justice" as a *mirage*. Hayek observed that there is no entity called "society" to redistribute wealth, or to re-calibrate the social order. There are only individuals belonging to political factions that vie for power and then wield it through their power in the state.[2] "Social justice," therefore, is necessarily the work of individuals driven by the same greed, prejudice, and habits of deceit that created the injustices progressives propose to repair. In its real-world practice "social justice" is, and can only be, the self-justifying rationale of a new despotism—worse than the old because its first agenda is a war against freedom, in particular the freedom of individuals to resist the social redeemers and their plans.

This was the conclusion I reached forty years ago under the influence of Hayek and the Polish philosopher Leszek Kolakowski, and why I resolved to devote the second half of my life—and eventually the nine volumes of this work—to analyzing and opposing this destructive cause.

Part One of this concluding volume features three essays on themes which have more or less defined my life's work. "The Fate of the Marxist Idea" originated as a chapter in *The Politics of Bad Faith* (1998). It is composed of two letters to former comrades announcing my break with the left, and explaining the reasons

---

[2] Friedrich von Hayek, *Law Legislation and Liberty: The Mirage of Social Justice*, Univ. of Chicago Press, 1976

why anyone concerned about humanity or justice should do the same. The first letter was written to Carol Pasternak Kaplan, a childhood friend whose father Morris was a cell leader in the local Communist Party. The second was written to Ralph Miliband, my political mentor and friend, as well as father of David Miliband, a future British Secretary of State for Foreign and Commonwealth Affairs, and of Ed Miliband, a future leader of the British Labour Party.

In the quarter-century since I published these reflections, there have been no attempts by progressives to answer them. This would be explicable if leftists considered my views unworthy of their attention. But that is not the case. I have been the subject of unflattering feature profiles in leftwing magazines such as *The Nation* and *Tablet*, and in papers of record (also on the left) such as *The New York Times*, the *Chronicle of Higher Education* and *The Washington Post*. The Internet is a repository of tens of thousands of leftist posts, including entire websites, filled with anti-Horowitz abuse. What is lacking is an intellectual argument to refute my views and specifically my reasons for rejecting the left; or reference to a historical record that would provide a critical response to the case I have made.[3]

"Slavery and the American Idea" is about the destructive ends to which progressive aspirations lead, in particular the determination to destroy the American social contract and the constitutional system that supports it. Race has been a primary weapon in this attack, which is why Volume 6 in this series is devoted to the

---

[3]In fact I have on occasion invited academic leftists into the pages of Frontpagemag.com to construct such arguments. But the exercise has merely demonstrated their inability to do so. This was the case with leftist historian Kevin Mattson, the author of *Rebels All!*, a book which describes me as a seminal figure of the modern right, an exemplar of "the post-modern conservative intellectual." Unfortunately, Mattson was incapable of getting the most basic elements of my conservative views straight, and was uninterested in correcting his mistakes when they were pointed out to him. See "Getting This Conservative Wrong," in Volume 1 of this series, pp. 121 et seq.

subject. This essay attempts to retrieve the historical record and celebrate the America Idea, which is responsible for *ending* slavery and encapsulates the vision that is opposed to all the destructive themes documented in these volumes. "Slavery and the American Idea" first appeared as the concluding chapter of *Uncivil Wars,* an account of the 2001 controversy I provoked by opposing the demand for reparations more than a century after slavery was abolished. It has been edited for inclusion in this volume.[4]

These two ideas—the American and the Marxist—may be said to constitute an ideological thesis and antithesis of the modern world. The resolution of the conflict between them will shape the course of human freedom for generations to come.

"America's Second Civil War" locates the source of the deep division of America's political life in the adoption of "identity politics" as the left's "progressive" creed. In this extension of Marx's faulty model of domination and oppression, the left is now committed to a political crusade that is racist and collectivist, and thus the antithesis of the principles that are the cornerstones of America's social contract.

"The Two Christophers" is an effort to define the parameters of the left through an essay on the life and thought of radical contrarian Christopher Hitchens, whom I first met in England in the 1960s and befriended in the last years of his life. Some have regarded Christopher's intellectual path as similar to mine because of his support for America's war in Iraq, and his belated recognition of the virtues of a country with which he was once at war. This is an unwarranted reading of Christopher's odyssey. In reflecting on Christopher's political course, I have attempted to show how utopianism and the romantic idea of a revolutionary transformation continued to shape his political choices and kept him from having consistent (or even coherent) second thoughts. His political trajectory clearly marks the differences between us,

---

[4]Volume 6 of this series, *Progressive Racism,* contains an account of my conflict with the left over reparations and the American idea.

and allows me to measure the distance I traveled in leaving the left. It thus provides a way to understand what it means to be the kind of progressive examined in these volumes, so it may function as a useful guide to the great schism of our times.

Part Two of *Ruling Ideas* provides several aids for readers of my work. The first is an account of my life and work by my friend and colleague, Dr. Jamie Glazov, appropriately the son of a courageous Soviet dissident. Dr. Glazov's article is an updated version of an essay that first appeared as the introduction to *Left Illusions,* an earlier collection of my writings published in 2003. Dr. Glazov's account is both accurate and insightful, and will be a helpful guide to those interested in my work.

The second is a bibliography of my writings compiled by Mike Bauer, who has also provided invaluable help in editing all the texts in this series.

Finally, David Landau, who has copy-edited and indexed the entire series, has also prepared a summary index to all nine volumes.

PART ONE

The Fate of the Marxist Idea

People who identify with the left often ask the following question: How is it possible for decent human beings *not* to be progressive like us? How can they not share our concern for social justice or the better world we are attempting to create? The answers progressives give themselves are the following: Ignorance clouds the understanding of others; class interest or race or gender prejudice blocks their human compassion. In the eyes of progressives, their opponents are prisoners of a false consciousness that prevents them from recognizing, and thus embracing, human possibility. This false consciousness is rooted in the self-interest of a ruling class (or gender or race) which is intent on defending a system that secures its privilege. In other words, opposition to progressive agendas grows naturally from selfishness, myopia and greed. To progressives, theirs alone is the vocation of generosity, morality and reason.

Opponents of the left have questions, too: How is it possible for progressives to remain so blind to the grim realities their ideas have created? How can they overlook the crimes they themselves have committed against the very poor and oppressed, the "marginalized" and vulnerable they think they have set out to defend? How can they have learned so little from the dark history their revolutionary fantasies have engendered?

It is apparent to others that progressives have a false consciousness all their own. They are intoxicated with the scent of their own virtue. Being so noble in their own estimation, how could they *not* be blind? Their blindness is the result of insularity and arrogance—of the very contempt they have for those not gifted with progressive morality and insight. The vast literature of radicalism is to a large extent innocent of serious engagement with its critics. The names, let alone the works, of Mises, Hayek, Aron, Popper, Oakeshott, Sowell, Strauss, Bloom, Kirk, and other antisocialist thinkers are virtually unknown on the left and have been purged from the academic reading-lists of the institutions they dominate. The same judgment cannot be made about their political opponents. Because of the cultural dominance of the left, its critics are familiar with the currency of socialist ideas and the intellectual tradition that underpins them.

Even after the failure of the Soviet "experiment," the marginalization of conservative ideas in the academy and literary world is so complete that the conservatives whose ideas were vindicated by socialism's fall remain hopelessly obscure. As far back as 1922, Ludwig von Mises wrote a 500-page treatise predicting socialism would not work because socialist theorists had failed to recognize economic realities that would eventually bankrupt the future they were creating: the indispensability of markets for allocating resources, of the profit motive for ensuring economic efficiencies and providing the incentives that would drive the engines of *social* wealth. Von Mises observed that socialists showed no inclination to take seriously the problems their schemes created: "Without troubling about the fact that they had not succeeded in disproving the assertion of the [classical] liberal school that productivity under socialism would sink so low that want and poverty would be general, socialist writers began to promulgate fantastic assertions about the increase in productivity to be expected under socialism."[1]

As accurately as any predictive analysis could, von Mises's warning anticipated the next 70 years of socialist history. Under

---

[1] Ludwig von Mises, *Socialism*, Liberty Classics, Indianapolis, 1981, p. 159.

the Soviet Union's socialist plans, the Kremlin's rulers were indeed unable to allocate resources rationally, to accommodate innovation, or to replace the profit motive with viable social incentives. As a result, the socialist economy was unable to keep abreast of technological changes that would power the capitalist West into a new post-industrial era, or even induce sufficient economic growth to feed its own people. Thus, grain—an export staple of Czarist Russia—was perpetually in shortage after the Bolsheviks took power, a direct consequence of collectivization. The economic effects of socialist order were exactly as von Mises had predicted—to generalize poverty, while preventing Soviet Russia from entering the new information era and competing technologically with the West.

Even though Soviet developments dramatically confirmed von Mises's prediction, his intellectual contributions are as unknown in the culture of the post-Communist West as they were before the Communist fall. Von Mises's work should be a central text of academic discourse on socialism and related social issues; instead it is absent from the academic canon, as if it had never been written.

In contrast to von Mises's fate, Stalinist intellectuals like Antonio Gramsci, Walter Benjamin, Louis Althusser, Eric Hobsbawm and numerous others have become icons of the academy, their texts familiar to new generations of students, promoted by a professorial caste which is intent on reviving the socialist illusion. The discredited intellectual tradition of the left, of Marx and Hegel, of Althusser and Benjamin, of Foucault and Derrida, is dominant to an extent undreamed of before the Communist fall, as though the catastrophes these ideas produced had never taken place.

If von Mises remains an obscure figure in academic culture, so does Friederich von Hayek, who began his career as a socialist, had second thoughts, and joined von Mises as one of the most important 20th-century critics of the radical idea. The theoretical edifice Hayek created is as comprehensive as that of Marx. It has been vindicated by the same history that has refuted Marxist ideas. Yet the name Hayek is all but invisible in the literature of the left or in the academic curriculum the left has imposed on institutions of higher learning. Typically, Hayek's works on capitalism and socialism—*The Constitution of Liberty, The Mirage of Social Justice* and *The Fatal Conceit*—are barely acknowledged in the progressive intellectual culture and their arguments rarely confronted.

In short, an intellectual *omertà* has been the left's principal response over the generations to its vindicated critics, especially those like Hayek who have emerged from its own ranks. It is an intellectual version of Stalin's attempt to transform his political opponents into un-persons in order to obliterate their influence and ideas. The historian Aileen Kraditor, to cite one example, was once a star in the firmament of the academic left. The books she wrote—*The Ideas of the Woman Suffrage Movement, Means and Ends in American Abolitionism* and *The Radical Persuasion*—were once widely cited by Sixties progressives as models of radical scholarship. But then Kraditor had second thoughts and departed the radical ranks.

As a pioneer in feminist scholarship, Aileen Kraditor should have been a prime candidate for high honors in today's politically correct academy. But instead it is as though she never existed and never wrote a line. Her last book was based on her own radical experience as a member of the Communist Party, during the height of the Cold War. It sets out to describe the intellectual worldview of American Communists. *"Jimmy Higgins": The Mental World of the American Rank-and-File Communist, 1930–1958* [2] is the definitive study of its subject. Yet, despite an explosion of academic interest in the history of American Communism in the last two decades, Kraditor's work is almost never referred to and almost

---

[2] New York: Greenwood Press, 1988.

never cited; its insights are never engaged by the academic left. Intellectually, Aileen Kraditor has become an un-person.

This intellectual censorship and self-enforced ignorance insulates the left from uncomfortable encounters with former comrades and necessary truths. Defectors from the radical ranks quickly find that—as with von Mises, Hayek and Kraditor—their ideas are *verboten* and their realities erased. This is the unwritten law of the radical intellect: once the revolutionary idea is called into question, the questioner must cease to exist. Whether by personal smear or by intellectual exclusion, suppression of the heretical idea is necessary to preserve the faith. To the religious mind, the thought of God's death is unthinkable; in the radical mindset, the idea of revolution—of creating a new world—is the equivalent of a divine inspiration.

The two letters that follow were attempts to pursue a dialogue about these subjects beyond the revolutionary grave, as it were. They were attempts to communicate a sobering experience to former comrades who remained still intoxicated by the radical faith. Both attempts failed. The first elicited the threat of a lawsuit; the second was answered by an insult and silence. Although both were published in *The Politics of Bad Faith* (1998), and thus available to a wide array of radicals and "progressives," I am unaware of any responses to the arguments and evidence they set forth.

● ● ●

Unnecessary Losses

> *"All that lives, deserves to perish."*
> —Mephistopheles, *Faust*

> *"Communism is the philosophy of losers."*
> —Daniel, *The Book of Daniel*

April 1987

Dear Carol,[3]

I'm sorry it has taken me so long to answer your letter. When I returned to California after my father's funeral, I spent a long time thinking about what happened during that weekend in New York. I thought about my phone call to you on Friday after I came back from the cemetery; how I had invited you to the memorial service we had planned for Sunday at my mother's house; how you had said you would come and how comforting that felt; how our conversation had turned to politics and changed into an argument, and our voices had become angry; how I had begun to feel invisible, and how the loneliness this caused in me became so intense I said we should stop; and how, when we could not stop, I hung up.

I thought about my feelings when you did not call back that day or the next; and when you did not come to my father's memorial on Sunday as you had said you would. I thought about our quarrel on the plane ride back home, and began to realize how deep the wound in our friendship had become.

I thought about how our friendship had begun nearly half a century before at the Sunnyside Progressive Nursery School—so embedded in memory that I have no image of a youth without it. In the community of the left, I guess, it is perfectly normal to erase the intimacies of a lifetime over political differences. On the long plane ride home, it gave me great pain to think that I might never hear from you again.

And then, a week after my return, your letter arrived in the mail. You were sorry, you said, about the way our phone call ended. *Because of our common heritage* [you said] *the personal and the political cannot so easily be separated.* Your words reminded me of the "Khrushchev divorces" of 1956—the twenty-

---

[3]Carol Pasternak, a childhood friend. This letter originally appeared as a chapter of Peter Collier and David Horowitz, *Destructive Generation: Second Thoughts About the Sixties,* Summit Books, 1989; 2nd ed., Encounter Books, 1995.

year marriages in our parents' generation that ended in disputes between the partners over the "correct" political position to take towards his secret report on the crimes of Stalin. As though a political idea defined their personal realities.

But then, as though a political idea defined our reality too, your letter suddenly forgot about what had happened between us as friends, and reopened the wound to resume the argument:

Dear David,

I was sorry that your call ended the way it did. It was not my idea to get into a political argument, but apparently you had a need to provoke it. I would have preferred to talk more about personal matters. But because of our common heritage the personal and the political cannot really be separated. And that is why I can't help thinking that the views you now hold are psychological rather than intellectual in origin.

I want to add some things to clarify my position. I still consider myself part of the left, but my views have changed significantly over the years. I haven't been a Stalinist since I visited the Soviet Union in 1957, when I was nineteen. After that, like you, I became part of the New Left. I no longer consider the Soviet Union a model for the socialist future. But after all the garbage has been left behind I do hold certain basic tenets from my old left background. The first is that there are classes and the rich are not on the same side as the rest of us. They exploit. The second is that I am still a socialist. I still believe in theory socialism is better than capitalism. If it has not worked so far, it is because it has not really been tried.

What concerns me about you is that you have lost the compassion and humanism which motivated our parents to make their original choice. There can be no other explanation for your support of the vile policies of Ronald Reagan. Except that you are operating from an emotional position which surpasses rational thinking. Also, by assuming that because you are no longer "left" you must be "right," you appear to be lacking a capacity to tolerate ambiguity; and the real world is indeed

ambiguous. Why do you feel the need to jump on establishment bandwagons? I assume they are paying you well for your efforts. Your old friend (one of the oldest),
Carol

The wound in our friendship is really a mirror of the wound that a political faith has inflicted on our lives; the wounds that political lives like ours have inflicted on our times.

Let me begin with a concession. It is probably correct of you to blame me for our argument. *Apparently you had a need to provoke it.* I probably did. I had just buried a father whose politics was the most important passion in his life. Political ideas provided the only truths he considered worth knowing, and the only patrimony he thought worth giving. When I was seventeen and had political ideas of my own for the first time, politics made us strangers. The year was 1956. My father and I were one of the Khrushchev divorces.

We never actually stopped speaking to each other. But the distance was there just the same. After I had my own children and understood him better, I learned to avoid the areas where our conflicts flourished. I was even able to make a "separate peace," accepting him as the father he was rather than fighting to make him the one I wanted him to be. But he never was able to make the same peace with me. In all those thirty years that were left to us after I left home, there was not a day I was not aware of the line that politics had drawn between us, not a day that I did not feel how *alien* my ideas made me to him.

Emotions of grief and mourning make a perverse chemistry. If I provoked you to attack me on my father's burial day, perhaps I had a need for it: to do battle with the ideas which in ways and at times seemed more important to him than I was; to resume the combat that was his strongest emotional connection to other human beings and to me. Perhaps I thought I could resurrect his ghost in you, one of my oldest and dearest friends, who despite "all the garbage" you have left behind remain true enough to the faith of our fathers to act as his stand-in.

I don't mean to excuse my provocation, but only to remind you of what you forgot in your political passion that evening and in the silence that followed. Me. David. An old friend in need. I had been obliterated by a political idea. I felt like those ideological enemies of the past whom Stalin had made into "un-persons" by erasing the memory of who they had been. Which is what happened to my father at his own memorial that Sunday you did not come.

For nearly fifty years our parents' little colony of "progressives" had lived in the same ten-block neighborhood of Sunnyside in Queens. And for fifty years their political faith had set them apart from everyone else. They inhabited Sunnyside like a race of aliens—in the community but never of it; in cultural and psychological exile. They lived in a state of permanent hostility not only to the Sunnyside community but to every other community that touched them, including America itself.

The only community to which they belonged was one that existed in their minds: the international community of the Progressive Idea. Otherwise they lived as internal exiles, waiting for the time when they would be able to go home. "Home," to them, was not a *place* like Sunnyside or America; "home" was a *time* in the future when the Sunnyside and America they knew would no longer exist. No compromise with their home ground could put an end to their exile; only a wave of destruction that would sweep away the institutions and traditions of the communities around them, and allow the international community of the Progressive Idea to rise up in their place.

To my father and his comrades, the fantasy of this future was more important than the reality around them. All the activities of the Sunnyside progressives—the political meetings they attended five and six nights a week, the organizations they formed, the causes they promoted—were solely to serve their revolutionary Idea. The result was that, after five decades of social effort, there was not a single footprint to show that they had really lived in our little ten-block neighborhood. When my father's life came to its close, he was buried as a stranger in the community where he had spent his last fifty years.

My father lived the sinister irony that lies at the heart of our common heritage: the very humanity that is the alleged object of its "compassion" is a humanity it holds in contempt. This irony defined my father's attitude towards the people around him, beginning with those who were closest—the heirs of his Jewish heritage, whose Community Center he would never be part of and whose synagogue he would never enter. Every Friday night his own mother still lit the *Shabbat* candles, but as a progressive he had left such "superstitions" behind. To my father, the traditions his fellow Jews still cherished as the ark of their survival were but a final episode in the woeful history of human bondage—age-old chains of ignorance and oppression from which they would soon be set free. With the members of the real communities around him, my father was unable to enjoy the fraternity of equals based on mutual respect.

The only community my father respected was the community of other people who shared his Progressive Idea, people like your parents. To my father and his Sunnyside comrades, this meant the orthodoxies that comprised the Stalinist faith. But when he was just past fifty, a Kremlin earthquake shattered the myth that held together the only community to which my father belonged. The year was 1956. It was the year my father's world collapsed.

By the time I reached Sunnyside from California my mother had already decided that his burial arrangements would be made by the Shea Funeral Home on Skillman Avenue. The Shea Funeral Home had been the last stop for the Catholics of the neighborhood for as long as I could remember. My father hated its very name. To him, the little storefront was a symbolic fortress of the enemy forces in his life—the Christian persecutors of the ghetto past he tried to forget, the anti-Communist crusaders of his ghettoized present. My father took his hate to the grave. But for his widow the battles were already forgotten, the political passions dead with the past. What was alive was her new solitude and grief, and her terror in the knowledge that everything had changed. To my mother the Shea Funeral Home was an ark of survival, as familiar and comforting as the neighborhood itself.

My father's burial was attended only by his immediate family. We were accompanied to the cemetery by a rabbi I had somewhat disloyally hired to speak at the graveside, after confirming with my mother that she would find his presence comforting too. Having been primed with a few details of my father's life, the rabbi observed that death had come to him the week before Passover whose rituals commemorated an exodus to freedom not unlike the one that had brought him as an infant from Russia 81 years before. Not unlike the dream of a promised future that had shaped his political life.

The place of burial was Beth Moses, a Jewish cemetery on Long Island fifty miles away from Sunnyside, the last of my father's exile homes. It was an irony noticed only by me that my father, who had struggled so hard in life to escape from his past, should find peace in a cemetery called the "House of Moses." And that this final compromise should have been made for him by the international community of his political faith. The grave where my father was buried among strangers was in a section of the cemetery reserved for Jews who had once belonged to the International Workers Order, a long-defunct Communist front which had sold the plots as fringe benefits to its members.

On Sunday, the last of my father's surviving comrades assembled in my mother's living room for the memorial. No ceremony had been planned, just a gathering of friends. Those present had known my father—some of them for more than fifty years—with the special intimacy of comrades who shared the scars of a common battleground—lifetime cohabitants in a community of exiles.

I could remember meetings when the same room had reverberated with their political arguments in the past. But now that the time had come to speak in my father's memory, they were strangely inarticulate. As though they were unequal to the task before them: to remember my father as a man.

My father was a man of modest achievements. His only real marks were the ones he made in the lives of the individuals he touched. The ones who were there now. The memories of the people who had gathered in my mother's living room were practically the only traces of my father still left on this earth. But when they finally began to speak, what they said was this: *Your father was a man who tried his best to make the world a better place ... your father was a man who was a teacher to others ... your father was a man who was socially conscious; progressive ... who made a contribution.*

And that was all they said. People who had known my father since before I was born, who had been his comrades and intimate friends, could not really remember him. All that was memorable to them in the life my father had lived—all that was real—were the elements that conformed to their Progressive Idea. My father's life was invisible to the only people who had ever been close enough to see who he was.

The obliteration of my father's life at his own memorial is the real meaning of what you call "our common heritage."

Our common heritage. Such a precious evasion. Our common heritage was totalitarianism, was it not? Our parents and their comrades were members of the Communist Party, were they not? Your need for this Orwellian phrase is revealing. It can hardly be for the benefit of an old comrade like me. In fact, its camouflage is for you. "Our common heritage" betrays your need to be insulated from your own reality—the reality of your totalitarian faith.

I'm sure this charge upsets you. In your own mind, the only elements that survive of our heritage are the innocent ones: *I haven't been a Stalinist since I visited the Soviet Union in 1957, when I was nineteen.... I no longer consider the Soviet Union a model for the socialist future.*

But which leftists who are able to enjoy the privileges of bourgeois democracy in the West think of themselves as Stalinists anymore, or the Soviet Union as a socialist model? Such vulgar convictions are reserved for the revolutionary heroes of the Third

World who actually wield the power—the Vietnamese and Cuban and Nicaraguan comrades—to whom you and other left-wing sophisticates pledge your loyalties and faith. *They* are Stalinists even if you are not.

Not an intention, but a totalitarian *faith* is what creates the common bond between revolutionary cynics like Stalin and Fidel and the Sandinista *comandantes* and progressive believers like yourself.

Totalitarianism is the possession of reality by a political Idea— the Idea of the socialist kingdom of heaven on earth, the redemption of humanity by political force. To radical believers this Idea is so beautiful it is like God Himself. It provides the meaning of a radical life. It is the solution that makes everything possible; it is the end that justifies the regrettable means. Belief in the kingdom of socialist heaven is the faith that transforms vice into virtue, lies into truth, evil into good. For in the revolutionary religion the Way, the Truth and the Life of salvation lie not with God above, but with men below—ruthless, brutal, venal men—on whom the faith confers the power of gods. There is no mystery in the transformation of the socialist paradise into communist hell: liberation theology is a Satanic creed.

Totalitarianism is the crushing of ordinary, intractable, human reality by a political Idea.

Totalitarianism is what my father's funeral and your letter are about.

Your letter indicts me because my ideas have changed. But the biggest change in me is not in any new political convictions I may have. It is in a new way of looking at things. The biggest change is seeing that reality is more important than any Idea. Reality—the concreteness of events and of people. In the years since we were close, I have gained respect for the ordinary experience of others and of myself. It is not a change I wanted to make. It is something that happened to me despite my resistance. But it is a change that has allowed me to learn from what I know. To connect, for example, the little episodes of our progressive heritage—like my father's memorial—with the epic inhumanities that its revolutions inspire. It is because you have not changed that these connections remain invisible to you.

What concerns me about you is that you have lost the compassion and humanism which motivated our parents to make their original choice.

You say their *original choice.* Another Orwellian evasion. Their "original choice" was Communism, was it not? Our parents were idolators in the church of a mass murderer named Joseph Stalin. They were not moralists but Marxist-Leninists. For them the Revolution *was* morality (and beauty and truth as well). For them, compassion outside the Revolution was mere bourgeois sentimentality. How could you forget this? Compassion is not what inspired our parents' political choices. Nor is compassion what inspired the left to which you and I both belonged—the *New Left* which forgot the people it liberated in Indochina once their murderers and oppressors were red; which never gave a thought to the Cubans it helped to bury alive in Castro's jails; which is still indifferent to the genocides of Marxist conquest—the fate of the Cambodias and Tibets and Afghanistans.

Compassion is not what motivates the left, which is oblivious to the human suffering its generations have caused. What motivates the left is the totalitarian Idea. The Idea that is more important than reality itself. What motivates the left is the Idea of the future in which everything is changed, everything *transcended.* The future in which the present is already *annihilated.* In which its reality no longer exists.

What motivates the left is an Idea whose true consciousness is this: *Everything human is alien.* Because everything that is flesh-and-blood humanity is only the disposable past. This is the consciousness that makes mass murderers of well-intentioned humanists and earnest progressives, the Hegelian liberators of the socialist cause.

In the minds of the liberators, it is not really *people* who are buried when they bury their victims. Because it is not really who stand in their way. Only "agents of past oppressions"—only "enemies of the progressive Idea." Here is an official rationale, from a Cheka official of the time of Lenin, for the disposal of 30 million human souls: "We are not carrying out war against individuals. We are exterminating the bourgeoisie as a class. We are not looking for evidence or witnesses to reveal deeds or words against the Soviet power. The first question we ask is—to what class does he belong, what are his origins, upbringing, education or profession? These questions define the fate of the accused. This is the essence of the Red Terror."

The Red Terror is terror in the name of an Idea.

The Red Terror is the terror that "idealistic" Communists (like our parents) and "anti-Stalinist" leftists (like ourselves) have helped to spread around the world. You and I and our parents were totalitarians in democratic America. The democratic *fact* of America prevented us from committing the atrocities willed by our faith. Impotence was our only innocence. In struggles all over the world we pledged our faith and gave our support to the perpetrators of the totalitarian deed. Our solidarity with them, like the crimes they committed, was justified in the name of the revolutionary Idea. Our capabilities were different. Our passion was the same.

And yours is still. You might not condone some of the crimes committed by the Kremlin or Castro or the Nicaraguan *comandantes.* But you would not condemn the criminals who are responsible for the deed. Or withhold from them your comradely support. Nor, despite all your enlightenment since the time of Stalin, are your thoughts really very different from theirs.

Does it occur to you that you condemn me in exactly the same terms that dissidents are condemned by the present-day guardians of the Soviet state? *There can be no other explanation for your support of the vile policies of Ronald Reagan. Except that you are operating from an emotional position which surpasses rational thinking.* In other words, the only explanation for my anti-Communist convictions is that I am "anti-social" (lacking compassion) or insane.

What kind of revolution do you think you and your radical comrades would bring to the lives of people—ordinary people who supported the "vile policies of Ronald Reagan" in such unprecedented numbers—people for whom you have so little real sympathy and such obvious contempt? The answer is self-evident: exactly the same kind of revolution that radicals of our "common heritage" have brought to the lives of ordinary people every time they seized power. For when the people refuse to believe as they should, it becomes necessary to make them believe by force. It is the unbelieving people who require the "Revolutionary Watch Committees" to keep tabs on their neighborhoods; the gulags to dispose of their intractable elements; the censors to keep them in ignorance and the police to keep them afraid. It is the reality of ordinary humanity that necessitates the totalitarian measures; it is the people that requires its own suppression for the revolution that is made in its name. To revolutionaries, the Idea of "the people" is more important than the people themselves.

The compassionate ideas of our common heritage are really masks of hostility and contempt. We revolutionaries are the enemies of the very people we claim to defend. Our promise of liberation is only a warrant for a new and more terrible oppression.

These are the realizations that have changed my politics. They were not clever thoughts that one day popped into mind, but—as you know and choose to forget—conclusions I was able to reach only at the end of a long period of reconsideration and pain.

Until then I had shared your conviction that we all were radicals for compassionate reasons, to serve benevolent ends. However perverted those ends might have become in the past, however grotesque the tragedies that occurred, I believed in the revolutionary project itself. I believed in it as the cause of humanity's hope. And I was confident that we could learn from history and would be able to avoid its destructive paths. I believed we could create a *new* left that would be guided by the principles of the revolutionary ideal—that would reject the claims of dictators like Stalin who had perverted its goals in the past.

After 1956 I joined others who shared this dream in the first attempts to create a new left in America and for nearly twenty years was part of the efforts to make it a reality. But eventually I realized that our efforts had failed. I gave up my political activities and embarked on a quest to understand why. When it was over, I saw that what we had dreamed in 1956 was not really possible. I saw that the problem of the left did not lie in sociopathic leaders like Stalin or Castro, who had perverted the revolutionary Ideal. It was the revolutionary Ideal that had perverted the left.

Because you knew me from the very beginning, you were aware of the road I had traveled, the connection between what I had lived through and what I had come to believe. No matter how different the traveler appeared at the end of the journey, you were a witness to his true identity. To the reality he had lived. But it is clear now that this reality—*my* reality—is something you no longer want to know. You prefer to erase me instead. It is not unlike the erasure of my father's truth that occurred at his memorial service.

Let me tell you some things—things you once knew, but have tried to forget, about the person you accuse now of being unable to cope with real-life complexity; of responding to the loss of one ideological certainty by reflexively embracing its opposite.

The formative experience of my politics was the shattering of the Old Left's illusions by the Khrushchev Report and the events of 1956. You and I were seventeen at the time—suddenly suspended between a political past that was no longer possible and a future that was uncertain. Our parents' political faith had been exposed as a monstrous lie. It was impossible for us to be 'left' in the way that they had been. But I did not assume therefore that I had to be 'right.' I swore I would never be part of another nightmare like theirs. But I didn't want to give up their beautiful Idea. So I joined the others in our generation who were setting out to rescue the Idea from the taint of the past and create a left that was new.

In the years that followed, I could always be seen in the ranks of the New Left, standing alongside my radical comrades. But in all those years there was a part of me that was always alone. I was alone because I never stopped thinking about the ambiguous legacy that we all had inherited. I was alone because it was a legacy that my New Left comrades had already decided to forget.

It was as though the radicals who came to politics in the Sixties generation wanted to think of themselves as having been born without parents. As though they wanted to erase the bad memory of what had happened to their dream when it had become reality in the Soviet past. To them the Soviet Union was "not a model" for the revolutionary future, but it was also not a warning of a revolutionary fate. It was—in the phrase of the time—"irrelevant."

All during the Sixties, I wrestled with the troubling legacies that my comrades ignored. While others invoked Marxism as a political weapon, I studied the four volumes of *Capital* to see "how much of the theory remained viable after the Stalin debacle," as I explained in the preface to a book I wrote called *The Fate of Midas*. For most New Left radicals who were impatient to "bring the System down," Marxism provided the convenient ax. Even if Marx was wrong, he was right. If Marxism promoted the desired result, what did it matter if the theory was false? But to me it mattered. All the nightmares of the past cried out that it did.

In the mid-Sixties I moved to London and came under the influence of Isaac Deutscher, an older Marxist who had written panoramic histories of the Russian Revolution and the lives of its protagonists Stalin and Trotsky. For me Deutscher was the perfect mentor, fully aware of the dark realities of the revolutionary past but believing still in the revolutionary Idea.

Inspired by my new teacher, I expanded my study of revolutionary history and intensified my search for a solution to the problems of our political inheritance. Before his untimely death in 1967, Deutscher encouraged me to expand one of my essays into a full-length literary effort. When *Empire and Revolution* was completed in 1968, it represented my "solution" to the radical legacy. I had confronted the revolutionary Idea with its failures, and I had established a new basis for confidence in its truth. In Europe my book joined those of a handful of others that shared its concerns, but in America *Empire and Revolution* stood all by itself. I don't think you will find another book like it written by an American New Leftist during that entire radical decade. In living with the ambiguities of the radical legacy, in my generation I was virtually unique.

When it was published in America, *Empire and Revolution* made no impression. The willful ignorance of New Left activists was an unshakable faith that long since had ceased to be innocent. Alliances had been struck with totalitarian forces in the Communist bloc; Stalinist rhetoric and Leninist vanguards had become the prevailing radical fashions. Even a New Left founder like Tom Hayden, previously immune to Marxist dogmas, had announced plans to form a new "Communist Party." As though the human catastrophes that had been caused by such instruments had never occurred.

In the face of these developments, I had begun to have doubts as to whether a New Left was possible at all. Whether the very nature of the left condemned it to endless repetitions of its past. But I deferred my doubts to what I saw at the time as a more pressing issue—the issue of America's anti-Communist war in Vietnam. Opposing the war was a moral obligation that in my mind took precedence over all other political tasks. The prospect of revolution which was the focus of my doubts was a reality remote by comparison. Even though I was uncomfortably allied with "Marxist-Leninists" whom I found politically dangerous and personally repellent, I didn't break ranks. As long as the Vietnam War continued, I accepted the ambiguity of my political position and remained committed to the radical cause.

But then the War came to an end and my doubts could no longer be deferred. The revolutionaries we had supported in Indochina were revealed in victory as conquerors and oppressors: millions were summarily slaughtered; new wars of aggression were launched; the small freedoms that had existed before were quickly extinguished; the poverty of the peoples increased. In

Asia, a new empire expanded as a result of our efforts, and over the peoples of Laos and Cambodia and South Vietnam fell the familiar darkness of a totalitarian night.

The result of our deeds was devastating to all that we in the left had said and believed. For some of us, this revelation was the beginning of a painful reassessment. But for others there were no second thoughts. For them, the reality in Vietnam finally didn't matter. All that mattered was the revolutionary Idea. It was more important than the reality itself. When they resumed their positions on the field of battle, they recalled "Vietnam" as a radical victory. The "Vietnam" they invoked in their new political slogans was a symbol of their revolutionary Idea: *Vietnam has won, El Salvador will win.* The next generation of the left had begun. The only condition of its birth was forgetfulness, forgetting what really had happened in Vietnam; erasing the memory of its own past.

But even before history had run its course in Vietnam, the refuge I had reserved for myself all these years in the left had already been cruelly destroyed. The murder of an innocent woman by people whom the New Left had celebrated as revolutionary heroes, and whom I had considered my political comrades, finally showed me how blind I had been made by my radical faith.

The murder was committed by the leaders of the Black Panther Party. Throughout the Sixties, I had kept my distance not only from the Panthers but from all the Leninists and their self-appointed vanguards. But at the same time I shared the reasoning that made gangs like the Panthers part of the left. According to this logic, the Panthers had become "politically aware" as a result of the "struggle" and had left their criminal past behind. By the same reasoning, their crimes were not something shameful; they were "pre-political" rebellions against their oppression as blacks. I accepted this logic for the same reason everyone else did, because it was the most basic tenet of our radical faith: reality was defined by politics, and could be changed by political ideas.

When the decade was over, and the war that had fueled its radical passions had begun to draw to an end, the political apocalypse suddenly receded. Almost overnight the "revolution" disintegrated. Its energies were exhausted, its organizations in varying stages of dissolution, its agendas put on hold. The Panthers survived to embrace the change with a new slogan proclaiming that "It's time to put away the gun" and, as their actions showed, to put away the Leninist posturing too. It was a time for practical community efforts, a time for reality. For me, it seemed a time to end my long alienation in the left. In 1973 I began a project with the Panthers to create a Community Learning Center in the heart of the East Oakland ghetto.

I allowed myself to be persuaded by the Panthers that they did not intend to use the center as a Panther enclave, but to turn it over to the ghetto community as a model of what good intentions could do. And I had persuaded myself that my intentions in working with the Panthers to accomplish this end were truly modest: to help the people in the community it would serve. But afterwards, I could see that my intentions were not modest at all. Every aspect of what I did was informed by the revolutionary Idea. That was the bond which connected me to the Panthers in the first place—which made what we were going to do resonate with the socialist future. That was what made me so ready to trust intentions I should not have trusted, and to forget the violent realities of the Panthers' past. That was what inspired me to ignore the surface betrayals of character that provided warnings to others but were dismissed by me as the legacies of an oppression that radical politics would overcome.

So I raised the necessary funds and bought a church facility in East Oakland to house a school for 150 children. I organized technical support systems and teacher-training programs and a variety of community services for the center, and I found a bookkeeper named Betty Van Patter to keep its accounts.

In the winter of 1974, the Panthers murdered Betty Van Patter and ended my career in the left. I suspected, and was later told by the Panthers, that they had committed the crime. There were others in the left who suspected them, too—people who knew that Betty was not the only person the Panthers had killed.

The Panthers were still, as they had always been, a criminal gang extorting the ghetto. But as a vanguard of the left they were a far more dangerous gang than when they had been street toughs. Whenever the police accused the Panthers of criminal activity, the left responded with cries of "racism" and "fascist repression," defending their innocence in the same way as the left in our parents' generation had defended the innocence of Stalin. For the left, the facts were not what mattered. What mattered was the revolutionary Idea.

It was a familiar pattern: the cynical exploiters of the revolutionary cause; the faithful defenders of the revolutionary name; the "political" silences that erased the truth; the blindness of believers like you and me. The legacy that I had tried so hard to leave by joining the New Left had now become the very center of my life.

The summer after Betty was murdered, you and I shared a tragedy of our own. Our friend Ellen Sparer, who had grown up with us in that over-rich political soil of Sunnyside, was brutally raped and strangled by a black youth in her Englewood, New Jersey home. We all had been members of the Sunnyside Young Progressives, which we founded when we were twelve years old under the covert auspices of the Communist Party. The premier issue of our *S.Y.P. Reporter* featured an editorial I wrote quoting a Negro Communist poet—"We, as a youth club, express our feelings best in the words of the great poetess Beulah Richardson, who said 'let our wholehearted fight be: peace in a world where there is equality'—and an original poem by Ellen herself about a Negro named Willie McGee, who had been executed in the South for raping a white woman:

> Did he have a fair trial?
> Did they have any Negroes in the jury?
> Did they have any proof of his guilt?
> NO!
> The only proof they had was that he was a Negro. A NEGRO!

In the years that followed, Ellen had been more faithful than either of us to the heritage we shared—joining the Communist Party *after* the invasion of Czechoslovakia. She was a missionary to the people she considered to be most oppressed, naming her third child "Martin" after Martin Luther King. As a high school teacher, she was devoted beyond the call of professional duty to black youngsters whose problems others considered difficult if not intractable. "She had the most intense rescue fantasies of anyone I have ever known," you wrote me after her death. To Ellen these were not individuals with problems, but victims of a racist system that she was determined to change. She would not let her own children play with toy guns or watch TV cartoons because they were violent; but she took real felons, who had committed real crimes with real guns, into the bosom of her family, "understanding" their actions and then disregarding the implications because the criminals were black.

She took them all on as a cause, and was willing to incur risks that others would not, making available not only her talents and intellect but her paycheck and her household as well. In your own words, "she was a sucker for a good sob story," losing over $1,000 by *twice* co-signing a loan for one of her students who conned her. On another occasion, she came close to losing her job when one of her outraged neighbors went to the school principal to complain that Ellen had abetted her daughter's flight from home.

On that fateful summer night, it was one of those troubled students, whom Ellen had taken up as a cause and set out to redeem, who returned to her house to murder her in her bed.

That summer you and I were able to share our grief over the friend we had lost, but we were never able to share an understanding of why she was dead. In your eyes, Ellen died a victim of circumstance; in mine she died a martyr of a political faith that had made her blind.

Because of this faith, Ellen's middle-class existence was constantly beset by unsuspected enemies and unseen perils. As a young instructor at Queens College, she helped black militants take over the SEEK program which employed her, but which they had targeted as racist. By publicly confirming the charge and personally betraying her professional colleagues, she was able to provide the radicals with the keys to their triumph. But, as you noted, "it also ultimately led to the loss of her job—because once the Black and Puerto-Rican Coalition came into power, they did not want any troublemakers around to disturb *their* comfortable sinecures!"

Even though her three children were asleep, Ellen had left her house unguarded. In our dialogues, you managed to find a way around this fact, and around everything else you knew about Ellen—including the battles you had had with her over locking her doors after her house was broken into, and her unwillingness to keep her boyfriend's dog in the house when she was alone. "I guess the fact is that Ellen was not killed by her heroics, naiveté, innocence, trust in human nature ... or idealism. She had the bad luck to be alone that night ... and had refused to keep Mel's very vicious German Shepherd at the house because the neighborhood kids were always in and out." Well, it was a psychotic neighborhood kid who had been "in and out" who finally killed her. And if Ellen had kept Mel's guard dog that night, she would be alive today.

To me, it is evident that Ellen's house was unguarded not by chance, and certainly not because the neighborhood was safe, but because of a political Idea. An Idea that to Ellen was more important than reality itself. The same Idea was expressed in the choice she had made of a place to live—one of the first integrated neighborhoods in America. To Ellen, Englewood was a social frontier that showed blacks and whites could live together. Over the years, experience had chastened Ellen enough for her to begin to lock her doors and to allow Mel's dog to stay when he stayed over. But in her heart, locked doors and guard dogs were still symbols of racist fear, of a world divided. The night Ellen was killed her home was unguarded because of her faith in the Progressive Idea. The Idea of the future that progressives like her were going to create: the future in which human conflicts would vanish as part of the oppressive past, and there would be "peace in a world where there is equality."

In months past, incidents of violence had been reported in the neighborhood and rumors had made its inhabitants afraid. As a good soldier of the faith, Ellen would not allow herself to surrender fully to this fear. Her house had been recently broken into and she was alone with her children but she refused to keep the dog that would have saved her life. On the night she was killed, Ellen's house was left unguarded *because* it was unsafe.

Ellen had no more understanding of the black people who lived in her neighborhood than she did of the black militants whom she had helped to dismiss her or the troubled teenager who finally killed her. Ellen had made all of their causes her own; had befriended them and given them her trust until finally she gave them her life. But Ellen never once really understood who they were. How could she possibly have understood? It was not because of who they were that Ellen had reached out to the black people she had tried to help. It was not because of their *reality* as individuals. It was because of an Idea she had of them as people who were "oppressed."

The night Ellen was killed, the black people in her neighborhood locked their doors. While Ellen was setting a progressive example, her black neighbors worried among themselves about the recent incidents and talked about them even more ominously than the whites. Ellen's black neighbors knew their fear was not symbolic and what threatened them was not an idea. They had special reason to worry that a dangerous criminal was stalking their neighborhood, because all his previous victims had been black.

In Ellen's fate I saw a mirror of mine. Our progressive mission had been destructive to others and, finally, destructive to us. It had imbued us with the greatest racism of all—a racism that was *universal*, never allowing us to see people as they really were, but only as our political prejudices required. With Ellen's death I had come to the last step in my political journey, which was to give up the progressive Idea—the fantasy of a future that made us so blind.

Why was this Idea so hard to give up? Since 1917, perhaps 100 million people had been killed by socialist revolutionaries in power; the socialisms they created had all resulted in new forms of despotism and social oppression, and an imperialism even more ruthless than those of the past. But the weight of this evidence had failed to convince us. We were able to hold on to our faith by rejecting this experience as a valid test. The ugly socialism of record, we explained to ourselves, was not "really" socialism. It was not our *Idea*. Listen to yourself: "*If it has not worked so far, it is because it has not really been tried.... In theory socialism is better than capitalism....*" If there was any validity to the Idea at all, to give up on it seemed an unthinkable betrayal, like turning one's back on humanity itself.

And so the last question I came to ask was whether there was any reality to the socialist Idea. In 1973, a conference was held at Oxford University with this very question as its main agenda. The organizer of the conference was a Marxist philosopher who was one of the founders of the European New Left and had traveled a road that ran parallel to my own.

When Eastern Europe's satellites rebelled against their Soviet oppressors in 1956 in the aftershocks of the Khrushchev Report, Leszek Kolakowski was one of their New Left leaders. The rebellions were brutally crushed by the Soviet armies, but Kolakowski remained a New Leftist until 1968. That summer, Soviet tanks again crossed into Eastern Europe to quell dissident Communists in Prague and Leszek Kolakowski fought a last- ditch defense of his New Left faith. For his efforts, he was expelled from his Party and driven into exile in the West.

When Kolakowski organized the Oxford conference on the socialist Idea, nearly twenty years had passed since he had joined the struggle to create a New Left in the Communist world. For two decades he had led efforts to create a new "humanistic Marxism" and to liberate socialism from its totalitarian fate. But by the time of the conference, Kolakowski could no longer ignore what his experience had shown. He was ready to admit defeat and give up the attempt to resolve the ambiguities we all had inherited.

The paper Kolakowski read at the conference examined the idea of a classless, unified human community—the progressive goal to which we had dedicated our lives.[4] The catastrophic experience of Marxist societies, he showed, had not been an accident. It was implicit in the socialist Idea. The forces required to impose the radical equality that socialism promised inevitably led to a new *inequality* and a new privileged ruling elite. The socialist unity of mankind we all had dreamed of could only be realized in a totalitarian state.

Kolakowski's arguments had already been made by critics of socialism in every generation since the time of Marx himself. In every generation since, the societies that Marxists created had only served to prove them right. And now they had been proven right in mine. In the light of all I had come to experience and know, Kolakowski's arguments were utterly and tragically correct. But I was still not ready to embrace their conclusions, whose consequences seemed as unthinkable as before. I decided to suspend judgment and take Kolakowski's arguments to my comrades in the left. I wanted to know how they would respond and whether they had the answers that I did not.

I initiated discussions in radical circles and even organized a seminar addressed to the question: "Is Socialism a Viable Idea?" The reactions I encountered proved personally frustrating, but finally instructive. Most radicals, I discovered, did not see the issue as important at all: people whose lives were absorbed in efforts to replace an "unjust" society with one that was better were not interested in whether their efforts might actually make things worse. The few who recognized the gravity of the issue

---

[4] "The Myth of Human Self-Identity" in Leszek Kolakowski and Stuart Hampshire, eds., *The Socialist Idea*, Basic Books, 1974.

reacted to my questions with suspicion and mistrust. To ask whether the socialist Idea was more than a fantasy was like asking believers about the existence of God.

My search finally ended when I was visited by a British New Leftist who had been one of my earliest mentors. In the days when we were all setting out on our journey, Ralph Miliband had guided me in my first encounters with the troubling legacies of the radical past. After Isaac Deutscher's death in 1967, Miliband was the Marxist whose intellect and integrity I respected most. I had not seen him for more than a decade, but I still read the socialist journal he edited. It was the only socialist publication that had printed Kolakowski's recent ideas.

After we had caught up on the years that had passed, I told him about the crisis I had reached. I recalled the impact of Kolakowski's arguments and the resistance I had met when I confronted other leftists with the issues they raised. I told Miliband it seemed irresponsible for radicals like us to call ourselves "democratic socialists" while Kolakowski's arguments remained unanswered and—even worse—when most of the left didn't care if his arguments could be answered at all. I didn't see how I could justify a commitment to a political movement with a history like the left's, which was dedicated to destroying society without a viable plan for what would come next. I was still ready, I said, to oppose injustices wherever I perceived them; but I could not be part of a movement that would not examine its goals.

When I was finished, I waited for an answer. Not an answer to Kolakowski, which I knew by then did not exist, but the answer I had been looking for all along. The one that would say: *David, you are not as alone as you think. The experiences of these years since we all began have indeed shown that the crisis of the socialist Idea is the crisis of the left itself. If this crisis can't be resolved, if socialism is not a viable future, then our radicalism is really nothing more than a nihilistic passion and the left a totalitarian force. But there is another possibility. The possibility that answers can be found; that a viable conception of socialism will result; a new agenda for the radical forces and a renewal of the radical hope. Ours may be a small contingent in the radical ranks, but the consequences of failure are too great to give up without trying.*

If my old teacher had answered me like this, perhaps the illusion would have been given new life. But when I was finished, Ralph Miliband said: "David, if those are your priorities, you are no longer a man of the left."

What my old teacher had told me was that the left was really a community of faith, and that I was no longer part of it.

My conversation with Ralph Miliband occurred sometime in the summer of 1979. I did not then leap to the right side of the political spectrum, but waited another five years before casting a vote for Ronald Reagan and the policies that you consider so "vile." During that time, as for 24 years previous, I had lived in the teeth of political ambiguity—never free from doubts about the left, but never feeling I had to resolve my doubts by embracing the views of the opposite side. Your image of me not only denies the meanings of my life but actually reverses them.

And finally misunderstands them. If I had to label the perspective my experience has given me, I would call it "conservative." And by that I would mean respect for the accumulated wisdom of human traditions; regard for the ordinary realities of human lives; distrust of optimism based on human reason; caution in the face of tragedies past. Conservatism is not the other side of the coin of radicalism, any more than skepticism is the mirror of faith. I have not exchanged one ideology for another; I have freed myself from the chains of an Idea.

Why was my freedom so hard to win? Why is the Idea so difficult to give up? When I asked myself these questions afterwards, I realized that to do so had seemed to me, at the time, like giving up something I could not do without—hope itself. Life without the Idea of the socialist future felt to me like life without meaning. It was then that I realized the reason the Idea is so hard is to give up is that a radical faith is like any other faith: it is not a matter of politics but of self.

The moment I gave up my radical beliefs was the moment I had to look at myself for the very first time. At *me*. As I really was—not suspended above everyone else as an avatar of their future salvation but standing beside them as an equal, as one of *them*. Not one whom History had chosen for its vanguard, but a speck of ordinary human dust. I had to look at the life ahead of me no longer guided and buoyed by a redeeming purpose; no longer justified by a missionary faith. Just a drop in the flow to the common oblivion. Mortal, insignificant, inconceivably small.

Marx was a rabbi after all. The revolutionary Idea is a religious consolation for earthly defeat. For the Jews of our Sunnyside heritage, it is the consolation for internal exile; the comfort and support of a marginal life. A passage home. Belief in the Idea is the deception of self that made people like my father and you and me feel real.

Self-deception is what links you to the "common heritage" which is so difficult for those who inhabit it to name. Communism was the center of my father's world, but the word never passed the lips of the comrades who rose to speak at his memorial. A political faith dominated both their lives and his, but in the end the faith could not be named. To name it would make their lives too uncomfortably real.

In their silence was their truth. What my father and his comrades were finally seeking in their political faith was not a new reality for the world but an old illusion for themselves. What they found was comfort for their lives of pain.

For my father it was the pain of a chosen son. My father was the only male child of poor immigrants who could not speak English and who were as fearful of the strange world they had reached as the one they had fled. His own father had failed as a provider, and when my father was still only a child he realized the family had already placed its fate in his hands. From that time until his death, he felt like a man treading in water that was over his head, with the shore forever out of sight.

At the age of nineteen my father found a means to support his parents, and a life raft for himself, in a job teaching English to other immigrant youngsters at Seward Park High School on the Lower East Side. But until he was thirty he continued to live in his parents' apartment and his own life remained dangerously adrift. Clarity entered my father's life through the Communist Party and the socialist Idea. The moment he joined the Party, he felt himself touch the shore of a land-mass that circled the globe and extended into the future itself. As a soldier in the Party's vanguard and a prophet of its truth, my father gained wisdom and power beyond his faculty, and finally achieved what his own father had not: his self-esteem as a man.

But in the memorials of his comrades, there was no mention at all of the Party that had given my father so great a gift. It was like a secret they all were keeping from themselves. And my father would have wanted them to keep their secret. Because he had a secret, too.

My father had left the Communist Party more than thirty years before.

It was only towards the end of his life that my father felt able to tell me his secret, and then in a voice full of emotion and pain, as if it had all not happened so many years past. The events had taken place in 1953, when I was fourteen and my father was approaching fifty (which is my age now). The anti-Communist crusade of the early Cold War was reaching its height, and my father was about to lose the first life raft that had kept him afloat. For twenty-nine years he had remained a teacher of English at the same high school on the Lower East Side, but now a new law had been passed that barred Communists from his lifetime vocation.

In the ordinary business of his life outside politics, my father had remained timid like his father before him, clinging all that time to his very first job. But in the drama of history which he now entered, my father was the tall man his faith had made him. He was ready to stand up to his inquisitors and bear the blows they were about to give him. To defend his Party and its cause, my father was even ready to give up his raft of survival and to swim for the first time in uncharted seas. It should have been my father's moment of glory, but instead it became his hour of shame.

For "political reasons" the Party had decided that my father would not be allowed to make his stand as a man on trial for his political beliefs. Instead he would have to defend himself as the victim of an "anti-Semitic" campaign. All my father's pride as a man lay in the cause that he had joined, in the fact that he had reached the shores of progressive light and had left his Jewish ghetto behind. Even in the best of circumstances, the lie that the Party now required would have been excruciating for a man of my father's temper. But when the court of history called him to account, there was no place for my father to hide.

When his moment came, my father followed the Party line as he always had done. In his moment of glory my father colluded in his own public humiliation and was fired as a Communist from his only profession, protesting his rights as a Jew.

When my father was betrayed by the Party he loved, he was forced to look at the truth. The Party was everything to him, but to the Party he was nothing at all. His faith in the Party had not really given him power; it had only made him a political pawn. The secret my father could only reveal to me late in his life was the terrible truth he had seen.

The truth made it impossible for my father ever to go back, but he did not have the strength to go forward. He could not leave—any more than you can leave—the faith that was the center of his life. It was a dilemma my father resolved—as you do—with a strategic retreat. He quietly left the Party that had betrayed him, but he kept his political faith. He was never again active in a political way; but every day of the thirty years that remained to him, he loyally read the Communist press and defended the Party line.

All those years my father kept his secret as though he were protecting a political cause. But in fact, as anyone else could see, all those years my father was keeping his secret in order to protect himself.

My father's deceit was small. The hurt it caused was only to him and his family. But my father's deceit is a metaphor for all the lies of the political faithful—the lies of self-deceit and the deceit of others that have made their cause a blight on our time.

The immediate intent of my father's deceit was to conceal the reality of his political cause—its casual inhumanities and devious methods, its relentless betrayal even of its own. But the real purpose of my father's deception was to avoid the reality that made his faith necessary in the first place, that makes the Idea so hard to give up. The reality my father could not confront was his own.

It is the same with you. When you deny my reality for a political Idea, what you really don't want to confront is your own. *I assume they are paying you well for your efforts.* Can you really think I sold out my faith for money? How can you, who know the price I had to pay for what I have learned, point such an accusing finger at me? Only if you feel so deprived in your own life that your words really mean this: *I am not being paid well for mine.*

The rich are not on the same side as the rest of us. They exploit. The radical truth— still your truth—is the *class war* of the social apocalypse, the war that divides humanity into the "Haves" who exploit and the "Have Nots" who are oppressed; into those who are paid well for their efforts and those who are denied; into the Just and the Unjust; into *their* side and *ours*. The radical truth is the permanent war that observes no truce and respects no law; whose aim is to destroy the only world we know.

This is the "compassionate" cause that makes radicals superior to ordinary humanity and transforms the rest of us into "class enemies" and un-persons and objects of contempt.

Take a careful look at what you still believe, because it is a mirror of the dark center of the radical heart: not compassion, but resentment—the envious whine of *have not* and *want*; not the longing for justice but the desire for revenge; not a quest for peace but a call to arms. It is war that feeds the true radical passions, which are not altruism and love but nihilism and hate.

The farcical surfaces of the political divorces over the Khrushchev Report masked a deeper reality of human pain. Consider what terrors of loneliness inhabit the hearts of people whose humanity must express itself as a political construction. Consider what passions accumulate in such unsatisfied souls.

This is the poisoned well of the radical heart: the displacement of real emotions into political fantasies; the rejection of present communities for a future illusion; the denial of flesh-and-blood human beings for an Idea of humanity that is more important than humanity itself. This is the problem of "our common heritage," as you so delicately name it, and it is our problem as well.

Your old friend and ex-comrade,

David

• • •

The Road to Nowhere

The self-deification of mankind, to which Marxism gave philosophical expression, has ended in the same way as all such attempts, whether individual or collective: it has revealed itself as the farcical aspect of human bondage.

—Leszek Kolakowski

October 1990

Dear Ralph,[5]

It has been over a decade since this silence as durable as an iron curtain descended between us. In these circumstances, I have had to depend on others to learn how you regard me these days: How, at a recent social gathering, you referred to me as "one of the two tragedies of the New Left"—the other being a former Brecht scholar who now publishes guides to the nude beaches of America; and how my apostasy has inflicted an emotional wound, as though

---

[5] Ralph Miliband, an English Marxist, author of *Parliamentary Socialism* and other works, who was my mentor during the years I was in England (1963–1967).

in changing my political views and leaving the left I had personally betrayed you.

I understand this. How could it be otherwise for people like us, for whom politics—despite our claim to be social realists—was less a matter of practical decisions than moral choices? We were partisans of a cause that confirmed our humanity, even as it denied humanity to those who opposed us. To leave such ranks was not a simple matter, like abandoning a misconception or admitting a mistake. It was more like accusing one's comrades. Like condemning a life.

Our choice of politics was never a matter of partial commitments. To choose the left was to define a way of being in the world. (For us, the personal was always political). It was choosing a future in which human beings would finally live as they were meant to live: no longer self-alienated and divided, but equal, harmonious and whole.

Grandiose as this project was, it was not something we had invented, but the inspiration for a movement that was coterminous with modernity itself. As you had taught me, the left was launched at the time of the French Revolution by Gracchus Babeuf and the Conspiracy of the Equals. In Marx's own words: "The revolutionary movement, which began in 1789 ... and which temporarily succumbed in the Conspiracy of Babeuf, gave rise to the communist idea.... This idea ... constitutes the principle of the modern world."[6] With a terrible simplicity the Babouvists pledged themselves to "equality or death," swiftly finding the latter—in a prophetic irony—on the Revolution's own busy guillotine.

The victorious radicals had proclaimed a theology of Reason in which equality of condition was the natural and true order of creation. In their Genesis, the loss of equality was the ultimate source of mankind's suffering and evil, just as the arrogant pride of the primal couple had provoked their Fall in the religious myths

---

[6]Karl Marx and Friedrich Engels, *The Holy Family*.

now discarded. The ownership of private property became a secular version of original sin. Through property, society re-imposed on every generation of human innocence the travails of inequality and injustice. Redemption from worldly suffering was possible only through the Revolution that would abolish property and open the gates to the socialist Eden—to Paradise regained.

The ideas embodied in this theology of liberation became the inspiration for the new political left, and have remained so ever since. It was half a century later that Marx first articulated the idea of a historical redemption, in the way that became resonant for us:

> *Communism* is the *positive* abolition of *private property*, of *human self-alienation*, and thus the real *appropriation* of *human* nature through and for man. It is therefore the return of man himself as a *social*, i.e., really human, being....[7]

This was our revolutionary vision. By a historical coup we would create the conditions for a return to the state of true humanity whose realization had been blocked by the alienating hierarchies of private property. All the unjust institutions of *class* history that had distorted, divided, and oppressed mankind would be abolished; and human innocence would be reborn.

In the service of this cause, no burden seemed too onerous, no sacrifice too great. We were the Christopher Columbuses of the human future, the avatars of a new world struggling to emerge from the womb of the old. How could I divorce myself from a mission like this without betraying those whom I had left behind?

Without betraying *you*, my political mentor and closest comrade. We had met in London at the beginning of the Sixties and you quickly became my guide through the moral wilderness created by the disintegration of the Old Left. I was the scion of Communists, troubled by the crimes the "Khrushchev Report" had recently unveiled; you had distanced yourself from official

---

[7] Karl Marx, *Economic and Philosophical Manuscripts.*

Communism, becoming a charter member of the New Left in the spring of 1956. Even as the unmarked graves of Stalin's victims were re-opened and their wounds bled afresh, the New Left raised its collective voice to proclaim the continuing truth of its humanitarian dream. Stalinism had died, not socialism. In the moral and political confusion of those years, it was you more than anyone else who helped to restore my radical faith.

To be sure, I was a willing disciple. To abandon the historic project of the left required a moral stoicism that I lacked. No matter how great the enormities perpetrated in the name of socialism, no matter how terrible the miseries inflicted, the prospect of a world without this idea, and its promise of justice, was unthinkable to me. To turn one's back on socialism would not be like abandoning a misconception or admitting a mistake. It would be like turning one's back on humanity. Like betraying myself.

And so I, too, refused to give up on this idea that inspired and ennobled us. I joined you and the pioneers of a New Left who had condemned Stalinism and its brutal past and pledged to keep the faith.

But we did not then ask ourselves a question that seemed unavoidable to me later: What was the meaning of this refusal to admit our defeat? For thirty years, with only a minority in dissent, the best, most vital and compassionate minds of the left had hailed the flowering of the progressive state in Soviet Russia. They had made the defense of Soviet "achievements" the *sine qua non* of what it was to be socially conscious and morally correct. Now the Kremlin itself had acknowledged the monstrous "mistakes" of the progressive experiment, confirming the most damning accusations of its political adversaries. In the face of such epic criminality and collusion, what was the urgency of our renewed dedication to the goals that had proved so destructive in the first place? Why were the voices of our enemies not more worthy of a hearing in the hour that seemed to vindicate them so completely? Why were we so eager to hurry past the lessons they urged on us, in order to resume our combat again?

Our radical generation was hardly the first (and not the last) to repent in such careless haste. The cycle of guilt was integral, in fact, to the progress of the left. It had begun with the radical birth in 18th-century Paris—that dawn of human Fraternity and Reason which devolved into fratricidal terror and imperial ambition. How had the redemptive illusions that inspired the left been so relentlessly renewed in radical generation after generation, despite the inexorable rebuke of human tragedy that attended each of its triumphs? How had the left negotiated these rebirths?

In the interlude following Stalin's death, when our generation was reviving its political commitments and creating the New Left, we did not stop to ask ourselves such questions. We were all too busy being reborn. But two decades later, when I had reached the end of my radical journey and had my second thoughts, I was able at last to see how our own modest histories provided the text of an answer.

Meanwhile, you have have had no such second thoughts. Even as I write, you and your comrades are engaged in yet another defiant resurrection—the birth of a new generation of the left, as eager to believe in the fantasy of a new world as we were then. In this *annus mirabilis,* when the socialist idea is being repudiated throughout the whole expanse of the Soviet empire by the very masses it claimed to liberate, you and your comrades are still finding ways to deny what has happened.

For you and the prophets of the next left, the socialist idea is still capable of an immaculate birth from the bloody conception of the socialist state. You seek to evade these lessons of the revolutionary present by writing the phrase "actually existing socialism" across its pages, thus distinguishing the socialism of your faith from the socialism that has failed. The historic bankruptcy of the planned societies created by Marxist dictators, a human catastrophe extending across nearly three quarters of a century and encompassing hundreds of millions of ruined lives, will not be entered in the balance sheet of the left. This would require of you and your comrades a fearless accounting and an agonizing self-appraisal. You prefer, instead, to regard the bankruptcy as someone else's.

There is nothing new in this shell game. It is the same operation we ourselves performed after 1956, when our slogan was: Stalinism is dead, long live socialism. Today you see the
demonstrations for democracy bringing an end to Communist history, and you are certain that this has no relevance to the ideas
that inspired that history in the first place. Here is your most
recent defense of the past:

> Communist regimes, with the notable exception of Yugoslavia
> after 1948, never made any serious attempt, or indeed any
> attempt at all, to break the authoritarian mould by which they
> had been cast at their birth. Conservative ideologists have a sim-
> ple explanation of this immobility: its roots are to be found in
> Marxism. In fact, Marxism has nothing to do with it.[8]

"Actually existing Marxism" is dead, long live Marxism. This
is the political formula of the left—of your left—today. Veterans of
past ideological wars, like yourself, will be crucial in selling this
hope to a new generation. The moral weight of this future will be
on your shoulders.

In reading your words, I could not help thinking how thirty
years ago there was an individual who provided the same hope for
you, and who since then has become the intellectual model for my
own second thoughts. Perhaps you are tempted to bury this connection. For there were not two, but three New Left apostasies
that touched you directly, and of these the defection of Leszek
Kolakowski was by far the most painful.[9]

---

[8]"The Crisis of Communist Regimes," *New Left Review*, September–
October 1989. As New Left professor Michael Burawoy actually wrote in
a special issue of *Socialist Review*: "Marxism is dead, long live Marxism!" *Now What? Responses to Socialism's Crisis of Meaning*, Volume
20 No. 2, April–June 1990.
[9]Acknowledging the "sharpness of tone" in your review of Kolakowski's
trilogy on Marxism, you explained: "I think this is in part attributable to
a strong personal sense of disappointment at Kolakowski's political evolution. I have known Kolakowski since the fraught days of 1956 and have
always thought him to be a man of outstanding integrity and courage,
with a brilliant and original mind. His turning away from Marxism and,

A philosopher of exceptional brilliance and moral courage, Kolakowski had been the intellectual leader of our political generation. Even the titles of his writings—"Responsibility and History," "Towards a Marxist Humanism"—read like stages of our radical rebirth. By 1968 those stages had come to an abrupt conclusion. When the Czechs' attempt to provide Communism with a human face was crushed by Soviet tanks, Kolakowski abandoned the ranks of the left. And he did more. He fled—unapologetically— to the freedoms of the West, implicitly affirming by his actions that the Cold War did indeed mark a great divide in human affairs, and that the left had chosen the wrong side.

Kolakowski's apostasy was challenged by Edward Thompson, then the foremost English New Leftist, in a 100-page "Open Letter" which you published in the *Socialist Register 1973*. Written in the form of a plea to Kolakowski to return to the radical fold, the letter began by paying homage to the example he had set for us all seventeen years before, and which Thompson now claimed as a "debt of solidarity":

> What we dissident Communists [of '56] did in Britain ... was to refuse to enter the well-worn paths of apostasy. I can think of not one who took on the accepted role, in liberal capitalist society, of Public Confessor and Renegade. No-one ran to the press with his revelations about Communist "conspiracy" and no-one wrote elegant essays, in the organs published by the Congress for Cultural Freedom, complaining that God had failed.... We refused to disavow "Communism" because Communism was a complex noun which included Leszek Kolakowski.

—Continued
as I see it, from socialism has been a great boon to the reactionary forces of which he was once the dedicated enemy, and a great loss to the socialist cause, of which he was once the intrepid champion. I felt that loss very keenly...."Ralph Miliband, *Class Power and State Power*, Political Essays, Verso 1983, pp. 226–27.

Here Thompson put his finger on a central reflex of the New Left revival: our refusal to break ranks with our comrades and join the camp of our Cold War opponents; in short, our ability to repudiate the catastrophic outcome of a generation of radical effort without abandoning the radical cause. Not even the crimes of Stalin could break the chain of our loyalties to the revolt against bourgeois society that had been launched at its inception by the Conspiracy of the Equals.

Because Communism was a "complex noun" which included Kolakowski, we were able to preserve our allegiances to an Idea that still included Communism, if only as a deformed precursor of the future to which we all aspired. Because Communism was a complex noun we refused to concede that Marxism or Socialism—integral elements of the Communist Idea—were themselves condemned by the Stalinist nightmare. Kolakowski provided the bridge across which New Leftists could march in a popular front with Communists to carry on a struggle that they had begun nobly, but soon distorted and then tragically perverted. Because Kolakowski was himself a complex noun, having spoken out for intellectual honesty and humanist values while he remained a Communist, we could do this without giving up our critical distance or self-respect.

Kolakowski, of course, was not alone. A generation of Kolakowskis had appeared after '56 to incite and inspire us. When you and I met in London in 1963, it occurred to me that if someone as morally serious and intellectually dedicated as you could still devote himself to Marxism and the cause of the left—despite Stalinism and all that it had engendered—it was possible for me to do so too.

There was one question that Thompson had failed to ask, however, which occurred to me only later: When had Communism *not* been a complex noun that included individuals like Kolakowski (and you)? Even in the most grotesque night of the Stalinist abyss, the Communist movement had included the complexity of intellects as subtle and independent as Trotsky and Lukacs, Varga and

Gramsci, not to mention the fellow-traveling chorus of "progressive" intellectuals who defended Stalinism while proclaiming their humanism from the privileged sanctuaries of the democratic West. Didn't this say something about the futility of such complexity, or its practical irrelevance?

In our minds, of course, the complexity of the Communist noun went beyond individuals to encompass the nature of reality itself. It was the Hegelian complexity that the idea of the future introduced into the present, that ultimately made us so willing to discount the evils of Stalinist rule. This complexity was a creation of our Marxist perspective, which decreed a divorce between appearance and reality, between present reality and the future to come; between class history ruled by impersonal forces and revolutionary history ruled by reason, and guided by the precepts of social justice.

This vision of the future was the heart of our radical illusion. We had rejected the crude determinism of our Stalinist precursors, but our confidence in the outcome of the historical process allowed us to put our talents on the Communist side of the global conflict, even though "really existing Communism" was an offense to the spirit of the socialism we believed in. In his "Open Letter" Thompson explained the paradox by which we gave our allegiance to an intellectual abstraction and wound up acting as partisans of a reality we disdained:

> In general, our allegiance to Communism was political: it arose from inexorable choices in a partisan world in which neutrality seemed impossible.... But our intellectual allegiance was to Marxism..... Thus there is a sense in which, even before 1956, our solidarity was given not to Communist states in their existence, but in their potential—not for what they were but for what—given a diminution in the Cold War—they might become.[10]

---

[10]E. P. Thompson, "An Open Letter to Leszek Kolakowski," *The Socialist Register*, 1973, pp. 1–100, https://www.marxists.org/archive/thompson-ep/1973/Kolakowski.htm

Our solidarity was given to Communist states *in their potential*. New Leftists like us refused to become anti-Communist cold warriors and offered "critical support" to repulsive Communist regimes because *we believed they would change*. It was the "humanist potential" of societies with socialist foundations, not their totalitarian realities, that claimed our allegiance. By the same reasoning, we were unimpressed by the democratic realities of the capitalist West, because private property rendered them incapable of such liberation.

We refused to join the attack on the Communist camp in Cold War battles, no matter how morally justified, because we did not want to aid those seeking to destroy the seeds of the future the left had sown in Soviet Russia. We were determined to defend what Trotsky had called "the gains of October"—the socialist edicts of the Bolshevik Revolution that had abolished private property and paved the way for a better world. It was our recognition of the epoch-making character of these "gains" that defined our radical faith.

By 1973 Kolakowski had rejected this faith and the politics it inspired. Thompson's "Open Letter" was a refusal to accept the rejection. It was an eloquent plea for the continuing vitality of the socialist future and for the left's enduring mission as the carrier of historical optimism: the idea that humanity could master its fate. It was, above all, a rebuke to the leader who had once inspired but now spurned the radicals of '56. "I feel," wrote Thompson, "when I turn over your pages a sense of injury and betrayal."

Kolakowski no longer believed in Communism as a complex noun. He no longer had faith in what he called the "secular eschatology" of the left—the political passion that sought to fuse "the essence of man with his existence," to assure that the timeless longings of humanity would be "fulfilled in reality."[11] He no longer believed in the reality of the socialist Idea.

---

[11]Leszek Kolakowski, "The Priest and the Jester" (1959) in *Towards a Marxist Humanism*, Grove Press, 1968.

Kolakowski replied to Thompson in the 1974 edition of the *Socialist Register*, which I read in America. Struggling, then, with my own doubts, I was drawn to his arguments which seemed to promise an exit from the ideological *cul-de-sac* in which I had come to feel trapped. In these passages he exposed the web of double standards that stifled radical thought and transformed it into a self-confirming creed.

As you know, there is no hallmark of left-wing discourse so familiar as the double standard. How many times had we been challenged by our conservative opponents for the support (however "critical") we gave to totalitarian states where the values we claimed to champion—freedom and human rights—were absent, while we made ourselves enemies of the Western democracies where (however flawed) they were defended. In the seventy years since the Bolshevik Revolution, perhaps no other question had proved such an obstacle to our efforts to win adherents to the socialist cause.

In his reply, Kolakowski drew attention to three forms of the double standard that Thompson had employed and that were crucial to the arguments of the left. The first was the invocation of moral standards in judging capitalist regimes on the one hand, while using historical criteria to evaluate their socialist counterparts on the other. As a result, capitalist injustice was invariably condemned by the left under an absolute standard, whereas socialist injustice was routinely accommodated in accord with the relative judgments of a historical perspective. Thus, repellent practices in the socialist bloc were placed in their "proper context" and thereby "understood" as the product of pre-existing social and political conditions—i.e., as attempts to cope with intractable legacies of a soon-to-be-discarded past.

Secondly, capitalist and socialist regimes were assessed under different assumptions about their futures. Capitalist regimes were judged under the assumption that they could not meaningfully improve, while socialist regimes were judged on the opposite assumption: that they *would*. Repressions by conservatives like

Pinochet in Chile were never seen in the terms in which their apologists justified them—as necessary preludes to democratic restorations—but condemned instead as unmitigated evils. On the other hand, the far greater and more durable repressions of revolutionary regimes, like the Castro dictatorship in Cuba, were invariably minimized as precisely that—necessary (and temporary) stages along the path to a progressive future.

Finally, in left-wing arguments the negative aspects of existing socialism were attributed to capitalist influences—survival of the elements of the old society, impact of anti-Communist "encirclement," tyranny of the world market, etc.—while the reverse possibility was not considered. Thus, leftist histories ritualistically invoked Hitler to explain the rise of Stalinism—the necessity of a draconian industrialization to meet the Nazi threat—but refused to see Stalinism as a factor contributing to the rise of Hitler.

Yet, beginning with the socialist assault on bourgeois democracy and the forced labor camps—which were a probable inspiration for Auschwitz—Stalinism was a far more palpable influence in shaping German politics in the Thirties than was Nazism in influencing Soviet developments. The "Trotskyite conspiracy with the Mikado and Hitler"—the cabal which the infamous show trials claimed to expose—was a Stalinist myth; but the alliance that German Communists formed with the Nazi Party to attack the Social Democrats and destroy the Weimar Republic was an actual Stalinist plot. Without this alliance, the united parties of the left would have formed a formidable barrier to the Nazis' electoral triumph and Hitler might never have come to power.

The same double standard underlies the left's failure to understand the Cold War that followed the allied victory. Leftist Cold War histories refuse to concede that the anti-Communist policies of the Western powers were a reasonable response to the threat they faced; instead, the threat itself is viewed as a fantasy of anti-Communist paranoia. Soviet militarism and imperialism, including the occupation of Eastern Europe, are dismissed as merely reactive; defensive responses to Western containment. But when the same Western actions produce the opposite result—Soviet withdrawal from Eastern Europe and, with that, an end to the Cold War—they are alleged to have had no influence at all.

In sum, positive developments in the Soviet bloc come from within; negative developments are the consequences of counter-revolutionary encirclement.

The double standards that inform the arguments of the left are really expressions of the left's false consciousness, the reflexes by which the left defends an identity rooted in its belief in the redemptive power of the socialist idea. *Of course the revolution cannot be judged by the same standards as the counter-revolution: the first is a project to create a truly human future, the latter only an attempt to preserve an anti-human past.* This is why, no matter how destructive its consequences or how absolutely it fails, the revolution deserves our allegiance; why *anti*-Communism is always a far greater evil than the Communism it opposes. Because revolutionary evil is only a birth pang of the future, whereas the evil of counter-revolution lies in its desire to strangle the birth.

It was this birth in which Kolakowski had finally ceased to believe. The imagined future in whose name all actually existing revolutions had been relieved of their failures and absolved of their sins, he had concluded, was nothing more than a mistaken idea.

When Kolakowski's reply to Thompson was printed in the *Socialist Register 1974,* you prefaced its appearance with an editorial note describing it as a "tragic document." At the time, I was in the middle of my own political journey and this judgment was the first stone in the wall that had begun to separate us. For already I had begun to realize just how much I agreed with everything Kolakowski had written.

It is clear to me now, in retrospect, that this moment marked the end of my intellectual life in the left. It occurred during what for me had been a period of unexpected and tragic events. In Vietnam, America had not stayed the course of its imperial mission, as we had said it would, but under pressure from our radical movement had quit the field of battle. Our theory had assured us the capitalist state was controlled by the corporate interests of a ruling class; but events had shown that the American government was responsive to the desires of its ordinary citizens.

Closer to home, a friend of mine named Betty Van Patter had been murdered by a vanguard of the left, while the powers of the state that we had condemned as repressive had been so impotent in reality as to be unable even to indict those responsible. These events—for reasons I need not review here—confronted me with questions that I could not answer, and in the process they opened my mind to thoughts I would previously have found unthinkable.

The shock of these recognitions dissolved the certainties that had previously blocked my sight. For the first time in my political life, I became inquisitive about what our opponents saw when they saw us. I began to wonder *what if*. What if we had been wrong in this or that instance, and what if *they* had been right? I asked these questions as a kind of experiment at first, but then with systematic determination until they all seemed to be pushing towards a single concern: What if socialism were not possible after all?

While I was engaged with these doubts, Kolakowski published *Main Currents of Marxism*[12]—a comprehensive history of Marxist thought, the world-view we all had spent a lifetime inhabiting. For three volumes and fifteen hundred pages, Kolakowski analyzed the entire corpus of this intellectual tradition. Then, having paid critical homage to an argument which for a hundred years had dominated so much of humanity's fate and his own as well, he added an epilogue which began with these words: "Marxism has been the greatest fantasy of our century." This struck me as the most personally courageous judgment a man with Kolakowski's history could make.

---

[12]Leszek Kolakowski, *Main Currents of Marxism*, 3 vols. Oxford University Press, 1978.

By the time I read your review of Kolakowski's book,[13] my own doubts had taken me to the perimeter of Kolakowski's position. Consequently, I approached your review in a mood of apprehension, even foreboding. For I already knew that this would be our final encounter on my way out of the community of the left—the last intellectual challenge I would have to meet.

It was appropriate that the final terrain of battle should be Marxism. Thompson had it right; our allegiance *was* to Marxism. Not to this particular thesis or that doctrinal principle, but to the paradigm itself: politics as civil war; history as a drama of social redemption.[14] If we remained in the ranks of the Marxist left, it was not because we failed to recognize the harsh facts that Marxists had created, but because we did not want to betray the vision that we shared with the creators.

And so the question that would irrevocably come to divide us was not whether Marxists had committed a revolutionary crime, or whether the revolutionary solution had veered off course; it was whether the Marxist Idea itself could be held accountable for the revolutions that had been perpetrated in its name. In the end, it was ideas that had made us what we were, and had given us the power of perennial rebirth. Movements rose and fell, but the ideas that generated them were immortal. And malleable as well. How easy it had proved in 1956 to discover humanitarian sentiments in Marx's writings and thus distance ourselves from Stalin's crimes; how simple to append the qualifier "democratic" to "socialist,"

---

[13]"Kolakowski's Anti-Marx," *Political Studies*, vol. XXIX, no. 1 (1981). Kolakowski's reply, "Miliband's Anti-Kolakowski," is printed in the same issue. A revised version of Miliband's review is printed in Ralph Miliband, *Class Power and State Power*, Verso Books, 1983.

[14]"At the core of Marxist politics, there is the notion of conflict [as] civil war conducted by other means. [Social conflict] is not a matter of 'problems' to be 'solved' but of a state of domination and subjection to be ended by a total transformation of the conditions which give rise to it." Ralph Miliband, *Marxism and Politics*, Oxford University Press, 1977, p. 17.

and thus escape responsibility for the bloody tyrannies that socialists had created.

It was on this very point that Kolakowski had thrown down his
gauntlet, declaring that Marx's ideas could not be rescued from the
human ruins they had created—that "the primordial intention" of
Marx's dream was itself "not innocent." History had shown, and
analysis confirmed, no reason to expect that socialism could ever
become real "except in the cruel form of despotism."[15] The idea of
socialism could not be freed from the taint incurred by its actual
practice and thus revitalized, as Thompson and the New Left proposed, because it was the idea that had created the despotism in
the first place. Marxism, as Kolakowski had announced at the outset of his book, was a vision that "began in Promethean humanism and culminated in the monstrous tyranny of Stalinism."

You understood the gravity of the challenge. The claim that the
Promethean project of the left led directly to the socialist debacle
depended on making two historical connections—between Marxism and Leninism, and between Leninism and Stalinism—thus
establishing the continuity of the radical fate. You were contemptuous in your response:

> To speak of Stalinism as following naturally and ineluctably from
> Leninism is unwarranted. However, to speak of Stalinism as 'one
> possible interpretation of Marx's doctrine' is not only unwar-
> ranted but false.

A decade has passed since you wrote this. In the East it is the
era of *glasnost*; the silence of the past is broken, the lies exposed.
The Soviets themselves now acknowledge the genesis of Stalinism
in Lenin. Yet, even if you were still tempted to resist this connec-

---

[15]Cited in Edward Palmer Thompson, *The Poverty of Theory*, Monthly
Review Press, 1978, p. 345. For Kolakowski's analysis of the impossibil-
ity of non-totalitarian Marxist socialism, see "The Myth of Human Self-
Identity" in Stuart Hampshire, ed. *The Socialist Idea*, Basic Books, 1975.
For Thompson's scholastic response to this argument, see Thompson,
op. cit.

tion, it would not detain us; for the real issue is the causal link between Marxism and Stalinism, encompassing both.

Stalinism is not a possible interpretation of Marx. What could you have been thinking to have written this, to have blotted out so much of the world we know? Forget the Soviet planners and managers who architected the Stalinist empire and found a rationale in Marx's texts for all their actions and social constructions—including the Party dictatorship and the political police, the collectivization and the terror, the show trials and the *gulag.* These, after all, were practical men, accustomed to bending doctrine in the service of real-world agendas. Consider, instead, the movement intellectuals—the complex nouns who managed to be Marxists *and* Stalinists through all the practical nightmares of the socialist epoch: Althusser and Brecht, Lukacs and Gramsci, Bloch and Benjamin, Hobsbawm and Edward Thompson too. Subtle Hegelians and social progressives, they were all promoters of the Stalinist cancer, devoting their formidable intellects and supple talents to its metastasizing terror. Were they illiterate to consider themselves Marxists *and* Stalinists? Or do you think they were merely corrupt? And what of the tens of thousands of Party intellectuals all over the world who were not so complex, among them Nobel Prize-winning scientists and renowned cultural artists who saw no particular difficulty in assimilating Stalin's gulag to Marx's utopia, socialist humanism to the totalitarian state? In obliterating the reality of these intellectual servants of socialist tyranny, you manifest a contempt for them far greater than that exhibited in the scorn of their most dedicated anti-Communist critics.

Stalinism is not just a *possible* interpretation of Marxism. In the annals of revolutionary movements it is without question the *prevailing* one. Of all the interpretations of Marx's doctrine since the *Communist Manifesto,* it is overwhelmingly the one adhered to by the most progressives for the longest time. Maoism, Castroism, Vietnamese Communism, the ideologies of the actually existing Marxist states—*these* Stalinisms are the Marxisms that shaped the history of the epoch just past. This is the truth that leftist intellectuals like you are determined to avoid: the record of the real lives of real human beings, whose task is not just to interpret texts but to move masses and govern them. When Marxism has been put into practice by real historical actors, it has invariably taken a Stalinist form, producing the worst tyrannies and oppressions that mankind has ever known. Is there a reason for this? Given the weight of this history, you should rather ask yourself: *How could there not be?*

What persuaded us to believe that socialism, having begun everywhere so badly, should possess the power to reform itself into something better? To pass through the *inferno* of its Stalinist tragedies to become the *paradiso* of our imaginations? To be something other than what it has always been?

For we did believe in such a transformation. We were confident that the socialized foundations of Soviet society would eventually assert themselves, producing a self-reform of the Soviet tyranny. This was our New Left version of the faith we inherited. This refusal to accept history's verdict made socialism a reality still. In the Sixties, when the booming capitalist societies of the West made radical prospects seem impossibly remote, we had a saying among us that the first socialist revolution was going to take place in the Soviet Union.

The lineage of these ideas could be traced back to our original complex noun, Trotsky: the legend of the revolution who had defied Stalin's tyranny in the name of the revolution. While the Father of the Peoples slaughtered millions in the 1930s, Trotsky waited in his Mexican exile for Russia's proletariat to rise up and restore the revolution to its rightful path. But as the waves of the Opposition disappeared into the *gulag,* and this prospect became impossibly remote, even Trotsky began to waver in his faith.

By the eve of the Second World War, Trotsky's despair had grown to such insupportable dimensions that he made a final wager with himself. The conflict the world had just entered would be a test for the socialist faith. If the great war did not lead to a new revolution, socialists would be compelled, finally, to concede their defeat—to admit that "the present USSR was the precursor of a new and universal system of exploitation," and that the socialist program had "petered out as a Utopia."[16]

Trotsky did not survive to see the end of the war and the unraveling of his Marxist dreams. In 1940 his dilemma was resolved when one of Stalin's agents gained entrance to the fortress of his exile in Mexico, and buried an ice pick in his head.

But the fantasy survived. In 1953 Stalin died and a new left generation convinced itself that the long-awaited metamorphosis was at last taking place.

With Stalin's death came the Khrushchev thaw, the famous speech lifting the veil on the bloody past, and a relaxation of the Stalinist terror. To those on the left who had refused to give up, these were signs that the totalitarian caterpillar, having lodged itself in the cocoon of a backward empire, was about to become the socialist butterfly of which they had dreamed.

We had our own complex noun to explain the transformation. Our mutual friend, Isaac Deutscher, had emerged from the pre-war battles over Trotskyism to become the foremost interpreter of the Russian Revolution to our radical generation. What made Deutscher's analysis so crucial to the self-understanding behind our revival was that he recognized the fact that Stalinism, in all its repugnance, was Marxist reality and had to be accepted as such. You, too, accepted this then, though it has become convenient for you to deny it now; just as you had embraced the Leninist version of Marx's doctrine as the only socialist outlook that actually produced a revolution.

There were social-democrat Marxists, of course, who opposed Lenin and Stalin from the beginning. But you dismissed them as sentimentalists—"socialists of the hearth," you called them—

---

[16]Leon Trotsky, *In Defence of Marxism*, cited in Isaac Deutscher, *The Prophet Outcast: Trotsky: 1929–1940*, Oxford University Press, 1963, p. 468.

reformers who were content to tinker with capitalism and lacked the fortitude to make a revolution.

Deutscher began with the reality that was given to us: the fact of Stalinism, as it had taken root in the Empire of the Czars. But instead of despairing like his mentor Trotsky, Deutscher began to explain why Stalinism, in spite of itself, was being transformed into socialism. In Trotsky's own theories Deutscher had found an answer to Trotsky's pessimism. While Trotsky worried that there would be no revolution from below, Deutscher explained to us why it was coming from above.

Stalinism, Deutscher wrote, was "an amalgamation of Marxism with the semi-barbarous and quite barbarous traditions and the primitive magic of an essentially pre-industrial [society]." In short, Stalinism was the fulfillment of Lenin's famous prescription: *With barbarism we will drive barbarism out of Russia.*

> Under Stalinism ... Russia rose to the position of the world's second industrial power. By fostering Russia's industrialization and modernization Stalinism had with its own hands uprooted itself and prepared its 'withering away.'[17]

The backwardness of Russian society had provided the Bolsheviks not only with a revolutionary opportunity but also with an historical advantage. They could avail themselves of modern technologies and social theories. Instead of relying on the anarchic impulses of capitalist investment, they could employ the superior methods of socialist planning. The result of these inputs would be a modern economy more efficient and productive than those of their capitalist competitors.

---

[17]Isaac Deutscher, "The Meaning of De-Stalinization," *Ironies of History*, Oxford University Press, 1966, p. 21. Cf. Deutscher, *The Prophet Outcast*, op. cit. p. 521: "Through the forcible modernization of the structure of society Stalinism had worked towards its own undoing and had prepared the ground for the return of classical Marxism." Lenin cited in Kolakowski, op. cit. Vol. II, p. 486.

According to Deutscher, in mid-century the socialist bloc, which had hitherto provided such grief for radicals like us, was poised for a great leap forward:

> With public ownership of the means of production firmly established, with the consolidation and expansion of planned economy, and—last but not least—with the traditions of a socialist revolution alive in the minds of its people, the Soviet Union breaks with Stalinism in order to resume its advance towards equality and socialist democracy.

The ultimate basis of this transformation was the superior efficiency of socialist planning:

> [Superior] efficiency necessarily translates itself, albeit with a delay, into higher standards of living. These should lead to the softening of social tensions, the weakening of antagonisms between bureaucracy and workers, and workers and peasants, to the further lessening of terror, and to the further growth of civil liberties.[18]

Deutscher wrote these words in 1957, a year in which the Soviets celebrated the fortieth anniversary of the revolution by launching the first space satellite into orbit. The feat dramatized the progress that had been achieved in a single generation and heralded the end of the Soviets' technological "apprenticeship" to the West. The message of Sputnik to the faithful all over the world, Deutscher predicted, was "that things may be very different for them in the second half of the century from what they were in the first."

For forty years, their cause had been "discredited ... by the poverty, backwardness, and oppressiveness of the first workers' state." But that epoch was now coming to an end. With the industrial leap heralded by Sputnik, they might look forward to a time when the appeal of Communism would be "as much enhanced by Soviet wealth and technological progress as the attraction of bour-

---

[18]Deutscher, *Ironies of History*, op. cit. p.58.

geois democracy has in our days been enhanced by the fact that it has behind it the vast resources of the United States."[19]

This was the vision of the socialist future that the Soviet leadership itself promoted. In 1961, Khrushchev boasted that the socialist economy would "bury" its capitalist competitors and that by 1980 the Soviet Union would overtake the United States in economic output and enter the stage of "full communism," a society of true abundance whose principle of distribution would be "from each according to his ability, to each according to his needs."

As New Leftists, we took Khrushchev's boast with a grain of salt. The Soviet Union was still a long way from its Marxist goals. Moreover, as Deutscher had warned, any future Soviet progress might be "complicated, blurred, or periodically halted by the inertia of Stalinism, by war panics, and, more basically, by the circumstance that the Soviet Union still remains in a position of overall economic inferiority vis-à-vis its American antipode."[20]

Actual socialism was still a myth that Stalinism had created. But it had a redeeming dimension: the myth had helped "to reconcile the Soviet masses to the miseries of the Stalin era" and Stalinist ideology had helped "to discipline morally both the masses and the ruling group for the almost inhuman efforts which assured the Soviet Union's spectacular rise from backwardness and poverty to industrial power and greatness."[21]

To us, Deutscher's assessment was even more intoxicating than the Khrushchev myth. Its mix of optimism and "realism" became the foundation of our political revival. The turn Marxism had taken in 1917, creating a socialist economy within a totalitarian state, had posed a seemingly insoluble riddle. How could

---

[19]Deutscher, *Ironies of History*, op cit. "Four Decades of the Revolution," p. 58.
[20]Ibid. p. 58.
[21]"The Irony of History in Stalinism" (1958) in *Ironies of History*, Oxford University Press, 1966.

socialist progress be reconciled with such a stark retreat into social darkness? What did this portend for Marx's insight that the mode of production determined the architecture of social relations? Building on Trotsky's prior analysis, Deutscher pointed to what seemed to be the only way out of the dilemma that would preserve our radical faith.

And no doubt that is why, thirty years later, even as the tremors of *glasnost* and *perestroika* were unhinging the empire that Communists had built, you returned to Deutscher's prophecy as a revolutionary premise. "Much that is happening in the Soviet Union constitutes a remarkable vindication of [Deutscher's] confidence that powerful forces for progressive change would eventually break through seemingly impenetrable barriers."[22]

Nothing could more clearly reveal how blind your faith has made you. To describe the collapse of the Soviet Empire as a vindication of Deutscher's prophecies—and so of the Marxist tradition that underpins them—is to turn history on its head. We are indeed witnessing a form of "revolution from above" in the Soviet Union, but it is a revolution that refutes Deutscher *and* Marx. The events of the past years are not a triumph for socialism. The rejection of planned economy by the leaders of actually existing socialist society; the pathetic search for the elements of rule by law, following the relentless crusades against "bourgeois rights;" the humiliating admission that the military superpower is in all other respects a third-world nation; the incapacity of the socialist mode of production to enter the technological future; and the unseemly begging for the advanced technology that it has stolen for decades from the capitalist West—all this adds up to a declaration of socialism's utter bankruptcy and historic defeat. This bankruptcy is not only moral and political, as before, but now economic as well.

---

[22]Ralph Miliband, Leo Panitch, John Saville, "Problems of Socialist Renewal: East and West," *Socialist Register*, Vol. 24, 1988, http://social-istregister.com/index.php/srv/article/download/5910/2806.

It is precisely this economic bankruptcy that Deutscher did not foresee, and that forecloses any possibility of a socialist revival. For all of these post-Khrushchev decades, that revival has been premised on the belief in the superiority of socialist economics. This is the meaning of the claim, so often repeated in leftist quarters, that the "economic rights" and "substantive freedoms" of socialist states took precedence over the political rights and merely procedural freedoms guaranteed by the capitalist West. Faith in the socialist future had come to rest on the assumption that abundance would eventually flow from the cornucopia of socialist planning and that economic abundance would then lead to political deliverance—the Deutscherian thesis.

In our New Left fantasies the political nightmare of the socialist past was to be redeemed by the *deus ex machina* of socialist plenty. The present economic bankruptcy of the Soviet bloc puts this faith finally to rest and brings to an end the socialist era in human history.

This is the reality you have not begun to face.

It is important to understand this reality, which signals the close of an historical era. But this can be accomplished only if we do not deny the history we have lived. You can begin this retrieval of memory by recalling your critique of Kolakowski ten years ago, which set down the terms of your defense of the cause to which we were all so dedicated.

Your complaint against Kolakowski, you remember, was that in demolishing the edifice of Marxist theory he had slighted the motives of those who embraced it and thus failed to explain its ultimate appeal. Kolakowski had portrayed Marxism as the secular version of a religious quest that went back to the beginning of human history: how to reconcile contingent human existence to an essence from which it was estranged—how to return humanity to its true self. For Kolakowski, Marxism was the messianic faith of a post-religious world.

Naturally, such an explanation would be insulting to you. You rejected it as "superficial," inadequate (you said) to explain Marxism's attraction to "so many gifted people." In your view, Marxism's appeal was not to those hungry for religious answers, but to people who responded to the call "to oppose great evils and to create conditions for a different kind of world, from which such evils would be banished." The call to fight these evils was the crucial factor in enlisting people in the cause of the left, and you named them: "exploitation, poverty and crisis, war and the threat of war, imperialism and fascism, the crimes of the ruling classes."[23]

Let us pass for a moment over the most dramatic of these evils—exploitation, crisis, war, imperialism, fascism, and the crimes of "ruling classes," including the vast privileges of the *nomenklatura*—from which you will agree Marxist societies themselves have not been free since their creation. Let us consider, rather, the simple poverty of ordinary people, whose redress was the most fundamental premise of the revolutionary plan. Let us look at what has been revealed by *glasnost* about the quality of the ordinary lives of ordinary people after 70 years of socialist effort—not forgetting that 40 million human beings (the figure is from current Soviet sources) were exterminated to make possible this revolutionary achievement.

Official statistics released during *glasnost* indicate that after 70 years of socialist development, 40 percent of the Soviet population and 79 percent of its older citizens live in poverty.[24] (Of course, judged by the standards of "exploitative" capitalist systems, the entire Soviet populace lives in a state of poverty.)

---

[23]"Kolakowski's Anti-Marx," op. cit.
[24]Zbigniew Brzezinski, *The Grand Failure: The Birth and Death of Communism in the Twentieth Century*, Charles Scribner's Sons, 1989, p. 237; For facts about Soviet society cited below, cf. also "Social and Economic Rights in the Soviet Bloc," special issue of *Survey Magazine*, Issue 127, August 1987; Richard Pipes, "Gorbachev's Russia: Breakdown or Crackdown?" *Commentary*, March 1, 1990, https://www.commentary-magazine.com/article/gorbachevs-russia-breakdown-or-crackdown/; Walter Laqueur, *The Long Road to Freedom: Russia and Glasnost*, Scribner, 1989; *Wall Street Journal*, June 28, 1989.

Thus, the Soviet Union's per capita income is estimated by Soviet economists as about one-seventh that of the United States, somewhere on a par with Communist China.[25]

In the Soviet Union in 1989 there was rationing of meat and sugar, *in peacetime;* the rations revealed that the average intake of red meat for a Soviet citizen was *half* of what it had been for a subject of the czar in 1913. At the same time, a vast supermarket of fruits, vegetables and household goods, available to the most humble inhabitant of a capitalist economy, was permanently out of stock and thus out of reach for the people of the socialist state. Indeed, one of the principal demands of a Siberian miners' strike in 1989 was for an item as mundane and basic to a sense of personal well-being as a bar of soap.

In a land of expansive virgin forests, there was a toilet paper shortage. In an industrial country with one of the harshest and coldest climates in the world, two-thirds of the households had no hot water, and a third had no running water at all. Not only was the construction of housing notoriously shabby; space was so scarce, according to the government paper *Izvestia*, that a typical working-class family of four was forced to live for 8 years in a single 8-by-8-foot room, before marginally better accommodation became available. The housing shortage was so acute that at all times 17 percent of Soviet families had to be physically separated for want of adequate space.

After 50 years of socialist industrialization, the Soviet Union's per-capita output of non-military goods and services placed it somewhere between 50th and 60th among the nations of the world. More manufactured goods were exported annually by Taiwan, Hong Kong, South Korea and Switzerland, while blacks in apartheid South Africa owned more cars per capita than did citizens of the socialist state.

---

[25]Robert Heilbroner, "After Communism," *The New Yorker*, September 10, 1990, p. 91, http://www.newyorker.com/magazine/1990/09/10/after-communism.

The only area of consumption in which the Soviets excelled was the ingestion of hard liquor. In this they led the world by a wide margin, consuming 17.4 liters of pure alcohol or 43.5 liters of vodka per person per year, which was five times what their forebears had consumed in the days of the czar. At the same time, the average welfare mother in the United States received more income in a month than the average Soviet worker could earn in a year.

Nor was the general deprivation confined to households and individual consumption. The "public sector" was equally desolate. In the name of progress, the Soviets devastated the environment to a degree unknown in other industrial states. More than 70 percent of the Soviet atmosphere was polluted with five times the permissible limit of toxic chemicals, and thousands of square miles of the Soviet land mass was poisoned by radiation. Thirty percent of all Soviet foods contained hazardous pesticides and six million acres of productive farmland were lost to erosion. More than 130 nuclear explosions had been detonated in European Russia for geophysical investigations to create underground pressure in oil and gas fields, or just to move earth for building dams. The Aral Sea, the world's largest inland body of water, was dried up as the result of a misguided plan to irrigate a desert. Soviet industry operated under no controls and the accidental spillage of oil into the country's ecosystems took place at the rate of nearly a million barrels a day.[26]

Even in traditional areas of socialist concern, the results were catastrophic. Soviet spending on health was the lowest of any developed nation, and basic health conditions were on a level with those in the poorest of third world countries. A third of the hospitals had no running water, the training of medical personnel was

---

[26]"No other great industrial civilization so systematically and so long poisoned its air, land, water and people. None so loudly proclaiming its efforts to improve public health and protect nature so degraded both. And no advanced society faced such a bleak political and economic reckoning with so few resources to invest toward recovery." Murray Feshbach and Alfred Friendly, Jr., *Ecocide in the USSR*, Basic Books, 1992, Ch. 1, p. 1.

poor, equipment was primitive and medical supplies scarce. US expenditures on medical technology alone were twice as much as the entire Soviet health budget.

The bribery of doctors and nurses to get decent medical attention and even amenities like blankets in Soviet hospitals was not only common, but routine. So backward was Soviet medical care, 30 years after the launching of Sputnik, that 40 percent of the Soviet Union's pharmacological drugs had to be imported, and much of these were lost to spoilage due to primitive and inadequate storage facilities.

Bad as these conditions were generally, in the ethnic republics they were even worse. In Turkmenistan, fully two-thirds of the hospitals had no indoor plumbing. In Uzbekistan, 50 percent of the villages were reported to have no running water and 93 percent no sewers. In socialist Tajikistan, according to a report in *Izvestia*, only 25-30 percent of the schoolchildren were found to be healthy. As a result of bad living conditions and inadequate medical care, life expectancy for males throughout the Soviet Union was 12 years less than for males in Japan, 9 years less than in the United States—and less for Soviet males themselves than in 1939.

Educational conditions were no less extreme. "For the country as a whole," according to one Soviet report, "21 percent of pupils are trained at school buildings without central heating, 30 percent without water piping and 40 percent lacking sewerage."[27] In other words, despite sub-zero temperatures, the socialist state was able to provide schools with only outhouse facilities for nearly half its children. Even at this impoverished level, only 9 years of secondary schooling were provided on average, compared to 12 years in the United States; while only 15 percent of Soviet youth were able to attend institutions of higher learning, compared to 34 percent in the U.S.

Education, housing and health are the areas traditionally emphasized by socialist politics because they affect the welfare of a people

---

[27]The USSR in Figures for 1987, 1988, p. 254.

and the foundations of its future. In Deutscher's schema, Soviet schools—"the world's most extensive and modern education system," as he described it—were the keys to its progressive prospect. But as *glasnost* revealed, Soviet spending on education had declined in the years since Sputnik, while US spending tripled. By the 1980s it was evident that education was no more exempt from the generalized poverty of socialist society than other non-military fields of enterprise. Seduced by Soviet advances in nuclear arms and military showpieces like Sputnik, Deutscher labored under the illusion of generations of the left. He too believed that the goal of revolutionary power was something other than power itself.

For years the left had decried the collusion between corporate and military interests in the capitalist West. But all that time the *entire* socialist economy was little more than one giant military-industrial complex. Military investment absorbed 25 percent of the Soviet gross product, compared to 6 percent in the United States; and military technology provided the only product competitive for export. Outside the military sector, as *glasnost* revealed, the vaunted Soviet industrial achievement was little more than a socialist mirage—imitative, archaic, inefficient and one-sided. It was presided over by a sclerotic *nomenklatura* of state planners, which was incapable of adjusting to dynamic technological change. In the Thirties, the political architects of the Soviet economy had over-built a heavy industrial base; and then, as if programmed by some invisible bureaucratic hand, rebuilt it again and again.

Straitjacketed by its central plan, the socialist world was unable to enter the "second industrial revolution" that began to unfold in countries outside the Soviet bloc after 1945. By the beginning of the 1980s, the Japanese already had 13 times the number of large computers per capita as the Soviets, and nearly 60 times the number of industrial robots— while the U.S. had three times the computer power of the Japanese.

"We were among the last to understand that in the age of information sciences the most valuable asset is knowledge, springing from human imagination and creativity," Soviet President Gorbachev complained in 1989. "We will be paying for our mistake for many years to come."[28]

While capitalist nations—including recent "third-world" economies like South Korea—were soaring into the technological future, Russia and its satellites, caught in the contradictions of an archaic mode of production, were stagnating into a decade of zero growth, becoming economic anachronisms; or what one analyst described as "a gigantic Soviet socialist rust belt."[29]

In the 1980s the Soviet Union had become a military superpower, but this achievement bankrupted its already impoverished society in the process. Nothing illustrated this bankruptcy with more poignancy than the opening of a McDonald's fast-food outlet in Moscow about the time the East Germans were pulling down the Berlin Wall. In fact, the semiotics of the two were inseparable. During the last decades of the Cold War, the Wall had come to symbolize the borders of the socialist world—the Iron Curtain that held its populations captive against the superiority of capitalist societies in the West. When the Wall was breached, the terror was over, and with it the only authority ever really commanded by the socialist world.

The appearance of the Moscow McDonald's revealed the prosaic truth that lay behind the creation of the Wall and the bloody epoch it had come to symbolize. Its Soviet customers gathered in lines whose length exceeded those waiting outside Lenin's tomb, the altar of the revolution itself. Here, the capitalist genius for catering to the ordinary desires of ordinary people was spectacularly displayed, along with socialism's relentless unconcern for the needs of common humanity. McDonald's executives even found it necessary to purchase and manage their own special farm in Russia, because Soviet potatoes—the very staple of the people's diet—were too poor in quality and unreliable in supply. On the

---

[28]Figures from Brzezinski, *The Grand Failure*, op. cit. p. 36 and George Gilder, "The American 80's: Disaster or Triumph?," in *Commentary*, September 1, 1990, https://www.commentarymagazine.com/article/the-american-80s-disaster-or-triumph/. Gorbachev cited by Gilder.

[29]Z (Martin Malia), "To the Stalin Mausoleum," *Daedalus*,, January 1990.

other hand, the wages of the Soviet customers were so depressed that a hamburger and fries cost half a day's pay. And yet this most ordinary of pleasures—the bottom of the food chain in the capitalist West—was still such a luxury for Soviet consumers that to them it was worth a four-hour wait and a four-hour wage.

Of all the symbols of the epoch-making year, this was perhaps the most resonant for leftists of our generation. Impervious to the way the unobstructed market democratizes wealth, the New Left had focused its scorn precisely on those plebeian achievements of consumer capitalism which brought services and goods efficiently and cheaply to ordinary people. Perhaps the main theoretical contribution of our generation of New Left Marxists was an elaborate literature of cultural criticism made up of sneering commentaries on the "commodity fetishism" of bourgeois cultures and the "one-dimensional" humanity that commerce produced. The function of such critiques was to let their authors feel superior to ordinary people governed by the principles of consumer sovereignty and market economy, which made them free.

For New Leftists, the leviathans of post-industrial alienation and oppression were precisely the "consumption-oriented" industries, like McDonald's, that offered inexpensive services and goods to the working masses—some, like the "Sizzler" restaurants, in the form of "all-you-can-eat" menus that embraced a variety of meats, vegetables, fruits and pastries virtually unknown in the Soviet bloc. These mundane symbols of consumer capitalism revealed the secret of the era that was now ending—the reason the Iron Curtain and its Berlin Walls were necessary.

The Cold War itself was an inevitable by-product of socialist rule. In 1989, for two hours' labor at the minimum wage, an American worker could obtain, at a corner "Sizzler," a feast more opulent, more nutritionally rich and gastronomically diverse than anything available to almost all the citizens of the socialist world, including the elite, at almost any price. In the counter-revolutionary year 1989, on the anniversary of the Revolution, a group of protesters raised a banner in Red Square that summed up an epoch:

Seventy Years on the Road to Nowhere. They had lived the socialist future and it didn't work.

This epic of human futility reached a climax that same year,
when the socialist state formally decided to return the land it had
taken from its peasants half a century before. The collectivization
of agriculture in the Thirties had been the very first pillar of the
socialist Plan and one of the bloodiest episodes of the revolutionary era. Armies were dispatched to the countryside to confiscate
the property of its recalcitrant owners, conduct mass deportations
to the Siberian gulag, liquidate the "kulaks" and herd the survivors into the collective farms of the Marxist future.

In this "final" class struggle, no method was considered too ruthless to midwife the new world from the old. "We are opposed by
everything that has outlived the time set for it by history," Maxim
Gorky wrote in the midst of battle. "This gives us the right to consider ourselves again in a state of civil war. The conclusion naturally
follows that if the enemy does not surrender, he must be destroyed."

The destruction of the class enemy—the most numerous and
productive element of Soviet society at the time—was accomplished
by massacres, by slow deaths in concentration camps and by deliber-
ately induced genocidal famine. In the end, more than 10 million
people were killed; more than had died on all sides in World War I.[30]

But the new serfdom the Soviet rulers imposed in the name of
liberation only destroyed the peasants' freedom and incentive, and
thus laid the foundations of the final impasse. Before collectivization, Russia had been the "breadbasket of Europe," supplying 40
percent of the world's wheat exports in the bumper years 1909 and
1910.[31] But socialism ended Russia's agrarian plenty and created
permanent deficits—not merely the human deficit of those who

---

[30]Robert Conquest, *The Harvest of Sorrow: Soviet Collectivization and
the Terror-Famine,* Oxford University Press, 1986; Nekrich and Geller,
*Utopia in Power: The History of the Soviet Union from 1917 to the Pres-
ent,* Summit Books, 1986.

[31]John Gray, "Totalitarianism, Reform and Civil Society," in *Totalitarianism at the Crossroads,* Ellen Frankel Paul, ed., Transaction Books, 1990.

perished because of Stalinist brutalities during the collectivization, but a deficit in grain that would never be brought to harvest
because of the brutality inherent in the socialist idea. Half a century after the socialist future had been brought to the countryside,
the Soviet Union had become a net *importer* of grain, unable to
produce enough to feed its own population.

These deficits eventually forced the state to allow a portion of the
crop to be sold on the suppressed private market. Soon, 25 percent of
Soviet grain was being produced on the 3 percent of the arable land
reserved for private production. Thus necessity had compelled the
Soviet rulers to create a dramatic advertisement for the system they
despised. They had rejected the productive efficiencies of the capitalist system as exploitative and oppressive. Yet the socialist redistrib-
ution of wealth had produced neither equity nor justice, but scarcity
and waste. At the end of the 1980s, amidst growing general crisis,
Soviet youth were using bread as makeshift footballs because its
price had been made so low—to satisfy the demands of social
equity—that it was now less than the cost of the grain to produce it.

This was a microcosm of socialist economy. Irrational prices,
bureaucratic chaos and generalized public cynicism—the actually
existing socialist ethos in all Marxist states—had created an environment in which 40 percent of the food crop was lost to spoilage
before ever reaching the consumer. And so, half a century after 10
million people had been killed to "socialize the countryside,"
those who had expropriated the land were giving it back.

The road to nowhere had become a detour. (*Soviet joke: What is
socialism? The longest road from capitalism to capitalism.*) Now
the Soviet rulers themselves had begun to say that it had all been a
horrible "mistake." Socialism did not work. Not even for them.

Of all the scenarios of the Communist *Götterdämmerung*, this
denouement had been predicted by no one. Ruling classes invariably held fast to the levers of their power. They did not confess
their own bankruptcy and then proceed to dismantle the social
systems that sustained their rule, as this one had. The reason for
the anomaly was this: the creators and rulers of the Soviet Union

had indeed made a mistake. The system did not work, not even in terms of sustaining the power of its ruling class.

The close of the Soviet drama was unpredicted because the very nature of the Soviet Union was without precedent. It was not an organic development but an artificial creation—the first society in history to be dreamed up by intellectuals and constructed according to plan. The crisis of Soviet society was not so much a traditional crisis of legitimacy and rule as it was the crisis of an *idea* – a monstrously wrong idea that had been imposed on society by an intellectual elite; an idea so passionately believed, and yet so profoundly mistaken, that it had caused more human misery and suffering than any single force in history before.

This suffering could not be justified by the arguments of the left that the revolutionary changes were "at least an improvement on what existed before." Contrary to the progressive myth that radicals invented to justify their failures, Czarist Russia was not a merely pitiful, semi-barbaric state when the socialists seized power. By 1917, Russia was already the fourth industrial power in the world. Its rail networks had tripled since 1890, and its industrial output had increased by three-quarters since the century began. Over half of all Russian children between eight and eleven years of age were enrolled in schools, while 68 percent of all military conscripts had been tested literate. A cultural renaissance was underway in dance, painting, literature and music; the names Blok, Kandinsky, Mayakovsky, Pasternak, Diaghilev, Rachmaninov and Stravinsky were already figures of world renown.

In 1905, a constitutional monarchy with an elected parliament had been created in which freedom of the press, assembly and association were guaranteed, if not always observed. By 1917 legislation to create a welfare state, including the right to strike and provisions for workers' insurance was already in force; and before it was dissolved by Lenin's Bolsheviks, Russia's first truly democratic parliament had been convened.[32]

---

[32]Nekrich and Geller, op. cit. pp. 15–17.

The Marxist Revolution destroyed all this, tearing the Russian people out of history's womb and robbing whole generations of their minimal birthright, the opportunity to struggle for a decent life. Yet even as this political abortion was being completed and the nation was plunging into its deepest abyss, the very logic of revolution forced its leaders to expand their lie: to insist that the very nightmare they had created was indeed the kingdom of freedom and justice the revolution had promised.

It is in this bottomless chasm between reality and promise that our own argument is finally joined. You seek to separate the terror-filled actualities of the Soviet experience from the magnificent harmonies of the socialist dream. But it is the dream itself that begets the reality, and requires the terror. This is the revolutionary paradox you want to ignore.

Isaac Deutscher had actually appreciated this revolutionary equation, but without ever comprehending its terrible finality. The second volume of his biography of Trotsky opens with a chapter he called "The Power and The Dream." In it, he described how the Bolsheviks confronted the situation they had created: "When victory was theirs at last, they found that revolutionary Russia had overreached herself and was hurled down to the bottom of a horrible pit." Seeing that the revolution had only increased their misery, the Russian people began asking: *"Is this ... the realm of freedom? Is this where the great leap has taken us?"* The leaders of the Revolution could not answer. "[While] they at first sought merely to conceal the chasm between dream and reality [they] soon insisted that the realm of freedom had already been reached—and that it lay there at the bottom of the pit. 'If people refused to believe, they had to be made to believe by force.'"[33]

---

[33]Isaac Deutscher, *The Prophet Unarmed: Trotsky: 1921–1929*, Vintage Books, 1965, pp. 1–2. The internal quote refers to a passage from Machiavelli that Deutscher had used as an epigraph to *The Prophet Armed:* "... the nature of the people is variable, and whilst it is easy to persuade them, it is difficult to fix them in that persuasion. And thus it is necessary to take such measures that, when they believe no longer, it may be possible to make them believe by force."

So long as the revolutionaries continued to rule, they could not admit that they had made a mistake. Though they had cast an entire nation into a living hell, they had to maintain the liberating truth of the socialist idea. And because the idea was no longer believable, they had to make the people believe by force. It was the socialist idea that created the terror.

Because of the nature of its political mission, this terror was immeasurably greater than the repression it replaced. Whereas the czarist police had several hundred agents at its height, the Bolshevik *Cheka* began its career with several hundred *thousand.* Whereas the czarist secret police had operated within the framework of a rule of law, the *Cheka* (and its successors) did not. The czarist police repressed extra-legal opponents of the political regime. To create the socialist future, the *Cheka* targeted whole social categories—regardless of individual behavior or attitude—for liquidation.

The results were predictable. "Up until 1905," wrote Aleksandr Solzhenitsyn in his monumental record of the Soviet *gulag,* "the death penalty was an exceptional measure in Russia." From 1876 to 1904, 486 people were executed—17 people a year, for the whole country—a figure which included the executions of non-political criminals. During the years of the 1905 revolution and its suppression, "the number of executions rocketed upward, astounding Russian imaginations, calling forth tears from Tolstoy [and] many others; from 1905 through 1908 about 2,200 persons were executed—forty-five a month. This, as Tagantsev said, was an *epidemic of executions.* It came to an abrupt end."[34]

But then came the Bolshevik seizure of power. "In a period of sixteen months (June 1918 to October 1919) more than sixteen thousand persons were shot, which is to say *more than one thousand a month.*" These executions, carried out by the *Cheka* without trial and by revolutionary tribunals without due process, were

---

[34]Aleksandr Solzhenitsyn, *The Gulag Archipelago,* Harper and Row, 1973, Vol. I. pp. 433 et seq.

executions of people exclusively accused of political crimes. And this was only a drop in the sea of executions to come. The true figures will never be known, but in the two years 1937 and 1938, according to the executioners themselves, half a *million* 'political prisoners' were shot, or 20,000 a month.

To measure these deaths on an historical scale, Solzhenitsyn compared them to the horrors of the Spanish Inquisition, which during the 80-year peak of its existence condemned an average of 10 heretics a month.[35] The difference was this: The Inquisition only forced unbelievers to believe in a world unseen; Socialism demanded that they believe in the very lie that the revolution had condemned them to live.

The author of our century's tragedy is not Stalin or even Lenin. Its author is the political left, the one we belonged to, which was launched at the time of Gracchus Babeuf and the Conspiracy of the Equals, and has continued its assault on bourgeois order ever since. The reign of socialist terror is the responsibility of all those who have promoted the Socialist idea, which required so much blood to implement, and then did not work in the end.

But if socialism was a mistake, it was never merely innocent in the sense that its consequences could not have been foreseen. From the very beginning, before the first drop of blood had ever been spilled, the critics of socialism had warned that it would end in tyranny and that economically it would not work. In 1844, Marx's collaborator Arnold Ruge warned that Marx's dream would result in "a police and slave state." And in 1872 Marx's arch-rival in the First International, the anarchist Bakunin, described with penetrating acumen the future that Marx had in mind:

> This government will not content itself with administering and governing the masses politically, as all governments do today. It will also administer the masses economically, concentrating in the hands of the State the production and division of wealth, the

---

[35]Ibid. p. 435n.

cultivation of land.... All that will demand ... the reign of *scientific intelligence,* the most aristocratic, despotic, arrogant, and elitist of all regimes. There will be a new class, a new hierarchy ... the world will be divided into a minority ruling in the name of knowledge, and an immense ignorant majority. And then, woe unto the mass of ignorant ones![36]

If a leading voice in Marx's own International could see with such clarity the oppressive implications of his revolutionary idea, there was no excuse for the generations of Marxists who promoted the idea even after it had been put into practice and the blood began to flow. But the idea was so seductive that even Marxists who opposed Soviet Communism continued to support it, saying this was not the actual socialism that Marx had in mind, even though Bakunin had seen that it was.

So powerful was the socialist idea that even those on the left who took their inspiration from Bakunin rather than Marx, and later opposed the Communists, could not bring themselves to defend the democratic societies of the capitalist West that the Marxists had put under siege. Like Bakunin they were sworn enemies of capitalism, the only industrial system that was democratic and that worked. Yet their remedy for its deficiencies—abolishing private property and the economic market—would have meant generalized poverty and revolutionary terror as surely as the statist fantasies of Marx. By promoting the socialist idea of the future, and by participating in the war against the capitalist present, these non-Marxist soldiers of the political left became partners in the very tragedy they feared.

Of all Marx's critics, it was only the partisans of bourgeois order who understood the mistake that socialists had made and thus appreciated the only practical, therefore real, bases of human freedom: private property and the market economy.

---

[36]Sam Dolgoff, ed. *Bakunin on Anarchy,* Alfred A. Knopf, 1972, p. 319; emphasis in original.

In 1922, as the Bolsheviks completed the consolidation of their political power, the Austrian economist Ludwig von Mises published his classic indictment of the socialist idea and its destructive consequences. Von Mises already knew that socialism could not work, and that no amount of bloodshed and repression could prevent its eventual collapse. "The problem of economic calculation," he wrote, "is the fundamental problem of socialism," and cannot be solved by socialist means. "Everything brought forward in favor of Socialism during the last hundred years, [all] the blood which has been spilt by the supporters of socialism, cannot make socialism workable." Advocates of socialism might continue "to paint the evils of Capitalism in lurid colors" and contrast them with an enticing picture of socialist blessings, "but all this cannot alter the fate of the socialist idea."[37]

Von Mises's thesis was elaborated and extended by the former socialist Friederich von Hayek, who argued that the information conveyed through the price system was so complex, and was changing so dynamically, that no planning authority, even with the aid of the most powerful computers conceivable, could ever succeed in replicating information that the market provided.[38]

Across the vast empire of societies that have put the socialist idea to the test, its fate is now obvious to all. Von Mises, Hayek, Polanyi and other prophets of capitalist economy are now revered throughout the Soviet bloc, even as the names of Marx, Lenin and Trotsky are despised. Their works—once circulated only in *samizdat* —were among the first to be liberated under *glasnost.* Yet in the socialist and Marxist press of the West, in articles like yours and in the efforts of your comrades to analyze the "meaning" of the Communist crisis, the arguments by capitalist critics of socialism, who long ago demonstrated its impossibility and who have

---

[37]Ludwig von Mises, *Socialism: An Economic and Sociological Analysis,* J. Cape, 1936.

[38]Gray, op. cit.; Friedrich Hayek, *The Constitution of Liberty,* University Of Chicago Press, 1978; Friedrich Hayek, *Law, Legislation and Liberty,* Routledge and Kegan Paul, 1973, and other works.

now been proven correct, are nowhere considered. As if they had never been made.

For socialists like you to confront these arguments would be to confront the enormity of the history that has passed: The socialist idea has been, in its consequences, the worst and most destructive fantasy ever to have taken hold of the minds of men.

And it *is* the idea that Marx conceived. For 200 years, the Promethean project of the left has been just this: to abolish property and overthrow the market, and thereby to establish the reign of reason and justice embodied in a social plan. "In Marxist utopianism, communism is the society in which things are thrown from the saddle and cease to ride mankind. Men struggle free from their own machinery and subdue it to human needs and definitions." That is Edward Thompson's summary of Marx's famous text in the first volume of *Capital:*

> The life-process of society, which is based on the process of material production, does not strip off its mystical veil until it is treated as production by freely associated men, and is consciously regulated by them in accordance with a settled plan.[39]

The "fetishism of commodities" embodied in the market is, in Marx's vision, the economic basis of the alienation at the heart of man's estate: "a definite social relation between men, that assumes, in their eyes, the fantastic form of a relation between things."[40] The aim of socialist liberation is humanity's re-appropriation of its own activity and its own product—the re-appropriation of man by man—which can only be achieved when private property and the market are replaced by a governing plan.

The slogan Marx inscribed on the banners of the Communist future—"from each according to his ability, to each according to his needs"—is but an expropriated version of Adam Smith's Invisible Hand, under which the pursuit of individual interest leads to

---

[39]Karl Marx, *Capital: A Critique of Political Economy*, Modern Library, Revised ed. 1906, p. 80.
[40]Ibid. p. 72.

the fulfillment of the interests of all. But in the socialist future there is no market to rule over individual human passions and channel self-interest into social satisfaction, just as there is no rule of law to protect individual rights from the passions that rule the state. There is only the unmediated power of the socialist vanguard, exercised from the sanctuary of its bureaucratic throne.

All the theorizing about socialist liberation comes down to this: The inhabitants of the new society will be freed from the constraints of markets and the guidelines of tradition and bourgeois notions of rule under the law. They will be masters in their own house and makers of their own fate. But this liberation is, finally, a Faustian bargain because it will not work. Moreover, the effort to make it work will create a landscape of human suffering greater than any previously imagined.

Towards the end of his life, our friend Isaac Deutscher had a premonition of the disaster that has now overtaken the socialist left. In the conclusion to the final volume of his Trotsky trilogy, *The Prophet Outcast,* he speculated on the fate that would befall his revolutionary hero if the socialist project itself should fail:

> If the view were to be taken that all that the Bolsheviks aimed at—socialism—was no more than a *fata morgana,* that the revolution merely substituted one kind of exploitation and oppression for another, and could not do otherwise, then Trotsky would appear as the high priest of a god that was bound to fail, as Utopia's servant mortally entangled in his dreams and illusions.

But Deutscher did not have the strength to see the true dimensions of the catastrophe that socialism had in store. Instead, his realism only served to reveal the depths of self-delusion and self-justifying romanticism that provide sustenance for the left. Even if such a failure were to take place, he argued, the revolutionary hero "would [still] attract the respect and sympathy due to the great utopians and visionaries...."

Even if it were true that it is man's fate to stagger in pain and blood from defeat to defeat and to throw off one yoke only to bend his neck beneath another—even then man's longings for a different destiny would still, like pillars of fire, relieve the darkness and gloom of the endless desert through which he has been wandering with no promised land beyond.[41]

This is the true self-vision of the Left: An army of saints on the march against injustice, lacking on its own side the capacity for evil. The left sees its revolutions as pillars of fire that light up humanity's deserts but burn no civilizations as they pass. It lacks the ability to make the most basic moral accounting—the awareness that the Marxes, Trotskys and Lenins immeasurably increased the suffering of humanity, and destroyed even those blooms that existing civilizations had managed to put forth.

Without socialism, the peoples of the Russian Empire might have moved into the forefront of the modern industrial world—as the Japanese have—without the incalculable human cost. Instead, even the most productive of the Soviet satellites, East Germany— once the Prussian powerhouse of European industrialism—is now condemned to a blighted economic standard below that of Italy, South Korea or Spain.

Consider the history of our century. On whose heads does responsibility lie for all the blood that was shed to make socialism possible? If the socialist idea is a chimera and the revolutionary path is a road to nowhere, can revolutions themselves be noble or innocent even in intention? Can they be justified by the lesser but known evils they sought to redress? In every revolutionary battle in this century, the left has been a vanguard without a viable future to offer, whose only purpose was to destroy whatever civilization actually existed.

Consider: If no one had believed Marx's idea, there would have been no Bolshevik Revolution. Russia might have evolved into a

---

[41]Deutscher, *The Prophet Outcast*, op. cit. pp. 510–511.

modern democracy and industrial state; Hitler would not have come to power; there would have been no cold war.

It is hard not to conclude that most of the bloodshed of the 20th century might have been avoided. For seventy years the revolutionary left put its weight on one side in the international civil war that Lenin had launched. The left put itself against the side that promoted human freedom and industrial progress. And it did so in the name of an idea that could not work.

The communist idea is not the principle of the modern world, as Marx supposed. It is its anti-principle, the reactionary rejection of political individualism and the market economies of the liberal West. Wherever the revolutionary left has triumphed, its triumph has meant economic backwardness and social poverty, cultural deprivation and the loss of political freedom for all those unfortunate peoples under its yoke.

This is the real legacy of the left of which you and I were a part. We called ourselves progressives, and others did as well; but actually we were the reactionaries of the modern world whose first era has now drawn to a close.

The iron curtain that divided the prisoners of socialism from the free men and women of the West has now been torn down. The iron curtain that divides you and me remains. It is the destructive utopian fantasy that you refuse to give up.

Your ex-comrade,

David

TWO

Slavery and the American Idea

Someone is always at my elbow reminding me that I am
the granddaughter of slaves. It fails to register depression
with me. Slavery is sixty years in the past. The operation
was successful and the patient is doing well, thank you.
The terrible struggle that made me an American out of a
potential slave said "On the line!" The Reconstruction
said "Get set!" and the generation before said "Go!"
I am off to a flying start and I must not halt in the
stretch to look behind and weep. Slavery is the price
I paid for civilization, and the choice was not with me.
It is a bully adventure and worth all that
I have paid through my ancestors for it.
—ZORA NEALE HURSTON, "HOW IT FEELS TO BE COLORED ME," 1927

Since the 1960s, radicals have waged a ferocious assault on America's conception of itself as a beacon of freedom. To fuel this assault, academic leftists have created a vast corpus of social theory that recasts old Marxist ideas in new "post-modern" forms and reinterprets the narrative of American freedom as a chronicle of race, gender and class oppression. A nation

---

See Volume 6 in this series, *Progressive Racism, Part III: Reparations for Slavery*, for further discussion of these matters, including the fate of the reparations legislation and claims.

conceived in liberty is described as "a nation conceived in slavery;" a "nation of immigrants" becomes a nation of victims.[1]

In 2001 I conducted a campaign against the demand of the left
that reparations be paid to African Americans for the crime of slavery. The idea that living generations of African Americans who
were not slaves should be paid reparations by Americans who were
not slaveowners makes sense only in the framework of the left's
indictment of America as an oppressor nation. The reparations
claim is designed to support the left's attack by challenging America's self-image as a nation dedicated to equality and liberty—in
Abraham Lincoln's words, "the last best hope of mankind." It is
because Thomas Jefferson and Abraham Lincoln are the indispensable shapers of this American narrative that they are also the
principal targets of the reparations left.

The modern reparations movement was launched in 1969 by a
Sixties radical named James Forman. Forman interrupted a Sunday
morning service at New York's Riverside Church to read a "Black
Manifesto," which demanded $500 million from churches and
synagogues as "a beginning of the reparations due us as people
who have been exploited and degraded, brutalized, killed and per-
secuted."[2] Despite the radicalized atmosphere of the time, the
manifesto's demands remained then, and for many years after, the
expression of a political fringe. No element of the civil rights leadership—neither the NAACP, nor the Urban League, nor the Congress for Racial Equality—took up Forman's claim.

---

[1] James W. Loewen, *Lies My Teacher Told Me*, New Press 1995, p. 182.
Loewen is a professor of sociology at the University of Vermont. Promi-
nent left-wing historians who provided the scholarly basis for his revi-
sionist text are Howard Zinn *(A People's History of the United States)*,
Ronald Takaki *(A Different Mirror)*, Gary Nash *(Red, White and Black)*,
Francis Jennings *(The Invasion of America)*, and Kirkpatrick Sale *(The
Conquest of Paradise)*. Support for this anti-American text was provided
via two postdoctoral fellowships granted to Loewen by the Smithsonian
Institution.

[2] James Forman, *The Making of Black Revolutionaries*, Macmillan Company, 1972, pp. 343–352.

In 1988, when Congress passed legislation to provide payment to Japanese-American citizens who had been relocated for security reasons during World War II,[3] reparations advocates saw an opening. The following year, Democrat John Conyers introduced bill HR 40 to create a commission parallel to the one that had paved the way for Japanese Americans. The bill's stated purpose was to "acknowledge the fundamental injustice, cruelty, brutality, and inhumanity of slavery in the United States and the 13 American colonies between 1619 and 1865 and to establish a commission to examine the institution of slavery, subsequent *de jure* and *de facto* racial and economic discrimination against African Americans, to make recommendations to the Congress on appropriate remedies, and for other purposes."[4]

Thirty-eight Democratic congressmen signed on as co-sponsors of the Conyers reparations bill and thrust the issue into the political mainstream. A decade later, the cause had won the support of leading black intellectuals and professionals; by June 2001 Randall Robinson could accurately claim that "there is no major black organization that does not support reparations."[5]

---

[3]The decision to pay reparations to Japanese Americans relocated for security reasons during World War II is a cautionary tale of what happens to issues of justice in an inflamed political environment. In fact, no Japanese American was required to enter a relocation camp; only to leave coastal regions threatened by Japan. Many of those interned rejected oaths of allegiance to the United States, requested repatriation to Japan and organized political protests against the American war effort. In its decision to award reparations, Congress ignored the intelligence reports on which the relocation order was based—instead deciding that it was based solely on racial and ethnic prejudice, and making no distinction among the recipients as to whether they had actually obstructed the American war effort or were in fact a threat to the national security: Lowell Ponte, "MAGIC & Manzanar," FrontPageMag.com, July 2, 2001, http://archive.frontpagemag.com/readArticle.aspx?ARTID=21698.

[4]Randall Robinson, *The Debt: What America Owes to Blacks*, Dutton Adult, 2000, p. 201.

[5]Tamar Lewin, "Calls for Slavery Restitution Getting Louder," *The New York Times*, June 4, 2001, http://www.nytimes.com/2001/06/04/us/calls-for-slavery-restitution-getting-louder.html.

This dramatic change in the attitude of black leadership can be attributed to changes that took place in the civil rights movement after the death of Martin Luther King. Under King's stewardship, the civil rights movement had pursued a quintessentially conservative goal: fulfilling the promise of equality in the American founding. It was a promise that slavery, segregation and Jim Crow had thwarted, denying full citizenship rights to black Americans. With the passage of the Voting Rights Act and the elimination of legal discrimination, the civil rights movement confronted a dilemma. The rights of African Americans were now backed by the full power of the federal government, and there were thousands of black elected officials at all governmental levels. Black Americans were the heads of police departments and big-city school administrations. Blacks had become the chief executives of major American cities—including New York, Los Angeles, Chicago, Detroit, Baltimore, Cleveland, Philadelphia, Atlanta, Houston, Washington DC and even Selma, Alabama, the symbol of segregation's last stand. There were no longer institutional barriers to black progress that required legal redress. Within a generation, three quarters of America's black population had risen out of poverty, and by the 1980s the black middle class would outnumber the black lower classes for the first time in American history.[6] Public opinion polls began to register a seismic shift in white attitudes towards blacks on issues like integration and inter-marriage, showing dramatic increases in levels of tolerance and social acceptance that seemed unimaginable only a decade before King's triumph.[7] These new attitudes were also reflected in the implementation of affirmative-action programs designed "to redress past social injustices" and in massive government efforts to assist the underclass in which black Americans had been disproportionately represented.

---

[6] This remarkable story is told in Stephen and Abigail Thernstrom, *America in Black and White*, Simon & Schuster, 1997.
[7] Ibid.

Despite these successes, a significant segment of the black community continued to lag behind, and the problem of racial "gaps" did not go away. Inequalities in education, economic status, and criminal incarceration rates persisted, confronting black leadership with a crisis of identity and purpose. It was in its resolution of this crisis that post-King civil rights leaders found a direction that brought them to the reparations cause. In explaining the remaining gaps, civil rights leaders turned to "continuing American racism" as the root cause of these intractable disparities. The explanation served to lift the burden of accountability off those African Americans who had fallen behind, while any other perspective was quickly dismissed as "blaming the victim." Martin Luther King had resisted this racial determinism. "We know that there are many things wrong in the white world," King said, "but there are many things wrong in the black world, too. We can't keep on blaming the white man. There are things we must do for ourselves."[8] But the new leadership of the civil rights movement was determined to blame the white man.

Shelby Steele has described the doctrine of King's successors as a "totalist" view. In a totalist perspective, victimization explains both "the hard fate of blacks in American history" and "the current inequalities between blacks and whites and the difficulties blacks have in overcoming them."[9] People also suffer, as Steele observed, "from bad ideas, from ignorance, fear, a poor assessment of reality and from a politics that commits them to the idea of themselves as victims." When the idea that people are agents of their fate is replaced by the idea that they are merely objects—that "*all* suffering is victimization"—the inevitable conclusion is that

---

[8] Quoted in Jason L. Riley, "Don't Replace Jesse Jackson," *The Wall Street Journal*, April 18, 2001, http://www.siliconinvestor.com/readmsg.aspx?msgid=15689907; W.E.B. DuBois had a similar attitude.

[9] Shelby Steele, *A Dream Deferred: The Second Betrayal of Black Freedom in America*, Harper, 1998, pp. 10; 8–9.

relief comes from outside—from "the guilty good-heartedness of others."[10] This is the perverse symbiosis at the core of the reparations idea.

"The yawning economic gap between whites and blacks in this country ... was opened by the 246-year practice of slavery," Randall Robinson declared in *The Debt,* a book regarded as the manifesto of the reparations movement. "It has been resolutely nurtured since in law and public policy. It has now ossified. It is structural. Its framing beams are disguised only by the counterfeit manners of a hypocritical governing class."[11]

Every claim advanced in this statement is false. Does Robinson really believe that, before the arrival of slaves in Jamestown in 1619, there was *no* economic gap between Europeans who lived in an era of nascent capitalism and scientific revolution, and Africans whose pre-literate tribal cultures were still mired in the Bronze Age? After billions spent on affirmative-action programs, federal anti-discrimination laws and extensive social programs aimed at addressing racial barriers and deficits, how is it possible to say that the gap between blacks and whites has been "resolutely nurtured" for the last 136 years by "a hypocritical governing class"? And what exactly does the gap mean? Thomas Sowell has observed that, while scholars have studied racial and ethnic groups around the world, they have not been able to come up with a single country where the different groups have the same incomes and occupations. "Why would people from Africa be the lone exception on this planet? Groups everywhere differ too much in too many ways to have the same outcomes."[12]

---

[10]Ibid. p. 10. Emphasis in original.

[11]Robinson, *The Debt,* op. cit. p. 204. Americans, he writes, must first "accept that the gap derives from the social depredations of slavery." Ibid. p. 173.

[12]Thomas Sowell, "Reparations for Slavery," *Jewish World Review,* July 17, 2000, http://www.jewishworldreview.com/cols/sowell071700.asp; Sowell himself is probably the leading academic expert on the subject.

The length to which Robinson is willing to take the view that the lives of blacks can be explained in terms of their victimization by whites is apparently without limit. "What can we say to the black man on death row? The black mother alone, bitter, overburdened and spent? Who tells them that their fate washed ashore at Jamestown with twenty slaves in 1619?"[13] These statements imply that a black murderer in the 21st century commits his crime because his ancestors were dragged to America in chains. Is Robinson aware how absurd this sounds, and how insulting it is to the vast majority of black Americans who are descended from slaves but manage to be law-abiding citizens as well?

Nonetheless, the view that every inequality African Americans experience is a legacy of slavery and of white racism is shared by all reparations proponents and is the basis of their lawsuit against the United States. Harvard Law Professor Charles Ogletree is head of the Reparations Coordinating Committee, a team of high-powered class-action lawyers who prepared the lawsuit. When asked by a reporter why he thought the government should pay reparations, Ogletree said: "It's been 250 years of slavery, 100 years of Jim Crow legal segregation and we have not fully addressed or remedied the 350 years of direct suffering that African Americans have endured in the United States." Asked what he thought some of the lingering effects of slavery were, Ogletree replied: "Racial profiling, selective incarceration, disparate sentencing, inner city poverty, limited opportunities, the whole issue of economic inequality, substandard health care and other life-threatening health issues. Discriminatory lending practices, red-lining, and a host of other issues that are directly related to race. They are as apparent in the 21st century as they were in the 17th century."[14]

To read these fevered statements by reparations advocates is to realize that slavery is invoked in them not as a dark episode in the

---

[13]Ibid. pp. 216–7.
[14]Interview with Alex Kellogg, BET.com, April 11, 2001; Associated Press, November 5, 2000.

American past, but as an emblem of America that defines its racial present. In response to an appearance of mine at Arizona State University to oppose reparations, Professor Michael Eric Dyson told students: "[Americans] can't talk about slavery because it indicts the American soul."[15] An indictment of the American soul sums up in a sentence the true agenda of the reparations advocates. Accordingly, Randall Robinson's manifesto opens with the following declaration: "This book is about the great still-unfolding massive crime of official and unofficial America against Africa, African slaves, and their descendants in America."[16] Throughout his book, the theme is pounded home: "At long last, let America contemplate the scope of its enduring human-rights wrong against the whole of a people. Let the vision of blacks not become so blighted from a sunless eternity that we fail to see the staggering breadth of America's crime against us."[17] And further: the "enormous human- rights crime of slavery (later practiced as peonage) [has been] overlapped and extended by a century of government-sponsored segregation and general racial discrimination." In short, while black Americans suffered, their white American masters reaped the rewards of that suffering: "Of course, benefiting intergenerationally from this weather of racism were white Americans whose assets piled up like fattening snowballs over three and a half centuries' terrain of slavery and the mean racial climate that followed it."[18]

Robinson's assessment of the scope of America's malignancy is apparently boundless: "The enslavement of blacks in America

---

[15]Kevin Grant, "Socialist Professor Addresses Student Audience on Reparations and Race Relations," *Arizona State Press*, April 24, 2001. Dyson, a leading African-American intellectual, is a professor at DePaul University and was flown in at ASU's expense to provide a rebuttal to my case against reparations. Dyson is the author of books on Malcolm X and Martin Luther King, Jr. and the honorary co-chair of the Democratic Socialists of America.

[16]Robinson, *The Debt*, op. cit. p. 8. Emphasis added.

[17]Ibid. p. 9.

[18]Ibid. pp. 226, 227.

lasted 246 years. It was followed by a century of legal racial segregation and discrimination. The two periods, taken together, constitute the longest running crime against humanity in the world over the last 500 years...."[19] In short, white America's crime is more heinous than the Nazi Holocaust, the Soviet gulag, the Armenian genocide, the Cambodian killing fields, or the slave system in Africa itself.

As a matter of historical record, Africa's *internal* slave trade, which did not involve the United States or any European power, extended throughout the entire 500 years mentioned by Robinson as well as during the 1,000 years preceding it. African slavery continues to this day. In the period between 650 and 1600, *before* any Western involvement, somewhere between 3 million and 10 million African slaves were bought by Muslim slavers for use in Saharan societies and in the Indian Ocean and Red Sea commerce.[20] By contrast, the enslavement of blacks in independent America lasted 89 years, from 1776 until 1865—not 246 years, as Robinson claims.

According to history, the combined slave trade to the British colonies in North America and later to the United States accounted for less than 3 percent of the global trade in African slaves. The total number of slaves imported to North America was 800,000—less than the number of slaves brought to the island of Cuba alone. If one takes into account the *internal* African slave

---

[19]This statement was made at a TransAfrica reparations forum attended by the chief counsel for the National Coalition of Blacks for Reparations in America, a representative of the NAACP Legal Defense and Educational Fund, Conyers, Ogletree, William Fletcher, Assistant to the President of the AFL-CIO, Dorothy Height, Chair of the National Council of Negro Women, Wade Henderson, Executive Director Leadership Conference on Civil Rights, and professors Charles Lawrence and Mari Matsuda (the legal architects of campus speech codes). The forum was broadcast on C-Span, http://www.c-span.org/video/?155972-1/black-reparations; The transcript is available at: http://www.mdcbowen.org/p2/rap/transafrica_transcript.htm.

[20]Paul Lovejoy, *Transformations In Slavery: A History of Slavery in Africa*, Cambridge University Press, 2000, p. 25.

trade—which began in the 7th century and persists to this day in the Sudan, Mauritania and other sub-Saharan states—the responsibility of American slave-traders amounts to a fraction of one percent of the black African slavery problem.[21]

That an anti-American animus, rather than a desire for justice, is driving the reparations movement is also the clear message of another of its leaders: Dorothy Benton-Lewis, whom I debated at MIT. Lewis summed up her views in this terse and telling formulation: "Slavery and white supremacy are alive and well in America and the issue of reparations is about dealing with the truth and exposing this country for what it is."[22]

For what it is. Challenging this slander was the real offense of the campus ad campaign I conducted in the spring and fall of 2001 against the reparations claims.[23] What reparations supporters most fiercely objected to were the ad's reminders of the contributions Americans have made to the cause of human freedom—and therefore to the freedom of African Americans themselves. For the same reason, prominently featured in their own campaigns were attacks on the American Founders and on the constitutional framework they created. "George Washington is not *my* ancestor, private or public," proclaimed Randall Robinson to make the point as bluntly as possible. The fact that Washington was a slaveholder is evidently more important to Robinson than anything else he may have done, including his decision to free his slaves. Yet that decision obviously

---

[21]Robert Fogel, *Without Consent or Contract: The Rise and Fall of American Slavery*, W. W. Norton & Company, 1992, p. 7; Thomas Sowell, Race and Culture, Basic Books, 1994, p. 188; "Over the centuries, somewhere in the neighborhood of 11 million people were shipped across the Atlantic from Africa as slaves, and another 14 million African slaves were taken across the Sahara Desert or shipped through the Persian Gulf and other waterways to the nations of North Africa and the Middle East.".

[22]A. S. Wang and Dana Levine, "Horowitz, Benton-Lewis Debate," *The Tech*, Vol. 121, Issue 16, April 6, 2001.

[23]See Volume 6 in this series, *Progressive Racism, Part III: Reparations for Slavery*. Also David Horowitz, *Uncivil Wars: The Controversy Over Reparations For Slavery*, Encounter Books, 2001.

said more about the nature of the man and his legacy than the fact that he had owned slaves as a subject of the British Empire.

The most venomous rage in Robinson's *The Debt* is reserved for Thomas Jefferson, the author of the document that made the premise of human equality central to the American idea. It is *because* Jefferson is the author of the words "all men are created equal" that Robinson and other reparations advocates are inspired to condemn him. "Jefferson," writes Robinson, "was a slave-holder, a racist and—if one accepts that consent cannot be given if it cannot be denied—a rapist."[24] This alludes to a sexual liaison that Jefferson is alleged to have had with his slave Sally Hemings. It is possible that Jefferson did have such a relationship, but there is no evidence to establish this as a fact. The closest historians have come in linking Jefferson sexually to Hemings is DNA evidence that shows a Jefferson male to have fathered one of her children. But Thomas Jefferson is not the only male family member who enjoyed the proximity and had the opportunity to impregnate her.[25] Moreover, even if it was Jefferson who fathered the ancestor of Eston Hemings, there is no basis for Robinson's accusation that Sally Hemings was "raped." The very premise of Robinson's allegation is false, since consent *can* be given even in circumstances where it cannot be denied. Hemings could have been in love with Jefferson despite the fact that she was his slave. And vice versa. Such hazards of the human heart are excised from the ideologically flattened and spiteful world that Robinson inhabits.

To seal his indictment, Robinson adds a gratuitous afterthought, suggesting that Jefferson "could have killed Sally and

---

[24]Robinson, op. cit. p. 52.

[25]Another family suspect, Jefferson's brother Randolph, was known to have spent time in the slave quarters at Monticello. Scholars have been able to place him at the estate at the times Sally was impregnated. Still, Jefferson cannot be excluded as the possible father of Eston's ancestor. A prudent attitude would be to suspend judgment; cf. *The Jefferson-Hemings Scholars Commission Report*, April 12, 2001, http://www.cap-press.com/pdf/1179.pdf. The Commission exonerated Jefferson. The above information is provided in the lone dissent by historian Paul Rahe.

faced no consequences." This malicious statement only reveals his ignorance of the complex reality of slavery in the United States. The founders generally, and Jefferson in particular, did not regard slaves as mere property. Even states of the Deep South, like North Carolina, made the murder of slaves by their owners a punishable crime. In *Federalist* 2754, which was published the year the Constitution was adopted, James Madison wrote:

> We must deny the fact, that slaves are considered merely as property, and in no respect whatever as persons. The true state of the case is, that they partake of both these qualities: being considered by our laws, in some respects, as persons, and in other respects as property. In being compelled to labor, not for himself, but for a master; in being vendible by one master to another master; and in being subject at all times to be restrained in his liberty and chastised in his body, by the capricious will of another, the slave may appear to be degraded from the human rank, and classed with those irrational animals which fall under the legal denomination of property. In being protected, on the other hand, in his life and in his limbs, against the violence of all others, even the master of his labor and his liberty; and in being punishable himself for all violence committed against others, the slave is no less evidently regarded by the law as a member of the society, not as a part of the irrational creation; *as a moral person, not as a mere article of property.* (emphasis added)[26]

As throughout *The Debt*, Robinson's attack on slavery is really an attack on America: "Does not the continuing un-remarked deification of Jefferson tell us all how profoundly contemptuous of black sensibilities American society persists in being? How deeply, stubbornly, poisonously racist our society to this day remains?"[27] Such a statement is neither syntactically nor logically sound. Obviously, Americans' reverence for Jefferson tells us

---

[26]February 12, 1788. I am grateful to Thomas West for this reference. In the same *Federalist*, Madison characterized as "barbarous" the policy of treating other human beings as property.

[27]Robinson, *The Debt*, op. cit. p. 52.

about white America's embrace of his egalitarian aspirations and honors the guilt he and the signers of the Declaration of Independence felt about the institution of slavery.

Over a century ago, the emancipated slave Frederick Douglass had a very different assessment of Jefferson and the founders: "The anti-slavery movement has little to entitle it to being called a new thing under the sun.... The patriots of the American Revolution clearly saw, and with all their inconsistency, they had the grace to confess the abhorrent character of slavery, and to hopefully predict its overthrow and complete extirpation. Washington and Jefferson, Patrick Henry and Luther Martin, Franklin, and Adams, Madison and Monroe, and a host of the earlier statesmen, jurists, scholars and divines of the country, were among those who looked forward to this happy consummation."[28] Douglass's view connects the destiny of liberated slaves to America's own aspirations as a nation, which is precisely the vision that anti-American ideologues like Robinson seek to suppress.

The hatred exhibited by Robinson and other reparations spokesmen for the author of the Declaration of Independence is complemented by a parallel antipathy towards the architect of emancipation and the "second American founding"—Abraham Lincoln. The intellectual generalship of this assault has fallen to historian Lerone Bennett, Jr., who is also the executive editor of the leading black magazine *Ebony*. Bennett was one of three witnesses to testify at the hearings preceding a Chicago City Council resolution on reparations. He told the council that American slavery was "the greatest crime in human history"[29]—a patent falsehood, since it was not even the greatest crime in the annals of black slavery. Recently, *Ebony*'s publishing company, which is the

---

[28]Philip S. Foner, ed. *Frederick Douglass: Selected Speeches and Writings*, Chicago Review Press, 1999, p. 31.

[29]"Politicians, Scholars Voice Support for Slavery Reparation," *Jetonline!*, May 15, 2000, http://www.highbeam.com/doc/1G1-62298398.html; Another witness was Congressman Bobby Rush, former head of the Black Panther Party in Chicago.

largest black publishing empire in America, released a 600-page crank history by Bennett called *Forced Into Glory: Abraham Lincoln's White Dream*. It presents the full-blown treatment of a thesis Bennett has been advocating in the pages of *Ebony* for more than three decades, claiming that Abraham Lincoln was a racist and a fraud—because he only pretended to free the slaves—and that "Lincoln must be seen as the embodiment, not the transcendence, of the American tradition of racism."[30]

Ironically, Bennett's view of Lincoln is shared by white racists as well. The right-wing polemicist Joseph Sobran and the intellectuals grouped around the Conservative Citizens Council regard Lincoln as a racist tyrant who conducted an illegal war against the South, while maintaining views of Negro inequality that made his proclamations and deeds to the contrary hypocritical. Sobran, who has been criticized by conservatives like Jack Kemp for being one of the current "assassins of Lincoln's character," is at work on his own book, *King Lincoln*. While praising Bennett's *Forced to Glory* for showing that the image of Lincoln as a "cherished crusader for equality—is a wholly imaginary being," Sobran has acknowledged that he has been able to add "only a few salient details" to Bennett's hatchet job.[31] The views of Bennett and Sobran stand in stark contrast to the testimony of Frederick Douglass, who visited Lincoln in the White House and was struck by the President's "freedom from popular prejudice against the colored people. He was the first great man that I talked with in the United States freely, who in no single instance reminded me of the difference between himself and myself, of the difference of color."[32]

---

[30]Lerone Bennett Jr., *Forced Into Glory: Abraham Lincoln's White Dream*, Johnson Publishing Company, 2000. Bennett comes to this conclusion by a sustained wrenching of Lincoln's statements and actions taken out of their historical context, completely ignoring the complex political coalition Lincoln had to lead in order to achieve emancipation.

[31]Joseph Sobran, "The Imaginary Abe," *Sobran's*, July 30, 2001, http://www.sobran.com/replyJaffa.shtml.

[32]Foner, op. cit. pp. 546–7.

A cardinal complaint of reparations partisans is the claim that "this country has never dealt with slavery," as Charles Ogletree put it, or confronted its evil.[33] But America *has* dealt with slavery—most significantly in the course of its bloodiest and most soul-wrenching conflict—a civil war in which more Americans were killed than in all America's other wars put together and the very existence of the nation was put at risk. America dealt with its legacies again in the civil rights movement that ended segregation, when individuals—white as well as black—put their lives on the line precisely to deal with the remnants of racial inequality.

The present government of the United States, which reparations lawyers propose to hold culpable for the crime of slavery, is lineally descended from the government that fought and bore the costs of the war that *ended* slavery. The recognition that slavery was a moral evil was the ultimate cause of that war, although reparations advocates tendentiously maintain that the Civil War was "not about slavery," but only about "saving the Union" and "economic interests." The same people who make this claim, however, protest the flying of the Confederate battle flag over government buildings as "racist," not because it is a symbol of "economic interests." The claim itself cannot withstand historical scrutiny. From its very inception as a nation, America's founders understood that the creed of liberty and equality, which had inspired its creation, inevitably brought it into collision with the system of human bondage it had inherited from the British Empire. In the Jefferson Memorial these words are enshrined: "God who gave us life gave us liberty. Can the liberties of a nation be secure when we have removed a conviction that these liberties are the gift of God? Indeed I tremble for my country when I reflect that God is just, that his justice cannot sleep forever. Commerce between Master and slave is despotism. Nothing is more certainly written in the book of fate than that these people are to be free."

---

[33]BET interview, op. cit.

The framers of America's Constitution omitted the words "slave" and "black" from its text because they believed that slavery was an immoral and dying institution and they did not want to recognize it more than absolutely necessary to achieve the compromise with the southern colonies they considered necessary to the survival of the Republic.[34] As Lincoln put it in 1854, "the thing is hid away in the Constitution, just as an afflicted man hides away a wen or a cancer, which he dares not cut out at once, lest he bleed to death; with the promise, nevertheless, that the cutting may begin at the end of a given time."[35] Beyond ending the slave trade, which they did in 1808, the Founders had no practical idea—short of a devastating war between the states—of how to abolish the institution itself.[36]

The flawed compromise with slavery in the American founding dictated by this prospect was the inescapable subtext of the national debates that that followed over more than half a century and finally led up to the war itself: whether liberty could or should be compromised in fugitive slave laws; whether the terrain of freedom should or should not be extended in the addition of new states; whether a nation could endure half slave and half free. In 1861, these questions were answered in a fratricidal resolution.

No figure in American politics so personified America's encounter with itself over the moral issue of slavery than its Civil War president, Abraham Lincoln. No political leader formulated the connection of slavery to the national issue so succinctly as Lincoln in a pre-war debate with Senator Stephen Douglas (1855): "Our progress in degeneracy appears to be pretty rapid. As a nation we began by declaring that, 'all men are created equal.' We now

---

[34]The dilemmas of the Founders are elegantly explored in chapter 3 ("The Silence") of Joseph Ellis's *Founding Brothers: The Revolutionary Generation*, Knopf, 2000.

[35]James McPherson, *Abraham Lincoln and the Second American Revolution*, Oxford University Press, 1991, p. 126.

[36]The rationales for the compromise are laid out in Ellis, *Founding Brothers*, op. cit.

practically read it 'all men are created equal, except Negroes.' When the Know-Nothings get control, it will read 'all men are created equal, except Negroes, and foreigners, and Catholics.' When it comes to this I should prefer emigrating to some other country where they make no pretense of loving liberty—to Russia, for instance, where despotism can be taken pure without the base alloy of hypocrisy."[37] As political scientist Harry V. Jaffa summarized Lincoln's pre-war role, "the assertion of equality in the Declaration of Independence was the prop and pillar of the antislavery cause. One might epitomize everything Lincoln said between 1854 and 1861 as a demand for recognition of the Negro's human rights, as set forth in the Declaration."[38]

It was the election of the man who held such views that triggered the secession of seven slave states and the formation of the Confederacy. The president of the Confederacy, Jefferson Davis, explained secession as an effort "to save ourselves from a revolution" that threatened to make "property in slaves so insecure as to be comparatively worthless."[39] The slaves themselves concurred, according to the testimony of Booker T. Washington: "During the campaign when Lincoln was first a candidate for the Presidency, the slaves on our far-off plantation, miles from any railroad or large city or daily newspaper, knew what the issues involved were. When war was begun between the North and the South, every slave on our plantation felt and knew that, though other issues were discussed, the primal one was that of slavery. Even the most ignorant members of my race on the remote plantations felt that

---

[37]McPherson, op. cit. p. 53. This small classic is the best introduction to the singular role that Lincoln played in freeing the slaves. Contrary views are invariably based on reading individual presidential statements or acts out of context, and failing to understand the complexities of the coalition Lincoln was leading or the perilous situation of the Northern cause at various stages of the conflict. McPherson's account admirably sets the record straight.

[38]Harry V. Jaffa, *A New Birth of Freedom: Abraham Lincoln and the Coming of the Civil War*, Rowman & Littlefield Publishers, 2000, p. 74.

[39]McPherson, op. cit. p. 27

the freedom of the slaves would be the one great result of the war, if the Northern armies conquered."[40]

Reparations partisans dismiss the Emancipation Proclamation as a mere expediency to win the war. But the Emancipation Proclamation was in fact the fulfillment of a design Lincoln had long held, which political circumstances prevented him from implementing. Lincoln's Republican Party was one of four contesting the election. Four border-states crucial to the Union cause were slave states. Lincoln could not have put together—or maintained—the coalition that won the war had he defined it as an anti-slavery cause at the outset. For the same reason the Emancipation Proclamation extended freedom only to slaves rebelling against the Confederacy. Preserving the Union was the war aim that united the coalition. But as the war progressed, Lincoln steadily redefined the Union war aims even as he redefined the American covenant and its "charter of freedom."

At Gettysburg, Lincoln declared the war a test to see "whether a nation conceived in liberty and dedicated to the proposition that all men are created equal" could endure. He proclaimed the war "a new birth of freedom," and identified the new freedom and the Union cause with the emancipation of the slaves. "Let us re-adopt the Declaration of Independence, and with it the practices and policy which harmonize it," Lincoln had said in the last debate with Douglas, before the war began. "If we do this, we shall not only have saved the Union; but we shall have so saved it, as to make, and keep it, forever worthy of the saving."[41]

Far from officially ignoring the evil of slavery or the need for reparation, Lincoln described the war as God's form of retribution—a payment in blood for the sins committed against African slaves. In 1864, in his second Inaugural address, he said: "American slavery is one of those offences which, in the providence of

---

[40]Booker T. Washington, *Up From Slavery*, introduction by Ishmael Reed, Penguin Books, 2000, pp. 5–6.
[41]McPherson, op. cit. p. 55. The evolution of Lincoln's political strategy with respect to slavery is outlined in this book.

God ... He now wills to remove [through] this terrible war, as the woe due to those whom the offence came.... Fondly do we hope—fervently do we pray—that this mighty scourge of war may speedily pass away. Yet if God wills that it continue, until all the wealth piled by the bondman's two hundred and fifty years of unrequited toil shall be sunk, and until every drop of blood drawn with the lash, shall be paid by another drawn with the sword, as was said three thousand years ago, so still it must be said 'the judgments of the Lord, are true and righteous altogether."[42]

To make up their rancid case against Lincoln, Robinson, Bennett and other reparations partisans ignore the human context of Lincoln's struggle against slavery. They suck the marrow out of a complex and heroic human drama, just as when they ignore the weight and consequence of Washington freeing his slaves. The Civil War was, as Frederick Douglass called it, "the abolition war," and no one has summed up Lincoln's calculation and achievement in successfully leading the free states to victory better than Douglass himself: "His great mission was to accomplish two things: first, to save his country from dismemberment and ruin; and, second, to free his country from the great crime of slavery. To do one or the other, or both, he must have the earnest sympathy and the powerful cooperation of his loyal fellow-countrymen. Without this primary and essential condition to success, his efforts must have been vain and utterly fruitless. Had he put the abolition of slavery before the salvation of the Union, he would have inevitably driven from him a powerful class of the American people and rendered resistance to rebellion impossible. Viewed from the genuine abolition ground, Mr. Lincoln seemed tardy, cold, dull, and indifferent; but measuring him by the sentiment of his country, a sentiment he was bound as a statesman to consult, he was swift, zealous, radical, and determined. Though Mr. Lincoln shared the prejudices of his white fellow-countrymen

---

[42]2nd Inaugural Address, March 4, 1864; *The Essential Abraham Lincoln*, ed. John Gabriel Hunt, Gramercy, 1993, p. 331.

against the Negro, it is hardly necessary to say that in his heart of hearts he loathed and hated slavery ... "[43]

More Americans died in the Civil War than in all other wars involving Americans combined. John Brown had said that the sin of slavery made it necessary to "purge this land with blood." More than three hundred and fifty thousand Americans lost their lives in the armies that vanquished the slave power. Was this not dealing with slavery, and a form of atonement?

When the economic and human costs of the war are added up, much—if not all—of the national wealth said to have been accumulated through slavery was spent or destroyed in the war that ended it. Retributive justice was ruthlessly exacted on the South: "When the Civil War became a total war the invading army intentionally destroyed the economic capacity of the south to wage war. Union armies ripped up thousands of miles of southern railroads and blew up hundreds of bridges; ... More than half of the South's farm machinery was wrecked by the war, two-fifths of its livestock were slaughtered, and one-quarter of its white males of military age—also the prime age for economic production—were killed, a higher proportion than suffered by any European power in World War I, that holocaust which ravaged a continent and spread revolution through many of its countries." The war destroyed 60 percent of southern wealth and "the value of southern agricultural land in relation to that of the North was cut by three-fourths."[44]

These historical realities refute the reparations claims that slavery was never confronted, or that a price for the sin of slavery was never paid. The Civil War was a second American Revolution. It not only redefined the founding covenant, making America the first multi-racial nation in the world; it was also a revolution in the strict sense, overthrowing the power of the slaveholding class. As a result of the war, the political supremacy of this class was destroyed. Thanks to the durability of the "Virginia Dynasty," the

---

[43]Foner, op cit., p. 621.
[44]McPherson, op cit., p. 38.

president of the United States had been a southerner and a slave-holder for forty-nine of the nation's first 72 years. After the War, it would be a century before another southerner was elected to the White House. Before the war, 23 of 36 Speakers of the House of Representatives had been southerners, along with 24 of 36 presidents *pro tem* of the Senate. For the next fifty years no southerner was elected leader of either chamber. Until the Civil War the South had a majority on the Supreme Court every year. During the next half-century only 5 of 26 justices were southerners.[45] As a result of the war, the power of the southern plantocracy that had fostered the three-fifths compromise, the fugitive-slave clause and the Dred Scott decision had been destroyed.

Reparations advocates like columnist Earl Ofari Hutchinson have asserted that "The U.S. government, not long-dead Southern planters, bears the blame for slavery." Hutchinson claims that the Constitution, in Article One, "designated a black slave as three-fifths of a person for tax and political representation purposes. It protected and nourished [slavery] in Article Four by mandating that all escaped slaves found anywhere in the nation be returned to their masters. In the Dred Scott decision in 1857, the U.S. Supreme Court reaffirmed that slaves remained slaves no matter where they were taken in the United States."[46]

True enough, but the planter class guilty of those crimes was extinguished in 1865. What is the rationale for holding the vanquisher liable?

Hyperbolic indictments of America have become such routine features of the political landscape that they have begun to eclipse the memory of the attitudes they displaced—attitudes once expressed by former slaves like Booker T. Washington: "Think about it: we went into slavery pagans; we came out Christians. We went into slavery pieces of property; we came out American

---

[45]McPherson, op. cit. p. 13.
[46]Earl Ofari Hutchinson, "Ten Reasons For Reparations" *Alternet*, April 2, 2001, http://www.alternet.org/story/10680/ten_reasons_for_reparations.

citizens. We went into slavery with chains clanking about our wrists; we came out with the American ballot in our hands.... When we rid ourselves of prejudice, or racial feeling, and look the facts in the face, we must acknowledge that, notwithstanding the cruelty and moral wrong of slavery, we are in a stronger and more hopeful position, materially, intellectually, morally, and religiously, than is true of an equal number of black people in any other portion of the globe."[47]

The case for slavery reparations, advanced more than a century after emancipation, is an attack not only on Abraham Lincoln and all he symbolized but on the America he was so instrumental in creating. The refusal of President Andrew Johnson to honor the promise of "40 acres and a mule" to freed slaves when the war concluded was certainly an injustice—and a costly one. So were the injuries inflicted by segregation and discrimination. When the Civil Rights Acts of the 1960s finally established full citizenship for black Americans, the government had a clear obligation to devise programs that would attempt to repair injuries these injustices had inflicted. The government—with the support of the American public—did just that. Yet Randall Robinson dismisses the efforts of the War on Poverty, the Great Society, and the Nixon affirmative action programs with an impatient gesture: "In 1965, after nearly 350 years of legal racial suppression, the United States enacted the Voting Rights Act and, virtually simultaneously, began to walk away from the social wreckage that centuries of white hegemony had wrought."[48]

The statement is a brazen falsehood. On June 4, 1965—following the passage of the Civil Rights Act—President Lyndon Johnson gave a famous commencement address at Howard University, vetted in advance by civil rights leaders, in which he described the vision inspiring his "War on Poverty" and "Great Society"

---

[47]Washington, op. cit. p. 11. Cf. also John Perazzo, *The Myths That Divide Us: How Lies Have Poisoned American Race* Relations, World Studies Books, 1998, p. 377.
[48]Robinson, *The Debt*, op. cit. p. 230.

programs. In this speech he made explicit—and official—the special obligation Americans had to make up for past injustices committed against black citizens: "This is the next and the more profound stage of the battle for civil rights. We seek not just freedom but opportunity. We seek not just legal equity but human ability, not just equality as a right and a theory but equality as a fact and equality as a result. For the task is to give 20 million Negroes the same chance as every other American to learn and grow, to work and share in society, to develop their abilities—physical, mental and spiritual, and to pursue their individual happiness."[49]

Freedom was "not enough," Johnson said. "You do not wipe away the scars of centuries by saying: Now you are free to go where you want, and do as you desire . . . You do not take a person who for years has been hobbled by chains and liberate him, bring him up to the starting line of a race and then say . . . 'you are free to complete with all the others,' and still justly believe that you have been completely fair."

This understanding was to become the rationale for affirmative action policies and all the racial preference programs for jobs, school placements and contract set-asides that would transfer wealth to black citizens over the next three decades. In the Howard speech Johnson also used the same terms to describe the anti-poverty welfare programs he set in motion. "For Negro poverty is not white poverty," he said; the differences between them were "not racial differences."[50] As if writing in advance the script later followed by Robinson and the reparations proponents, he explained: "They are solely and simply the consequence of ancient brutality, past injustice, and present prejudice. They are

---

[49]Lyndon B. Johnson, "To Fulfill These Rights," June 4, 1965, http://www.lbjlib.utexas.edu/johnson/archives.hom/speeches.hom/650604.asp.

[50]Compare Robinson: "Lamentably, there will always be poverty. But African Americans are over represented in that economic class for one reason and one reason only: American slavery and the vicious climate that followed it." *The Debt*, op. cit. pp. 8–9.

anguishing to observe. For the Negro they are a constant reminder of oppression. For the white they are a constant reminder of guilt. But they must be faced and they must be dealt with and they must be overcome, if we are ever to reach the time when the only difference between Negroes and whites is the color of their skin." Johnson concluded his vision of "the next and the more profound stage of the battle for civil rights" by setting it in its historical frame: "So it is the glorious opportunity of this generation to end the one huge wrong of the American Nation."

In other words, nearly forty years ago the American government set out on exactly the path of repairing the wrong of slavery and its legacies, an effort that Robinson and the reparationists maliciously deny was ever attempted.[51]

During those years, trillions of dollars were spent in means-tested poverty programs under the Great Society welfare project. These monies represented a net transfer of more than $1.3 trillion to African Americans.[52] Johnson thought that the various gaps between black and white incomes could be closed by external means; that the problem of lagging black indices came from being "buried under a blanket of history and circumstance." Subsequent experience has proven him wrong. The welfare programs devised by well-intentioned social reformers not only did not reduce black poverty, but exacerbated and deepened it.[53] This reality poses questions that the reparations crowd does not even begin to address, even though it is crucial to their case. If huge sums of government monies already expended have not made a dent in the solution to these problems, why should there be any basis for thinking that reparations might solve them in the future?

---

[51]"Those who exercise control over our public policy see no reason why they should care very much about taking steps to fix what America has done to blacks." Ibid. p. 238.

[52]As of 2001. The figure was calculated for this text by Robert Rector of the Heritage Foundation.

[53]Robert Rector and William F. Lauber, *America's Failed $5.4 Trillion War on Poverty*, Heritage Foundation, 1995.

Johnson's initiative in expanding the welfare state, and in directing anti-poverty efforts to inner-city areas with large concentrations of African Americans, was followed by Richard Nixon's reinvention of affirmative action as a racial preference program. With the "Philadelphia Plan," he launched an era of racial set-asides in government contracts, and racial preferences in hiring and in college admissions that resulted in a massive transfer of wealth to blacks.[54] Even though racial preferences violated the fundamental principle of neutral standards that had just been won by the civil rights movement, the Supreme Court defended them, when they were challenged at the end of the decade, as reparations for past injustices: "Government may take race into account," wrote Justice Brennan, "to remedy disadvantages cast on minorities by past racial prejudice...."[55] In a concurring opinion, Justice Thurgood Marshall justified racial preferences as an effort to "remedy the effects [of] centuries of unequal treatment."[56]

Robinson dismisses this entire history with a contemptuous sneer: "America followed slavery with more than a hundred combined years of legal racial segregation and legal racial discrimination of one variety or another.... The country then began to rub itself with the memory-emptying salve of contemporaneousness. If the wrong did not just occur, it did not occur at all in a way that would render the living responsible."[57] This denial of the American conscience—and of its manifest deeds of retribution—is integral to the portrait of America as an embodiment of racial evil. "America is one of the cruelest nations in the world when it comes to black folk," declared a leading reparations proponent, Chicago Alderman Dorothy Tillman, before a large audience of University of Chicago students and faculty, when the opposite is the truth. Tillman had been invited to the university by the

---

[54]And, ironically, slowed the progress of black advancement. Stephen and Abigail Thernstrom, op., cit., pp. 172–3.
[55]Ibid. p. 415.
[56]Ibid. p. 417.
[57]Robinson, op. cit. p. 230.

campus left to inoculate them against an appearance I was sched-
uled to make a few days later. It did not occur to Tillman or her
audience that American blacks are not noticeably fleeing a country that is so cruel to them; or that the Immigration and Natural-
ization Service has to turn away thousands of refugees from
black-run countries like Haiti, Ethiopia, Somalia, Rwanda and the
Congo who are seeking a safe haven in America because of the cruelty of *their* governments. Continuing her crude attack, Tillman
said: "America owes us a debt and we intend to collect. The white
ruling class accumulated enormous wealth from slavery, either
directly or indirectly. Virtually every white person in America
reaped some benefits by either owning slaves, investing in the
slave industry, or purchasing slave-produced products. Meanwhile,
blacks received absolutely nothing."[58]

This preposterous claim can be put alongside Robinson's
equally absurd statement that the economic gap between whites
and blacks "has been static since the Emancipation Proclamation."[59] The record says just the opposite. In the years between
1940 and 1995, the median income of black males rose from 41
percent to 67 percent of that of white males, while black females'
median income rose from 36 percent to 87 percent of that of white

---

[58]Vanessa Cordonnier, "Local Groups Plan to Protest Horowitz Visit,"
Chicago Maroon, May 8, 2001.
[59]Randall   Robinson,   Transafrica   Forum   transcript,   op.   cit.
http://www.mdcbowen.org/p2/rap/transafrica_transcript.htm, In the
last decade, a tendentious literature has appeared attempting to prove
the thesis: "The notion embodied in the 'sedimentation of racial
inequality' is that in central ways the cumulative effects of the past have
seemingly cemented blacks to the bottom of society's economic hierarchy." Melvin L. Oliver and Thomas M. Shapiro, *Black Wealth, White
Wealth: A New Perspective on Racial Inequality*, Routledge, 1995, p. 5.
Cf. Also Claud Anderson, *Black Labor, White Wealth: The Search for
Power and Economic Justice*, Powernomics Corp of America, 1994. The
Oliver/Shapiro study is far more substantial, but both arguments treat
blacks largely as the objects of impersonal forces, and fail to confront the
success of other highly discriminated-against and impoverished groups
like Jews and Asians, not to mention West Indian-born or -descended
blacks who perform at the American mean.

females.[60] In the same period, the percentage of black families with income below the poverty line declined from 87 percent to 26 percent.[61] The percentage of black males in middle-class occupations has increased *six times* in fifty years (from 5.2 percent in 1940 to 32 percent in 1990); for black females it has increased *nine times* over the same period (from 6.4 percent in 1940 to 58.9 percent in 1990).[62] As a result of these gains, 50 percent of black families are now solidly middle-class (as compared to only 1 percent in 1940) along with the vast majority of American families of all ethnicities and colors.[63] In 1994, black household earnings exceeded that of whites in 130 cities and counties across the nation.[64]

Despite these dramatic changes, poverty persists among a quarter of the black population. This poverty has been thoroughly analyzed, however, and has been shown to result from factors that are not determined by racial barriers. For example, poverty was once the result of low-paying jobs, and black poverty was powerfully affected by job discrimination. By the end of the 20th century, however, discrimination had been outlawed for decades. In contemporary America, poverty for all racial groups is almost entirely the result of failure to work. In 1995, only 2.5 percent of black men who were fully employed had incomes below the poverty line.[65]

---

[60]Ibid. p. 195. Ibid. p. 126. Cf. also, John McWhorter, *Losing the Race: Self-Sabotage in Black America*, Free Press, 2000, pp. 6–7.

[61]Stephen and Abigail Thernstrom, *America in Black and White: One Nation, Indivisible*, Simon & Schuster, 1997, p. 233.

[62]Stephan and Abigail Thernstrom, ,op. cit. Table, p. 185.

[63]Poverty in the United States: 1995, Washington DC US Govt Printing Office, September, 1996, p. D-7, http://www.census.gov/hhes/www/poverty/publications/p60-194.pdf; Cited in Stephan and Abigail Thernstrom, op. cit. The Thernstroms define "middle-class" as twice the income of the poverty level.

[64]John McWhorter, "What's Holding Blacks Back?" City Journal, Winter 2001, http://www.city-journal.org/html/11_1_whats_holding_blacks.html.

[65]Poverty in the United States: 1995, op. cit. Table 3. Stephan and Abigail Thernstrom, op. cit. p. 242.

It is a well-established fact that the black poverty gap is greatly impacted by astronomical out-of-wedlock birthrates for African Americans. Eighty-three percent of black children who are poor have been born out of wedlock and raised in homes with no fathers.[66] A child raised in a single-parent, female-headed household is 5 times more likely to be poor—regardless of race or ethnic background—than a child raised in a two-parent family.[67] This cannot be attributed to slavery (as it often is) because it is a recent phenomenon, post-dating the end of slavery by more than a hundred years.[68] As recently as 1960, two-thirds of all black children were born into two-parent families. Fifty years later, two-thirds of black children overall are born out of wedlock.[69]

"It is family structure that largely divides the haves from the have-nots in the black community," conclude Stephan and Abigail Thernstrom in their path-breaking study, *America in Black and White*. "The population in poverty is made up overwhelmingly of single mothers."[70] The broken family structure of the black community dates from the 1960s and the inception of government welfare programs which dramatically and adversely affected black families in particular. There is no obvious connection between *these* facts and slavery, or between these facts and *de jure* or *de*

---

[66]Irwin Garfinkel and Sara McLanahan, *Single Mothers and Their Children*, Urban Institute Press, 1986, pp. xix, 14–15, 30; cited in Dinesh D'Souza, *The End of Racism*, Free Press, 1995, p. 516.

[67]Horowitz, *Uncivil Wars*, op. cit. p. 129.

[68]Even the destruction of the black family in slavery has been significantly exaggerated in the rhetoric of the left. Cf. "The Myth of the Absent Family," in Eugene Genovese, *Roll, Jordan, Roll: The World the Slaves Made*, Random House, 1974, pp. 450 et seq. "Slaves created impressive norms of family life, including as much of a nuclear family norm as conditions permitted, and ... they entered the postwar social system with a remarkably stable base." Robert Fogel, ed., *Without Contract or Consent*, W. W. Norton & Company, 1992, p. 165 and Leon Litwack, *Been in The Storm So Long*, Alfred A. Knopf, 1979.

[69]Stephen and Abigail Thernstrom, *America in Black and White*, op. cit. p. 240.

[70]Ibid. p. 237.

facto discrimination; and no proponent of reparations has made any attempt to establish one.

The claim that *de jure* and *de facto* discrimination are responsible for the significant achievement gaps between blacks and other ethnic groups is a claim of ideology, not science. It is based on a Marxist-derived model that divides society into race victimizers and race victims. In this model, the accountable individual disappears into the group, and the members of victim groups are regarded as lacking either the free will or the ability to function as active subjects. They are perceived, instead, as the passive objects of historical forces over which they can have no control. This is a social elitism that denies the humanity of those it labels victims. "Lamentably, there will always be poverty," writes Randall Robinson. "But African Americans are over-represented in that economic class for one reason and one reason only: American slavery and the vicious climate that followed it."[71] This certainly can't be the case. For if three-quarters of all black families in America, subject to the same history and climate, have managed to raise themselves above the poverty line, what has prevented the other quarter from doing the same?

The presentation of the reparations claim as an economic demand diminishes and obscures the moral dimensions of the slavery issue. Slavery, as James Madison said, is "the most oppressive dominion of man over man," and as such is an offense to the human spirit.[72] Instead of focusing on *this* fact, reparations advocates treat slavery as a form of theft and urge their constituencies to line up for an overdue payday. As Dorothy Tillman summarized it: "America owes blacks a debt because when we built this country on free [i.e., unpaid] labor, ... wealth was handed down to the white community."[73] But, as already noted, the slave plantations

---

[71]Robinson, *The Debt,* op cit., p. 8.

[72]Thomas G. West, *Vindicating the Founders: Race, Sex, Class, and Justice in the Origins of America,* Rowman & Littlefield Publishers, 1997, p. 5.

[73]"Chicago City Council Votes to Urge Congress to Consider Slavery Reparations," *Jet Magazine,* June 5, 2000, p. 16.

were destroyed, with the private wealth from slavery largely con-
fiscated and used to pay off the costs of the war to end it. On the
other hand, the alleged contribution of the slave economy to
"white" wealth is greatly exaggerated, the claim that the slave system played a key role in the industrialization of the American
economy far from self-evident.

During the era of slavery, contemporary observers regularly
noted the economic backwardness of the South as compared to the
industrial development of the North. To this day, the question of
whether the slave economy was a drag on the Southern economy
is a point of historical contention. The post-slavery South has long
been the poorest region of the United States. The subject of
whether the slave economy was a net asset to the national economy as a whole is the center of an ongoing dispute among economic historians, which has not been resolved after a century and
a half of debate.[74]

If looked at from the perspective of the slaves themselves, the
economic argument for reparations does not become much
stronger. The claim that all of a slave's labor was "free labor" is a
simple misunderstanding of economic realities. During the 19th
century, most work—even of the labor force that was free—was
subsistence labor. Almost the entire income of a 19th-century free
laborer was spent in keeping himself and his family sheltered and
alive.[75] Slaves were housed, clothed and fed by their owners. Since
owners viewed their slaves as capital, they had a vested interest in
their health and well-being, and not in keeping them in the concentration camps fantasized by reparations advocates. Consequently,
the diet and shelter of slaves were often comparable to that of the

---

[74]Mark M. Smith, *Debating Slavery: Economy and Society in the Ante-*
bellum American South, Cambridge University Press, 1998, "Ch. 6: The
Profitability of Slavery As A System." Cf. also Robert Fogel and Stanley
Engermann, *Time On The Cross: The Economics of American Negro*
Slavery, Little Brown & Co., 1974, pp. 59 et seq.
[75]Horowitz, *Uncivil Wars,* op. cit. p. 129.

free labor force.[76] Because of the costs of this upkeep, owners did not begin to make a profit from the labor of an individual slave until he or she reached 26 years of age.[77] According to the calculations of econometricians Fogel and Engermann, over a slave's lifetime the amount of "wealth" the owner was able to appropriate from his or her labor (i.e., the amount of labor that was actually unpaid) was approximately twelve percent of the income the slave earned.[78] This is far less than the free labor that is currently expropriated by the federal government in the form of income taxes from the average U.S. citizen.[79] The relatively small percentage of actually expropriated slave income does not make slavery less repellent or the expropriation more acceptable; it merely serves to put in perspective the bogus claim for the return of stolen wealth.

An equally problematic issue for the reparations case is the current economic prosperity of African Americans, relative to that of black people anywhere else. The average income of a black person in America is twenty to fifty times the income of the contemporary inhabitants of the West African nations from which the slaves were taken. The average income in Benin, one of the principal slave-trading states, for example, is $380.[80] This does not even

[76]Fogel and Engermann, op cit., pp. 109 et seq. The richest, most informative book on slave conditions and slave life is Eugene Genovese, *Roll, Jordan, Roll: The World the Slaves Made*, Random House, 1974.

[77]Ibid. p. 153. "Prior to age 26, the accumulated expenditures by planters on slaves were greater than the average accumulated income which they took from them.".

[78]Ibid. Fogel and Engermann also showed that a significant number of planters actually developed forms of reward, profit-sharing and payment for their slaves, pp. 144 et seq.

[79]Including the taxes that funded the net transfer of approximately $1.5 trillion in welfare funds to African Americans in the last 35 years. According to statistics released by Americans for Tax Reform, the average American citizen is forced to work 187 uncompensated days a year to pay for government; press release, July 6, 2001.

[80]http://pdf.usaid.gov/pdf_docs/PNABP951.pdf; According to the Census Bureau, per capita income among blacks in the U.S. in 1999 was $14,397. ("Money Income in the United States," Washington: US Census Bureau, September, 2000, Table A, p. viii, http://www.census.gov/prod/2000pubs/p60-209.pdf).

take into consideration the social environment, the general inse-
curity of life in Africa, the political instability, and the prevalence
of epidemics—factors that have kept to an absolute minimum any
migration of African Americans to Africa. "Does anyone seriously
suggest that blacks in America today would be better off if they
were in Africa?" asks African-American economist Thomas Sowell, putting a bottom line on the issue. "If not, then what is the
compensation for?"[81]

There is a strong element of racism in the reparations claim. It
is reflected in the subtitle of Robinson's book—"What America
Owes to Blacks"—and the determined reference of reparations partisans to "246 years of slavery" as the baseline for their grievance
against the government of the United States. The United States
government was established in 1787 with the adoption of the Constitution. It was thus in existence for only 78 years before the 13th
Amendment abolished slavery. Robinson knows this, but like
every other reparations advocate he chooses to ignore it. What
could possibly be the motivation behind a sleight-of-hand that
makes America responsible for England's crimes, if not a determination to subordinate every other historical factor to race? This is
also the only possible inference of the following sentence from
The Debt: "Well before the birth of our country, Europe and the
eventual United States perpetrated a heinous wrong against the
peoples of Africa—and sustained and benefited from the wrong for
centuries."[82]

It is a striking fact that no American Indian nations are
indicted in *The Debt* or are named in any of the reparations claims
made on behalf of American blacks. The historical record shows
that Choctaws, Chicasaws, Cherokees, Creeks and Seminoles
owned black slaves; and that black slavery even persisted among
them until after the Civil War, when the United States govern-

---

[81]Thomas Sowell, "Reparations for Slavery," *Jewish World Review,* July
17, 2000, http://www.jewishworldreview.com/cols/sowello71700.asp.
[82]Robinson, *The Debt,* op. cit. p. 230.

ment forced the tribes to end the practice through a formal treaty.[83] What can explain this omission from the reparations indictment, except that the debt of slavery is less an issue for its proponents than the imagined debt of race? An African-American critic of reparations, Adolph Reed, concludes just that: "The deeper appeal of reparations talk for its proponents is to create or stress a sense of racial people-hood as the primary basis for political identity."[84]

The racist subtext of the reparations movement can be seen even more clearly in the claims advanced by African nations. These claims are supported by Robinson and other reparations advocates in the United States.[85] While African nations clamor for reparations from the western nations, which abolished slavery more than a century ago, there are still tens and perhaps hundreds of thousands of slaves in the African nations—the Sudan, Ghana, Mauritania, Benin, Gabon, Mali and the Ivory Coast.[86] By making no claims against African governments that participated (and still do) in the slave trade, reparations proponents make clear that their grievance is not against an institution—slavery—and those who benefited from it, but that slavery is a means for them to formulate an indictment against Europeans and their descendants—in a word, against whites.

Even as the successful efforts of Americans and white Europeans to abolish slavery are ignored or discounted, so is the fact that the suppression of the African slave trade was the work of the

---

[83]D'Souza, *The End of Racism*, op. cit. p. 75; Theda Perdue, *Slavery and the Evolution of Cherokee Society*, University of Tennessee Press, 1979, pp. 38–39.

[84]Adolph Reed, "The Case Against Reparations," *The Progressive*, December 2000, pp. 15–17. Reed refers to the claims advanced by the campaign as "racially defined reparations.".

[85]"And then, of course, there are the billions of dollars owed to Africa and the descendants of slaves for wealth lost in a post-slavery environment of government-approved discrimination." Robinson, *The Debt*, op. cit. p. 244.

[86]Jeffrey White, "Africans Undermine Reparations Claims," *National Post*, April 21, 2001.

colonial powers which accomplished the emancipation of African slaves against great resistance from Africans themselves. Slavery not only flourished in Africa after the American Civil War; it greatly increased, since slaves became cheaper when Caribbean and South American markets were closed. It was the actions of the European colonial powers that gradually eliminated most vestiges of slavery from the African continent.[87] British abolitionists in particular "forced anti-slavery treaties on hundreds of remote rulers, blockaded distant ports and rivers, boarded foreign ships at risk of war, bribed oriental chiefs and sultans, spent billions in today's currencies, years on monotonous patrols and died in their thousands of malaria and yellow fever" to suppress the slave trade. British and American gunboats destroyed the slave ports on Africa's western coast. When the trade was finally suppressed in 1808, there were riots protesting the suppression in the Gold Coast (now Ghana)—while the King of Bonny (now Nigeria) told the British: "Your country, however great, can never stop a trade ordained by God himself."[88] The present reparations movement in Africa—fully supported by its American counterparts—is thus directed at the very parties who righted the wrong, and did not institute it in the first place.

In advancing this double standard, reparations proponents employ an argument similar to the academic left's tendentious claim that only whites can be racists (because allegedly "only whites have power"). They argue that African slavery was not really slavery, or not really bad. Thus Robinson: "While King Affonso [of Kongo] was no stranger to slavery, which was practiced throughout most of the known world, he had understood slavery as a condition befalling prisoners of war, criminals, and debtors, out of which slaves could earn, or even marry, their way. This was nothing like seeing this wholly new and brutal commercial

---

[87]Horowitz, *Uncivil Wars*, op. cit. p. 131.
[88]White, op. cit.

practice of slavery where tens of thousands of his subjects were dragged off in chains."[89] Dorothy Benton-Lewis also argues that only American slavers were racist or brutal: "It is American slavery that put a color on slavery. And American slavery is not like the slavery of Africa and ancient times. This was dehumanizing, brutal and barbaric slavery that subjugated people and turned them into a profit."[90]

Both claims are false. Orlando Patterson, an academic expert (and African American) who has studied fifty-five slave societies, writes: "It has often been remarked that slavery in the Americas is unique in the primary role of race as a factor in determining the condition and treatment of slaves. *This statement betrays an appalling ignorance of the comparative data on slave societies....* Throughout the Islamic world, for instance, race was a vital issue. The light-skinned Tuareg and related groups had decidedly racist attitudes toward the Negroes they conquered. Throughout the Islamic empires, European and Turkish slaves were treated quite differently from slaves south of the Sahara Desert.... Slavery [in Africa] was more than simply 'subordination'; it was considered a degraded condition, reinforced by racist attitudes among the Arab slave owners."[91] (emphasis added)

The idea that African slavery was not "commercial" and therefore benign is an invention of reparations proponents like Robinson. No ownership of human beings is benign. The claim is based on the fact that some slave practices and some slave masters made life less onerous for their human chattel. But this was true in America as well. Moreover, plantation slavery, which reparations proponents regard as especially exploitative, was widespread in Africa: "In the nineteenth century, slaves on the East African coast became enmeshed in a developing plantation economy that in

---

[89]Robinson, *The Debt*, op. cit. p. 26.

[90]A. S. Wang and Dana Levine, "Horowitz, Benton-Lewis Debate," *The Tech*, Vol. 121, Issue 16, April 6, 2001.

[91]Orlando Patterson, *Slavery and Social Death: A Comparative Study*, Harvard University Press, 1982, p. 176, 193.

many ways resembled the plantation economies of the Western Hemisphere. Plantations were large-scale, specialized units that developed in order to serve the needs of a vast and widespread market for particular commodities."[92] Writing of African slavery before 1600, historian Paul Lovejoy notes: "For those who were enslaved, the dangers involved forced marches, inadequate food, sexual abuse, and death on the road."[93] Slaves in Africa were used for mining gold and salt, as well as for ritual sacrifices. Families were separated. Men were executed to make their women available for concubinage. Young males were castrated for court use and "death from unsuccessful operations could be as large as nine boys out of ten."[94]

This information is readily available. But advocates of reparations have chosen to ignore historical reality in order to prosecute their cause, and proceed with their indictment of white Americans. Black novelist Zora Neale Hurston had a dissenting view: "The white people held my people in slavery here in America. They bought us, it is true, and exploited us. But the inescapable fact that stuck in my craw was [that] my people had sold me.... My own people had exterminated whole nations and torn families apart for profit before the strangers got their chance at a cut. It was a sobering thought. It impressed upon me the universal nature of greed and glory."[95]

[92]Frederick Cooper, *Plantation Slavery on the East Coast of Africa*, Yale University Press, 1977, p. 3.
[93]Lovejoy, *Transformations In Slavery*, op. cit. p. 35.
[94]Ibid. Writing of gold mining in the period between 1600 and 1800, Lovejoy observes: "The practice of using slaves in gold production continued under Asante. The risk of death in the pits was considerable because of the environment and relatively low level of technology. The rainy season left the ground damp for months, thereby increasing the danger of cave-in. This risk was perhaps a major reason why custom forbade the Akan from mining gold themselves." Roger Morton, who studied Arab slavery in Kenya, observes: "Rendered inferior by birth, occupation, and color, slaves became natural objects of abuse for the Muslim free-born." Cited by Patterson, *Slavery and Social Death*, op. cit.
[95]Zora Neale Hurston, *Dust Tracks on a Road*, G K Hall & Co., 1997, p. 145. Cited in D'Souza, *The End of Racism*, op. cit. p. 74.

It was this kind of universalist outlook that inspired Americans from the beginning to enlarge their humanity and proclaim the principle of equality before the law. The reparations movement is an attempt to take a giant step backwards from this milestone of human progress.

Americans generally do not think of themselves as racists or oppressors, and there is no reason they should. America was a pioneer in ridding the world of African slavery, and in establishing the first multi-racial society in human history. During the last half-century, Americans have voted equal rights to African American citizens and supported massive compensations to African Americans and others who have lagged behind. To be indicted after such efforts is offensive and unjust. The reparations claim can only be understood as a hostile, historically ignorant and racially motivated assault on America and its heritage. Its divisive message and fallacious history can only have a profoundly adverse effect on those African Americans who embrace it, making it impossible for them to see their past clearly, or to find their way to an American future. Keith Richburg spent three years as a *Washington Post* reporter in Africa. He found that he shared little in common culturally with black Africans and came back with this self-understanding: "By an accident of birth, I am a black man born in America, and everything I am today—my culture and attitudes, my sensibilities, loves, and desires—derives from that one simple and irrefutable truth."[96]

If the negative claims of the reparations argument were true, black Americans would have no usable American past, and no element of the national heritage would be available to them to feel American in their soul. It is a short step from the reparations argument to the separatist idea that black Americans have no home in this country. This is in fact the threat just beneath the surface of Randall Robinson's text: "Until America's white ruling class

---

[96]Keith B. Richburg, *Out of America: A Black Man Confronts Africa*, Basic Books, 1997, p. 248.

accepts the fact that the book never closes on massive un-redressed social wrongs, America can have no future as one people."[97]

Thomas Sowell has pointed out that the victims of the reparations movement are actually blacks themselves: "Is anyone made better off by being supplied with resentments and distractions from the task of developing the capabilities that pay off in a booming economy and a high-tech world? Whites may experience a passing annoyance over the reparations issue, but blacks—especially young blacks—can sustain more lasting damage from misallocating their time, attention and efforts."[98] I was made painfully aware of these negative consequences in my encounters with black students at the colleges I visited during the reparations controversy. Many of their attitudes were expressed in a letter written to the editor of *The Lariat*, the student paper at Baylor University. The writer was a young woman who wanted to complain about my reparations ad: "My ancestors provided this nation with more than 200 years of hard, free labor and instead of their 40 acres and a mule, what did they get? Nothing. Nothing but 100 more years of hate, Black Codes, Jim Crow laws, the KKK, lynchings, segregation, miscegenation, oppression, poverty, fear and more hate."[99] This young woman was attending a university whose tuition and board was $20,000 a year, yet she was filled with such resentment and feelings of futility and victimization that she could not appreciate the fact that all that her ancestors really had to show for their suffering were the opportunities she had been given. Her ancestors had not been requited in their own lives and no longer could be. Her life, on the other hand, was before her, and as their descendant

---

[97]Robinson, *The Debt*, op. cit. p. 208.
[98]Thomas Sowell, "Reparations for Slavery," *Jewish World Review*, July 17, 2000, http://www.jewishworldreview.com/cols/sowell071700.asp.
[99]Pamela A. Hairston, letter to the editor of *The Baylor Lariat* ("Reparations fair, necessary response to injustices caused by Black Codes"), March 20, 2001, http://www.baylor.edu/lariatarchives/news.php?action=story&story=16707.

she had numerous blessings to count as a black woman in America. But in her anger, she could see none.

My futile efforts, to make this argument to most of the black students who attended my appearances, revealed how effective the suppression of ideas had become at the educational institutions that were shaping their futures. For observing that white Americans died to free America's slaves, and suggesting that a bond between them had been created in this sacrifice, I was tarred as a "racist." For attempting to restore Jefferson and Lincoln as heroes of liberty for all Americans, I was condemned as "anti-black." For arguing that America's promise can be real for everyone who embraces it, I was dismissed as "insensitive" to the descendants of slaves.

In contrast to the reparations advocates whose passions are disturbingly focused on race, I am convinced that the fault-line in American society is not racial but political, and that the great obstacle to a constructive approach to these issues is a leftist agenda that is hostile to America's democracy. Fortunately, there have been bonds forged out of the American heritage that stretch across racial lines. During my anti-reparations campaign I had defenders of all races—among them some who did not share my specific views, but believed in the value of engaging them with respect.

The present text was originally completed on the Fourth of July, 2001. On that day ceremonial tributes to the Fourth were published in newspaper columns across the country. Two that came to my notice were from the other side of the political spectrum and were written by journalists who were black. The fact that I found myself in wholehearted agreement with both of these writers provides a note of optimism with which to end this account.

The first was written by Clarence Page, whom I have known and respected, but who penned a harsh (and uncharacteristically unkind) attack on me in the midst of my battles against the reparations idea. To commemorate this national day, he wrote about a black state senator from Tennessee who had refused to pay homage to the flag, saying: "I can't pledge allegiance to a flag that represents the former colonies that enslaved our ancestors." In her separatism, the senator was not alone, Page observed. "Many African-Americans feel an odd disconnection around the flag, the Fourth of July and other expressions of patriotism to a country founded in significant part by, oh, yes, slaveholders." But then he added: "As a fellow descendant of slaves—and an Army veteran—I disagree.... The pledge is not a declaration of existing reality. It is an expression of one's commitment to a goal worth achieving. Sure, this country has yet to achieve perfection in the liberty and justice department, but we're working on it. I see the pledge as a promise to keep working on it. Further, I resent the implication that patriotism cannot really be, to coin a popular implication-loaded phrase, 'a black thing.' African-Americans have fought and sacrificed themselves in every American war—even under the command of that slaveholder George Washington. If anybody has reason to be patriotic, it is us.... The genius of our slaveholding Founders ... was in their having the foresight to create documents that had better values than those they practiced.... [They] set up a challenge for the people of this nation to never shirk from the task of making liberty and justice a reality for everybody. A flag that stands for those values is worth pledging allegiance to."[100]

In his column Page also mentioned a newly published book, written by a veteran civil rights activist and journalist, Roger Wilkins. It was called *Jefferson's Pillow: The Founding Fathers and the Dilemma of Black Patriotism.* Wilkins's uncle, Roy, had been head of the NAACP in the golden era of civil rights struggle, and like others of his generation the nephew had veered to the left in the years that followed. Roger Wilkins was always associated in my mind with a bottomless scowl as he talked about race in

---

[100]Clarence Page, "Patriotic Despite Sore Points," *Chicago Tribune,* July 5, 2001, http://articles.chicagotribune.com/2001-07-05/news/0107050153_1_patriotism-pledge-liberty-and-justice.

television interviews and newspaper columns. I vividly remember his comments on some anniversary of the civil rights struggles; perhaps it was in 1993, thirty years after Martin Luther King had his famous dream of a color-blind American future. Wilkins's eyebrows furrowed and his expression grew dark as he said how little had changed for black people in America, and how dire were the prospects they faced. His pessimism caused me to wonder about that American future of which King had dreamed. But on this July 4th, Roger Wilkins's views had undergone a dramatic change.

His column was titled "Black Patriotism Enlarges the American Tradition," and was excerpted from the final pages of his new book.[101] It began like this: "One famous African-American has been quoted recently as saying, 'At no time have I ever felt like an American.' Well, I have—all my life.... The privilege of defining me rests with my African ancestors, who had the fortitude to survive the Middle Passage and the 'seasoning' meted out by their American jailers. It rests with those enlightened philosophers who inserted the idea of human equality into the ideology of the West—including the founders of America, notably Thomas Jefferson, the quintessential man of ambiguity.... I have seen and participated in a remarkable enlargement of American opportunity and justice. From the one-room segregated schoolhouse in Missouri where I started school, through a lifelong friendship with [Supreme Court Justice] Thurgood Marshall and a rich variety of struggles for justice, I have had the fortune to participate in an astonishing American effort to adjust life, as it is lived, to the ideals proclaimed by the founders. While the transformation is far from complete, the change has nevertheless been so dramatic that my belief in American possibilities remains profound."

---

[101]Roger Wilkins, "Black Patriotism Enlarges the American Tradition," *The New York Times*, July 4, 2001, http://www.nytimes.com/2001/07/04/opinion/black-patriotism-enlarges-the-american-tradition.html.

These were testaments to the resilience of the American dream, and were reassuring as they came from descendants of slaves and critics of American life. They reaffirmed the possibility that the American founders had created a nation so steeped in its principles that it could—out of the multi-racial, multi-ethnic variety of this remarkable people—make the many into one.

End note

In 2001, Randall Robinson repudiated his American citizenship and left the country, a decision he chronicled in a book titled *Quitting America*. He returned shortly thereafter to take up a position as "Distinguished Scholar" at the Pennsylvania State University Dickinson School of Law, where he began teaching in 2008. The reparations movement was put on hold when Democrats won the House in 2006 and Rep. John Conyers, author of the reparations bill, became chairman of the House Judiciary Committee, which had oversight of his bill. Conyers never brought the bill to the floor, and it remained on the shelf when the first African American president of the United States took office in January 2009.

Five years later, in June 2014, the reparations cause was revived by a celebrated essay in the *Atlantic Monthly*, "The Case for Reparations" by Ta-Nehesi Coates. Coates' essay is heir to all the racial attitudes and false claims advanced in Robinson's *The Debt*, as evidenced in its sub-heading: "Two hundred fifty years of slavery. Ninety years of Jim Crow. Sixty years of separate but equal. Thirty-five years of racist housing policy. Until we reckon with our compounding moral debts, America will never be whole."

THREE

America's Second Civil War

Senator Kamala Harris is a rising star in the Democratic Party, frequently mentioned on the short list of contenders for the next presidential race. In a recent commencement speech at Howard University, Harris issued a call to arms, urging her audience to rally behind the Democrats' *resistance* to the Trump administration: "Graduates, indeed we have a fight ahead. This is a fight to define what kind of country we are, and it's a fight to determine what country we will be."

Ignore for a moment the impropriety of addressing a class of students as though they were Democratic Party operatives. Focus instead on the statement itself. The call "to define what kind of country we are" is an ominous agenda for America.

Compared to other nations, America is absolutely unique in one regard: it is a country *defined in its creation*. Normally, nations have been formed on the basis of common origins, ethnicities, and languages—a modern form of tribalism. In contrast, America was created by peoples of diverse origins and ethnicities and on principles that were universal. The American union was forged in a set of founding documents that insisted on the equality of citizens—regardless of origins. The idea that creates the identity "American" is summarized in America's *de facto* motto *E pluribus unum*—out of many, one.

These ideas are elaborated in my recent book, *Big Agenda: President Trump's Plan to Save America*, Humanix Books, 2017.

It took a Civil War and two hundred years of sacrifice and struggle to achieve a polity that approached this ideal. If one political faction were now able to redefine the ideal to conform to its own sectarian beliefs, the country we have known would cease to exist. But that is just what the current creed of the Democratic Party—"identity politics"—entails; and it is why the current divisions in our political life seem so intractable.

Identity politics is, in fact, the antithesis of the American idea. It is a reversion to tribal loyalties. It regards diverse origins—colors, ethnicities, genders and classes—as primary, and proposes a hierarchy of privilege based on them, which it justifies as a reversal of past oppressions.

It is not the proper role of an opposition party in a democracy to mount a "resistance" to a duly elected government and press for its overthrow at the very outset of its tenure. But that is precisely what the Democrats have done in the first months of the Trump administration.

For the second time in its history, the Democratic Party has opted to secede from the Union and its social contract. The first time was over the issue of slavery; now it is over the issue of whether Americans are to be divided by race, gender, sexual orientation and class. This time there is not going to be an actual civil war because the federal government is so powerful that whoever controls it will decide the outcome. The passions of an irreconcilable conflict are still present, but they are channeled into a political confrontation over the executive power.

In launching their resistance, Democrats rejected the honeymoon normally afforded to incoming presidents. Until now this tradition has functioned as something of a sacred political rite. Campaigns are by their nature divisive, and they inevitably exaggerate the differences between factions of the electorate. The presidential honeymoon is designed to reunite the contending factions as constituents of a shared constitutional republic. It allows an incoming president to take his place as the chief executive of all the people, to have his cabinet confirmed, and to launch his agendas before the normal contentions of a democracy resume. It ratifies the peaceful transition of power and reasserts the principle that as Americans we are one.

According to the Gallup organization, the normal duration of a presidential honeymoon in recent times has been seven months. The Democrats didn't give Trump seven seconds. While he was president-elect, they were already attacking him as a racist, a "white nationalist," anti-immigrant, and anti-Muslim; also as an anti-democratic "fascist," a would-be dictator. His election was called illegitimate; he was branded as the agent of a Russian conspiracy. This meme swiftly metastasized into one of the most bizarre witch-hunts in our political history, a "red scare" without actual reds, in which Democrat after Democrat stepped forward to allege that Trump had colluded with Vladimir Putin to steal the election.

Trump did not get confirmation hearings for the team he was hoping to put in place. He got a witch-hunt instead—a series of attempted character-assassinations directed at his nominees. Most outrageously, his candidate for Attorney General, Senator Jeff Sessions, was smeared as a "racist" by one Democratic senator after another, beginning with Minority Leader Chuck Schumer. Yet Sessions' public career reflected values that were quite the opposite. It included service as the attorney general of a deep Southern state, in which capacity he had prosecuted the Ku Klux Klan and desegregated the public schools. These acts reflected his actual commitment to civil rights. Schumer and his colleagues had served alongside Sessions for ten or twenty years, and knew very well that their accusations were defamatory and false. But they persisted in them anyway.

So that no one would mistake their hostile intent, the Democrats' attacks were accompanied by calls for Trump's impeachment, despite the fact that he had hardly been in office. These were echoed in massive street demonstrations, organized and funded by core Democratic groups, which featured chants of "Not My President," claims by celebrity speakers that Trump's election was "worse than being raped," and addled wishes to "blow up the White House." Each protest—no matter its official organizing premise—was orchestrated to underscore identity-driven accusations that the Trump regime was anti-woman, anti-black, anti-Muslim, and anti-immigrant. Trump and his supporters were in turn anathemized as members of a hostile tribe—"white nationalists."

Behind this Democratic rage is the conviction that the Trump administration represents a reactionary throwback to the *status quo ante* before Obama began "fundamentally transforming the United States of America," as the former president had promised on the eve of his election. The new order towards which progressives think they are marching is called "social justice." To Democrats the hierarchy of privileges they offer groups on the basis of ethnicity, skin color, and gender is "social justice." It defines the society they intend to create—a project which in their eyes is mortally threatened by the Trump regime and its conservative supporters.

During the second presidential debate, there was a seminal moment illuminating this conflict. It occurred when Trump turned to the fifty million viewers in the television audience and said: *"You have to understand, Hillary has tremendous hatred in her heart."* He was referring to Clinton's campaign remark that her opponents belonged in a "basket of deplorables—irredeemables," whom she went on to name: "Racists, sexists, homophobes, Islam-ophobes, xenophobes. . . ." Trump, she said, had "raised them up," and that made him "unfit" to be America's president.

The condemnation of her political opponents is not unique to Clinton but is shared by Democrats generally. There is hardly a conservative in the country who has been in an argument with a so-called liberal and not been called a racist, sexist, homophobe, *et cetera*—terms designed to drum them out of decent society. These insults are expressions of the hatred progressives feel towards any-one who opposes their crusade to re-define America's identity in the interests of "social justice."

The theory behind "identity politics" is an ideology the politi-cal left refers to as "cultural Marxism." This perspective takes Marx's view that society is divided into warring classes, and extends it to encompass races, genders, and ethnicities. It is a vision that regards one group's success as another group's oppression. "Social justice"—the proposed remedy for inequality and division—proposes to punish oppressor groups by redistributing their incomes and privileges to the "underrepresented," "marginalized" and otherwise oppressed. It is a vision that disregards the accountability of individuals and ascribes to group identities the inequalities that are alleged to be unjust.

The left has created a term of art—"people of color"—to promote its collectivist views on ethnicity and race. "People of color" is not grammatical English; we do not refer to "crayons of color" or "televisions of color." It is a French construction, reflecting the way French people speak (*gens de couleur*). "People of color" is an invention of ideologues; its purpose is to organize the world into the basic dichotomy of Marxism, oppressors and oppressed. To understand its usage one has only to look to Mexico, a country whose illegal migrants have been one of the flashpoints of the war against the Trump administration, as Democrats have rallied to their defense.

Mexico is composed of two main ethnic groups: the descendants of the Spanish conquistadors who enslaved and slaughtered the indigenous Indians; and the descendants of the Indians. In other words, actual oppressors and actual oppressed. When members of these two groups cross into the United States, however, they both become "people of color," therefore oppressed; therefore deserving of special sensitivities, special allowances, special privileges—all without regard to their individual histories and merits. That is why criminal migrants from Mexico, who are here illegally, can commit felonies against Americans, including rape and murder, and become a cause for progressives and Democrats, who create "sanctuary cities" and policies to protect them. Because they are people of color and allegedly oppressed.

Maharajahs in India are also "people of color." Islamic beheaders and crucifiers in Syria are "people of color" too. The whole world is "people of color" except for, the designated oppressors—white people.

Identity politics is both racist and totalitarian. It obliterates the individual in favor of the group. It removes the agency of individuals as subjects and turns them into objects. After this is understood, there is no longer any mystery as to why advocates of identity politics should come into existential collision with the American framework and its defenders, now personified by President Trump.

The 2016 platform of the Democratic Party vows "a societal transformation" that will "end institutional and systemic racism in our society." This is the ideology of cultural Marxism.

"Institutional racism" as a systemic American problem is a political fiction. Americans outlawed "institutional racism" half a century ago with the passage of the Civil Rights Acts of 1964 and 1965. Any incidence of institutional racism today is actionable in the courts—the ultra-liberal courts that threw out Trump's executive orders on extra-legal grounds, because of off-the-cuff remarks he had made on the campaign trail.

"Systemic racism" and "institutional racism" are anti-American mythologies that drive the Democratic Party's political agendas. The Democratic platform, and Democrats generally, regard every social disparity as *prima facie* evidence of racial or gender oppression, and attribute such disparities not to individual decisions and performances but to un-named "policies," which if they actually existed would be illegal. Consider this plank in the 2016 Democratic Party platform:

Closing the Racial Wealth Gap
America's economic inequality problem is even more pronounced when it comes to racial and ethnic disparities in wealth and income. It is unacceptable that the median wealth for African Americans and Latino Americans is roughly one-tenth that of white Americans. These disparities are also stark for American Indians and certain Asian American subgroups, and may become even more significant when considering other characteristics such as age, disability status, sexual orientation, or gender identity.

The platform then explains: "The racial wealth and income gaps are the result of policies that discriminate against people of color and constrain their ability to earn income and build assets to the same extent as other Americans."

If such policies existed, they would be illegal under the Civil Rights Acts of 1964 and 1965. The disparities, on the other hand, are realistically explained by individual details; for example, by the presence (or lack) of two-parent families, the degree of education, or whether (in the case of Latino Americans) English is spoken in the home. More generally, the ability to accumulate wealth is determined in large part by genes and by cultural attitudes that guide the choices families and individuals make. Otherwise Japanese Americans, who are people of color, would not be among America's richest (and therefore most privileged) economic groups.

The same mythology characterizes the Democrats' claims about gender disparities. The Clinton campaign presented itself as a quest for equality for women. According to candidate Clinton, women across America were being paid only 76 cents on the dollar for the same skills, job experience and work as men. But if this were so, it would also be illegal under the Equal Pay for Equal Work Act passed as long ago as 1963 by a Congress dominated by men. After the election, *The New York Times* published a column inspired by studies that ratified what conservatives had been saying for a generation: "The Gender Pay Gap Is Largely Because of Motherhood." The disparity exists because child-rearing takes women out of the work force for extended periods, and also causes them to seek flex-time occupations that pay less.[1]

Similarly, the animus behind Democratic assaults on Republicans and their support for law and order as "racist" is the direct consequence of viewing all social disparities through the distorted lens of oppression politics. Thus, the "over-representation" of African-Americans in the prison system is not due to systemic

---

[1] https://www.nytimes.com/2017/05/13/upshot/the-gender-pay-gap-is-largely-because-of-motherhood.html?_r=0

racism. Police forces have been integrated for decades, along with the entire criminal justice system. African-Americans are "over-represented" in the prison population because they are "over-represented" in the commission of actual crimes.

Democrats' embrace of the Black Lives Matter movement, and its efforts to cast career criminals as civil rights victims and law enforcement officials as villains, is an inevitable consequence of ignoring the specific circumstances of the incidents under review, and forcing them into the melodramatic framework of "racism" and "oppression."[2] The "social justice" future to which these attitudes lead can be seen on college campuses, the experimental laboratories of the left, which are now characterized by privileged admissions and tuition scholarships distributed on a racial basis; by "safe spaces" for people of color only; and, at Harvard, by segregated graduations for blacks.

Trump and his followers understand the fateful nature of the conflict triggered by decades of these assaults. Indeed, their campaign to "Make America Great Again" is a direct response to the Democrats' attacks. In his inaugural address Trump opposed to the progressive vision and its divisive consequences the American idea, *E pluribus unum*. Referring to those Americans who had been economically left behind, Trump said: "We are one nation and their pain is our pain. Their dreams are our dreams and their success will be our success. We share one heart, one home, and one glorious destiny. The oath of office I take today is an oath of allegiance to all Americans."

Trump then elaborated on the idea that Americans are united as equal citizens: "Through our loyalty to our country, we will rediscover our loyalty to each other. When you open your heart to patriotism, there is no room for prejudice." And finally: "It's time to remember that old wisdom our soldiers will never forget—that whether we are black or brown or white, we all bleed the same red

---

[2] For statistical confirmation, see Heather MacDonald, *Are Cops Racist?* 2016.

blood of patriots. We all enjoy the same glorious freedoms, and we all salute the same great American flag. And whether a child is born in the urban sprawl of Detroit or the windswept plains of Nebraska, they look up at the same night sky, they fill their heart with the same dreams, and they are infused with the breath of life by the same almighty Creator."

In spirit, this echoed the address by the last man to have war declared on his presidency by an opposition party even as he entered the office. "In your hands, my dissatisfied fellow country-men, and not in mine, is the momentous issue of civil war," Lincoln said in his first inaugural. "You have no oath registered in Heaven to destroy the government, while I shall have the most solemn one to 'preserve, protect and defend' it.... Though passion may have strained, it must not break our bonds of affection. The mystic chords of memory, stretching from every battlefield and patriot grave to every living heart and hearthstone all over this broad land, will yet swell the chorus of the Union when again touched, as surely they will be, by the better angels of our nature."

FOUR

The Two Christophers
{or, The Importance of Second Thoughts}

Ifirst met Christopher Hitchens in 1970 when I was editing *Ramparts Magazine,* which was then the largest publication of the left. Christopher was ten years my junior and fresh out of Oxford, embarking on his first adventure in the New World. When he stopped in at my Berkeley office looking for guidance, one of the questions he asked me in all seriousness was, "Where is the working class?" Only the devout left—the "holy rollers" as I regarded them by that time—could still think this mythical entity was an actual force in a nation where classes were social relics, and every man was king. But rather than make this an issue, I directed my visitor to the local Trotskyists, who were true believers, failing to realize that he was one of them.

Our next encounter took place a dozen years later, also in Berkeley, and was not nearly as pleasant. By then I had rejected most tenets of the radical faith, although I had not publicly left its ranks. We met at a small lunch attended by several *Nation* editors, among them Victor Navasky and Kai Bird. Before long the conversation turned to the Middle East and the war in Lebanon, and I found myself confronting what in those days we referred to as a political "gut check." What was my attitude, Christopher wanted to know, towards Israel's invasion of Lebanon?

The goal of the Israeli offensive was to clear out PLO terrorists who had entrenched themselves behind an international border in southern Lebanon and were shelling towns in northern Israel. The left's attitude was that Israel was an imperialist pawn of the United States and oppressor of Palestinians. Leftists therefore opposed Israel's effort to protect itself. My second thoughts had led me to the conclusion that I was not a leftist, and I rose imprudently to Christopher's provocation. "This is the first Israeli war I have supported," I said, which ended any fraternal possibilities for the remaining conversation.

Two years later, my co-author Peter Collier and I voted for Ronald Reagan, and three years after that we organized a "Second Thoughts" conference bringing together other former radicals who had become supporters of the anti-Communist cause. Christopher came to our conference with his *Nation* cohort Alex Cockburn to attack us. In the column he filed after our event, he described our suggestion that second thoughts might be superior to first ones as "smug," and singled out as "sinister" my remark that supporting America's enemies should be considered treason.[1] He subsequently elaborated his feelings about those who had abandoned the leftist cause in a brutal article about the writer Paul Johnson, sneering at his "well advertised stagger from left to right," which Christopher regarded as the venal maneuver of someone "who, having lost his faith, believes that he had found his reason."[2] (And why not?)

But times change, and subsequently Christopher himself became associated by others—not entirely correctly—with a generation of post-9/11 second-thoughters. Revising some of his attitudes towards the left and its loyalties, he vaunted a patriotism towards America he would once have thought of as, well, sinister. A climactic moment in this odyssey—or so it should have been— was the publication of an engrossing memoir of a life, heretical at both ends, which he called *Hitch-22*. Among its other virtues, the book provided a fertile occasion for those of us who preceded him to take another look at our own second thoughts and measure the

---

[1] Christopher Hitchens, "Minority Report," *The Nation*, November 7, 1987, http://www.mail-archive.com/pen-l@sus.csuchico.edu/msg26336.html.

[2] Christopher Hitchens, "The Life of Johnson," *Critical Quarterly*, 1989, FSA, p.260.

distances that we, and our one-time antagonist, had traveled.

The man his friends called "Hitch" was a figure of such unruly contradictions it may be said of him, as Dr. Johnson said of the metaphysical poets, that he had "the ability to yoke heterogeneous ideas by violence together." Opponent of America's war in Vietnam and supporter of America's war in Iraq; libertarian defender of free-market capitalism and impenitent admirer of Trotsky and Marx; pro-lifer and feminist doctrinaire; friend to both Paul Wolfowitz, neo-conservative hawk, and to Victor Navasky, apologist for Alger Hiss, the Rosenbergs, and Hamas.

Christopher eagerly embraced not only incompatible ideas and unlikely comrades but divergent modes of being: both a political renegade and keeper of the flame; fierce partisan and practiced ironist; post-modern skeptic and romantic nostalgist; one-dimensional polemicist and literary polymath; passionate moralist and calculating operator; hard-headed critic and dewy-eyed sentimentalist; serious thinker and determined attention-grabber; irreverent contrarian and serenader of the choir; self-styled Man of the People and accomplished social climber; and—most inexplicable of all—Oxonian gentleman and master of the vitriolic attack.

Among the things to be discovered reading Christopher's memoir is that there are not many things you will figure out about him that he had not already thought of himself. His chronicle opens with a superbly realized account of personal origins, containing portraits of his conservative Anglican father and his rebellious, romantic and secretly Jewish mother—"two much opposed and sharply discrepant ancestral stems: two stray branches that only war and chance could ever have caused to become entwined."[3] On one side his mother Yvonne, an alien who refused to know her place; on the other his father, a naval officer referred to by the son as "the Commander," who knew his place and served his country. "Sending a Nazi convoy raider to the bottom," his radical offspring

---

[3] Ibid., p. 46.

observes in a typically inscrutable Hitchens tribute, "is a better day's work than any I have ever done."[4]

Those familiar with Hitchens's writing have long appreciated his stylistic elegance. But it was not until the publication of his memoir that he showed he was also a wily operator, for whom Homer's epithet for Ulysses—"deep devising"—is particularly apt, using his roguish charm and sparkling literacy to eat his cake and have it too, stutter-stepping past potentially inconvenient truths.

At the outset, the reader is alerted to Christopher's conscious pursuit of "the Janus-faced mode of life," as he characterizes it.[5] The figure Janus was the Roman god of temple doorways, who looks both ways and is invariably depicted in his statuary with two faces. Grabbing the horns of his own enigma, Christopher observes that the doors of the temple were open in time of war, and that war "is a time when the ideas of contradiction and conflict are most naturally regnant." The most intense wars, he also notes, are civil and the most rending conflicts internal. "What I hope to do now," he says of the text to come, "is give some idea of what it is like to fight on two fronts at once, to try and keep opposing ideas alive in the same mind, even occasionally to show two faces at the same time."[6]

It is the initial salvo in a campaign to defend a life that aspired to moral authenticity but often seemed to skirt the edge of having it both ways, a tendency that provided his most determined enemies with an irresistible target. In the *New Statesman*, the Marxist literary critic Terry Eagleton castigated him thus: "It is as though he sees his own double-dealing as a rather agreeable versatility—as testimony to his myriad-mindedness rather than as a privileged, spoilt-brat desire (among other things) to hog it all."[7] Characteristically, Hitchens does not duck his contradictions in

---

[4]Ibid., p. 36.
[5]Ibid., p. 7.
[6]Ibid.
[7]Terry Eagleton, "Hitch-22: a Memoir," *New Statesman*, May 31, 2010, http://www.newstatesman.com/books/2010/05/christopher-hitchens-iraq-self.

this memoir but embraces them, making no effort to hide the determination to keep "double-entry books." Describing an occasion on which his radical comrades caught him fraternizing with John Sparrow, a notorious symbol of the reactionary ruling caste at Oxford, Christopher writes: "I could have taken refuge in some 'know your enemy' formulation but something in me said that this would be ignoble. I didn't want a one-dimensional politicized life."[8]

Whatever may be said of these choices, they are an undeniable source of Christopher's appeal as an *enfant terrible*, the reason he is far more interesting than Eagleton or any of his left-wing critics with whom, this memoir shows, he still shared fundamental beliefs. It is why reading his book—agree with the politics or find them repellent or merely confusing—is an enterprise that is rewarding and often a delight. But Christopher's express desire not to be confined to a single standard does not explain the life that unfolded along multiple paths, nor does it put to rest the ethical questions that dog it.

In attempting to understand Christopher's politics and to understand *him*, the reader of his book is continually frustrated by a troubling lacuna at the heart of the text—a Hitch-22 as it were. Inexplicably for a writer so keenly observant of the world around him, Christopher's attempt at a self-portrait lacks the introspective curiosity integral to such a task or the interior probing that would unwrap his mysteries both for himself and others.

A dozen years before Christopher's book appeared, I was at a similar age and also wrote a memoir. One of my purposes was to give an account of the path I had traveled away from the Marxist views and socialist crusade that had previously shaped my life. Here is the way I described the point at which I finally came to reject these beliefs: "In that very moment a previously unthinkable possibility ... entered my head: The Marxist idea, to which I had

---

[8] Christopher Hitchens, "The Life of Johnson," op. cit., p. 105.

devoted my entire intellectual life and work was false.... For the first time in my conscious life I was looking at myself in my human nakedness, without the support of revolutionary hopes, without the faith in a revolutionary future—without the sense of self-importance conferred by the role I would play in remaking the world. For the first time in my life I confronted myself as I really was in the endless march of human coming and going. *I was nothing."*[9]

The crisis that followed this realization became a crucible of despair from which I was able to free myself only when I was able to replace the myths that had sustained me with other reasons to go on. But in Christopher's account of his life there is no such moment of crisis and no such self-encounter, despite the fact that the journey he describes would seem to have warranted both.

The conclusion to be drawn from this void is that, through all his surface changes, Christopher never felt a real subtraction from himself. At every stage of his career he was in his own eyes exactly what he had always been, except more so. Each twist in the road presented an opportunity for the accretion of complexity, making an ever more intriguing spectacle for his observers. As my colleague Peter Collier put it, "Christopher was an oyster always working on his own pearl."

Even if there was no such dark night of the soul when Christopher decided to abandon his hostility to a nation he had long been at war with, and to defend a symbol of the system he despised, such a night certainly took place much earlier, when as a young man fresh out of college he was climbing onto the wave of the revolutionary future. The life-changing event was the suicide of his mother Yvonne, still a young woman. She had killed herself in a hotel room in Athens after making a pact with the clergyman she had run off with and taken as a lover. It was, Christopher concedes,

---

[9]David Horowitz, *Radical Son,* Free Press, 1997, p. 280.

a "lacerating, howling moment in my life."[10] He was all of twenty-four.

But in Christopher's memoir there is no elaboration of how this trauma might have affected him—no indication of how so searing a loss and maternal betrayal might have impacted the double lives he pursued, the personal and political triangles he indulged and the fracturing of commitments to comrades and friends that followed. It is left for the reader to speculate about these matters from a text that denies the very elements that are essential to the task.

Although Christopher was married twice and had other romantic attachments, including a briefly mentioned affair with the sister of novelist Martin Amis, not one really appears in the 400-page book he wrote about himself. Of Christopher's first wife, a Greek Cypriot lawyer and the mother of his two oldest children, we are told nothing, not even her name. Carol, his second wife, is mentioned several times in passing; but we are never introduced to her, and there are no descriptions to put flesh on the woman he shared the last decades of his life with, no attempt to convey how he actually felt toward her or for that matter toward marriage itself. Of his children he writes mainly to concede his guilt over his absence as a father.

But when it comes to Yvonne, whose chapter-length portrait opens the book, the texture is quite different and feelings rise rapidly to the surface. "Yvonne then was the exotic and the sunlit when I could easily have had a boyhood of stern and dutiful English gray. She was the cream in the coffee, the gin in the Campari, the offer of wine or champagne instead of beer, the laugh in the face of bores and purse-mouths and skinflints, the insurance against bigots and prudes."

In a single sentence that closes his account of her life and death he provides a glimpse of their influence on his own: "Her defeat

---

[10]Christopher Hitchens, "The Life of Johnson," op. cit., p. 22.

and despair were also mine for a long time, but I have reason to know that she wanted me to withstand the woe, and when I once heard myself telling someone that she had allowed me a 'second identity,' I quickly checked myself and thought no, perhaps with luck she had represented my first and truest one."[11]

His truest identity. At this point on the page a reader expects the author's gaze to continue inward, exploring the vein just opened. Instead the text abruptly interrupts itself and presents the reader with a set piece under this cold heading: "A *Coda* on the Question of Self-Slaughter"—as though the author were writing about anyone but his mother. In the ensuing passage, the reflections are abstract and the tone that of an academic paper on psychology and the sociology of suicide as perceived in the writings of Emile Durkheim, A.A. Alvarez and Sylvia Plath.

The author tells the reader that this research reflects a quest he has pursued over "four decades," revealing without actually conceding that the pain in fact did not go away. But why then engage in this pedantic distraction from the turmoil in his heart, which tells us nothing about the trauma to his soul? Partly because he is the enemy of moist sentiments; but also because this gratuitous erudition is a squid's ink to cover his decision not to use the hairpin his mother offered him, in her life and in her death, to pick his own lock. As a memoirist, Hitchens was as *sui generis* as he was in other avenues of his life—not really wishing to be known by others or by himself.[12]

In his portrait of Yvonne, the son describes his mother as the power behind his future throne. "If there is going to be an upper class in this country," she vows, "Christopher is going to be in it."[13] Despite the constraints of their circumstances, Yvonne sent Christopher to infiltrate England's Protestant establishment, first at a posh private school the family could barely afford, and then to Balliol College Oxford to join the upper crust. Yvonne was in her own person a

[11]Ibid., pp. 25–26.
[12]I owe these perceptions to my friend Peter Collier.
[13]Christopher Hitchens, "The Life of Johnson," op. cit., p. 13.

secret agent, a displaced Polish Jew who in marrying the Commander had infiltrated an alien, anti-Semitic culture, hiding her true identity from those closest to her in order to provide herself and her children opportunities they would otherwise have been denied.

How did this matrilineal romance and its tragic ending affect Christopher's attitude towards the sunny tomorrows his comrades pursued? How did it color his optimism about the quest for social justice? (Where, he might have asked, was the justice for *him*? For *Yvonne*?) Christopher is silent. Reflecting on the anarchistic upheavals in France in 1968, he writes: "If you have never yourself had the experience of feeling that you are hooked to the great steam engine of history, then allow me to inform you that the conviction is a very intoxicating one."[14]

What is the need of the individual soul for this intoxication? What was *Christopher's* need? What happens when the engine and the feelings stop? Christopher makes no attempt to provide answers, nor does it seem likely that he even asked himself the questions.

All the while he was making his way through private schools and burrowing into the inner sanctums of the establishment, Christopher was simultaneously becoming a social rebel, taking the very skills venerable institutions had placed in his hands and puting those skills into the service of the war that a radical generation was waging against them. Yet even his commitment to rebellion was only half-made, or not so much made as hedged: "I was slowly being inducted into a revolution within the revolution, or to a left that was in and yet not of the 'left' as it was generally understood. This perfectly suited my already-acquired and protective habit of keeping two sets of books."[15] Or of being a secret agent in a world he never allowed himself to fully assimilate to.

The leftist sect Christopher joined was actually more convoluted and insulated from normal accountabilities than his narrative suggests. It was a revolution *within* "the revolution within

---

[14]Ibid., p. 98.
[15]Ibid., p. 87.

the revolution." Trotskyism could be said to be a revolution within the revolution. But the International Socialists, whom Christopher joined, were a Trotskyist splinter consisting of a hundred or so members who were opposed not only to Stalinism but to the Trotskyist mainstream. They separated themselves from other Trotskyists (and from Trotsky himself) who attacked Stalinism but still defended the Soviet Union. Trotskyists who followed "the Old Man" regarded themselves as "Bolsheviks" and viewed Russia as a "deformed" socialist state. By contrast, Hitchens's sect regarded the Soviet Union as having reverted to capitalism and therefore as having joined the enemy. This allowed the group to continue their attacks on the democracies of the West without having to defend "actually existing" socialism in Russia and make excuses for the totalitarian state their fellow Marxists had created.

How does Hitchens view the scholastically precious politics of his youth, or interpret its significance in his memoir? Typically, he doesn't say. But there is another witness, a Hitchens foil so to speak, who provides a telling insight into this puzzle. Peter Hitchens is Christopher's younger brother by two years but like Christopher's wives is virtually invisible in Christopher's text, despite the fact that they followed similar political paths. Peter joined the same International Socialist sect in the same era and later came to have second thoughts. But unlike Christopher, Peter eventually became a religious conservative with no ambivalent attitudes towards his previous leftist commitments.

Peter's commentary on Christopher's Trotskyist sect is this: "The [mainstream Trotskyists] were more honest than we were. Ours was the extreme version of pretending that the USSR was not the fault of socialists, or even of Bolsheviks (which we wished to be). Of course it was their fault, the fault of people exactly like us, but we closed our minds to this with a web of excuses. We pretended not to be who we were, and that the USSR was not what it was."[16]

---

[16]Peter Hitchens, *The Broken Compass*, Bloomsbury Academic, 2009, p. 75.

Christopher does not acknowledge that he pretended not to be who he was, and expresses no such second thoughts. On the contrary, his text is rich in late attitudes that are strikingly consistent with the views he held as a youth. "Where it was easy to do so," brother Peter writes of the International Socialists, "we supported causes—the National Liberation Front in Vietnam in particular—whose objects were to extend Soviet power."[17] The fact that the Vietnamese Communists, whom the New Left idolized, were minions of the totalitarian empire that Stalin had built was one of the realizations that turned Peter Collier and myself to second thoughts. When America quit the field of battle in Vietnam under pressure from the antiwar left, and the Communists proceeded to slaughter millions of innocents without protest from that left, we recoiled in horror at what our campaigns had made possible, at what those commitments had proved to be, and we said goodbye to all that.

Not so Christopher, who remains loyal in his memoir to the "antiwar" positions he held at the time, regarding the Communists as liberators and the Americans who opposed them as oppressor villains: "The United States was conducting an imperialist war in Indo-China, and a holding action against the insistent demands of its own long-oppressed black minority at home."[18] These are troublingly deceitful remarks. What holding action would Christopher be referring to? The American civil rights movement was supported by the entire nation outside the Deep South, including the White Houses of both Kennedy and the southerner Lyndon Johnson. What America was resisting the insistent demands of the black minority at home? And what imperialist war could he be thinking of? The one bruited in a famous malapropism of Jane Fonda, who claimed that America was in Vietnam for the "tung and the tinsten"? Or is Christopher ventriloquizing Ho Chi Minh

---

[17]Ibid.
[18]Christopher Hitchens, "The Life of Johnson," op. cit., p. 106.

and claiming that Americans wanted to replace the French as colonial masters of Indochina?

Writing of his own participation in a "vast demonstration"
against the war, which took place in front of the American
Embassy in London, Christopher recalls "the way in which my
throat and heart seemed to swell as the police were temporarily
driven back and the advancing allies of the Vietnamese began to
sing, 'We Shall Overcome.'" He then pats himself on the back: "I
added to my police record for arrests, of all of which I am still rea-
sonably proud."[19]

But why would he be proud of his arrest in a demonstration
supporting the Communist conquerors of Cambodia and South
Vietnam? Christopher's antiwar comrades, the International
Socialists among them, were not "allies of the Vietnamese," as
Christopher writes, but allies of the Vietnamese *Communists*, as
brother Peter points out, and therefore of the Soviet empire behind
them. What these leftists and their Communist heroes actually
achieved in Indochina was one of the worst genocides in history,
and a long totalitarian night for the Cambodians and Vietnamese.

To have remained an unreconstructed New Leftist into the
21st century was a particularly problematic failing for a man
whose model was George Orwell and whose political persona was
consciously framed by a perceived moral authority. In a statement
that amounted to a one-sentence credo, Christopher writes in his
memoir: "The synthesis for which one aimed was the Orwellian
one of evolving a consistent and integral anti-totalitarianism."[20]
But apparently not for the Cambodians and Vietnamese.

Loyalty to bad commitments leads to moral incoherence, a
syndrome that manifests itself in Christopher's choices of friends
and enemies. The epic struggle against totalitarianism for much of
the 20th century was America's Cold War against the Soviet
empire. But during the last decades of this conflict, Christopher's

---

[19]Ibid., p. 108.
[20]Ibid., p. 181.

platform was *The Nation* magazine—America's leading journal of the "*anti*-anti Communist left"—the fellow-traveling left of apologists for the Communists' crimes, the very people whom Trotsky had referred to as "frontier guards" for the Soviet empire. Although Christopher expressed intermittent internal dissents from this orthodoxy, he remained in his own words a "comrade" of these enablers of the totalitarian cause.

Right to the end, Christopher's political friends were still generously drawn from the *Nation* editorial board and the English Marxists grouped around the *New Left Review,* whom he gushingly refers to in an endnote to his memoir as "heroes and heroines of the 'first draft' and of the work in progress."[21] Among these heroes are the aforementioned Victor Navasky, defender of Alger Hiss; Robin Blackburn, a Castro acolyte; and Perry Anderson, an anti-American Marxist who regarded both the 9/11 attacks and the war in Iraq as by-products of the "Israel Lobby's" stranglehold on American policy.[22] Although Christopher socialized and shared political sentiments with a number of conservatives, including myself, there was not a single conservative I was able to identify on this list of political intimates and trusted readers.

As a self-conceived revolutionist within the revolution, Christopher maintained his contrarian ways and kept his double books, avoiding a record as regrettable as his abiding loyalties might have led one to expect. But the actual record was bad enough. My own experience of Christopher's malodorous service during the Cold War was his presence on a media firing squad that came to our Second Thoughts Conference with the intention of stigmatizing and discrediting the small band we had gathered to announce our revulsion at the slaughter of innocents in Indochina and our rejection of the destructive commitments our socialist colleagues had made.

---

[21]Ibid, p. 424.

[22]Perry Anderson "Jottings on the Conjuncture," *New Left* Review, November-December 2007, http://newleftreview.org/II/48/perry-anderson-jottings-on-the-conjuncture.

Two years later, Christopher attacked me venomously over the account Peter Collier and I had recently published about our second thoughts, which we called *Destructive Generation*. The opportunity was provided when Lewis Lapham, the left-wing host of a PBS show called "Book Notes," invited me to discuss our book on his show and also invited Christopher to comment on what we had written. Christopher singled out a passage in which I had described a small memorial service held for my father in my mother's house. I had written of my distress at the totalitarian overtones of the service, which I felt erased my father's individual memory, reducing him to a symbol of the "struggle." His progressive friends and comrades who gathered for the occasion, and who had known him all his life, eulogized him as a servant of their political cause but couldn't remember a single aspect of the flesh-and-blood person he had been. Christopher's comment on this was: "Who cares about his pathetic family?"

Christopher had come to Lapham's studio accompanied by his friend David Rieff, the writer Susan Sontag's son, who lay in ambush for me in the green room for an alleged slight to his mother. I greeted him warmly, not suspecting that he was about to spit at me in a revenge moment the two had arranged. The attack was inspired by a passage in our book, where Collier and I had noted the way Sontag trimmed her sails after her famously telling remark that Communism was "fascism with a human face," when she allowed the book she had written fulsomely praising the North Vietnamese police state to be republished without revision.[23] I hold no grudge against Hitchens or Rieff for the incident, but it remains a sharp reminder of how fiercely partisan Christopher could be in behalf of an indefensible cause.[24]

A striking elision in Christopher's backward look—particularly for a Trotskyist who regarded the Soviet Union as an enemy—is his failure to note, except in passing, the fall of the Berlin Wall and

---

[23]Horowitz, *Radical* Son, op. cit., p. 382.
[24]Christopher Hitchens, "The Life of Johnson," op. cit., p. 139.

the defeat of the totalitarian empire. Equally striking is the fact that, to the extent that Christopher mentions the anti-Communist struggle of the Cold War at all, his heroes are East European Marxists like Adam Michnik and Jacek Kuron, admirable figures whose second thoughts about Communism led them to participate in the democratic struggle against the Soviet state. But contrast this with Christopher's view of the conservatives who led the anti-Communist struggle for nearly four decades. Of Ronald Reagan, the Free World leader who actually wielded the power that made the "velvet revolutions" of the Michniks and Kurons possible—or even thinkable—Christopher has this to say: "Even now, when I squint back at him through the more roseate lens of his compromise with Gorbachev, I can easily remember ... exactly why I found him so rebarbative at the time."[25] Rebarbative: *adj.*, repellent, unattractive, forbidding, grim.

And what, exactly, might Christopher have had in mind in referring to Reagan's "compromise" with Gorbachev? Could he have been suggesting that Gorbachev agreed not to send the Red Army to rebuild the Berlin Wall and crush the Eastern European revolt in exchange for Reagan's agreement not to *invade* Eastern Europe or the Soviet Union? Can he have actually believed this?

Possibly. For Christopher's text is not finished with Reagan: "There was, first, his appallingly facile manner as a liar"—"he was married to a woman who employed a White House astrologer"— "[he] was frequently photographed in the company of 'end-times' Protestant fundamentalists"—and so on, *ad nauseam.*[26] Christopher actually sanitized this litany from its original appearance in the malicious obituary he wrote when Reagan died in 2004, and from which much of the attack in his memoir is cribbed: "I only saw him once up close, which happened to be when he got a question he didn't like.... The famously genial grin turned into a rictus

---

[25]Ibid., p. 232.
[26]Ibid., pp 232–3.

of senile fury: I was looking at a cruel and stupid lizard."[27] This was how Christopher summed up a man who liberated hundreds of millions of victims of totalitarianism, and who is revered throughout the former Soviet empire as a hero for this service to the cause of freedom. An Orwellian synthesis of "consistent and integral anti-totalitarianism," indeed.

Contrast this contemptuous performance with Christopher's enduring sympathies for his long-admired but eventually discarded friend Noam Chomsky—a man who spent the Cold War years denying the Cambodian genocide, promoting a denier of the Jewish Holocaust, and comparing America, unfavorably, to the Third Reich. When Chomsky's extreme views came under attack from other leftists, Christopher actually defended him in a regrettable article that attempted to explain away Chomsky's apologetics for the Cambodian genocide. Christopher called his piece "The Chorus and Cassandra," as though Chomsky—one of the most cited intellectuals in the academic world—was a prophet of truth to whom no one would listen.[28]

Eventually the two fell out over Chomsky's justification of the 9/11 Islamic attack on the World Trade Center and his opposition to America's military rescue of Muslims in Bosnia. But in his memoir, written nearly ten years later, Christopher still managed to find Chomsky "a polemical talent well-worth mourning, and [a man with] a feeling for justice that ought not to have gone rancid and resentful."[29] As a leftist who had a similar falling out with Chomsky twenty years earlier over his insistence that America was no better than Russia and that *Pravda* was a "mirror image"

---

[27]Christopher Hitchens, "Not Even A Hedgehog: The Stupidity of Ronald Reagan." *Slate,* June 7, 2004, http://www.slate.com/articles/news_ and_politics/fighting_words/2004/06/not_even_a_hedgehog.html.

[28]Christopher Hitchens, "The Chorus and Cassandra," *Grand Street,* Autumn 1985, http://www.chomsky.info/onchomsky/1985——.htm; For a critique of Hitchens's article see, Bruce Sharp, "The Chorus and the Cassandra: A Response," *Cambodia,* July 11, 2010, http://www.mekong.net/cambodia/hitchens.htm.

[29]Christopher Hitchens, "The Life of Johnson," op. cit., p. 416n.

of *The New York Times*, I can testify that Chomsky's feelings were rancid and resentful long before 9/11, and that his commitment to justice was nil.[30]

A similar myopia draws a cloud over Christopher's otherwise admirable defenses of First Amendment freedoms. His long and courageous battle in behalf of Salman Rushdie, after the Ayatollah Khomeini had issued a *fatwa* calling for his murder, is one of several memorable passages in *Hitch-22* and a pivotal episode in the evolution of Christopher's current beliefs. The Rushdie case was, he writes, "a matter of everything I hated versus everything I loved. In the hate column: dictatorship, religion, stupidity, demagogy, censorship, bullying and intimidation. In the love column: literature, irony, humor, the individual and the defense of free expression."[31]

But in the next breath Christopher fawns over the late Jessica Mitford, a Communist hack who spent her life supporting dictatorships, stupidity, demagogy, bullying, intimidation and censorship. He calls her one of his "heroines." As it happens, this hypocrisy in Christopher's text has a resonance for me personally. When Peter Collier and I were still leftists we wrote an article about murders that had been committed by George Jackson and other Black Panthers, who to this day are regarded as progressive heroes. Leftists who were aware of these crimes suppressed the knowledge and withheld the facts in the name of a higher political truth. Peter and I published our article in the journal of a progressive writers' guild and did so at some personal risk, since members of the political gangs responsible for the murders were still active.

While our article was undergoing the usual editorial scrutiny, Jessica Mitford and *Nation* journalist Eve Pell led a campaign to stigmatize us as snitches and racists (since the perpetrators of the crimes were black), and to pressure the journal's editors into censoring what we had written. In a letter describing our article not as

---

[30]David Horowitz, "A Radical's Disenchantment," *The Nation*, December 8, 1979, pp. 586–588, http://www.unz.org/Pub/Nation-1979dec08-00586 (reprinted in Left Illusions as the chapter "Left Illusions").
[31]Christopher Hitchens, "The Life of Johnson," op. cit., p. 268.

untrue but as "appalling" and "atrocious" because it *was* true, Mitford said: "I deeply wish it had never been written." At a public meeting of the progressive guild, to which we also belonged, she told the writers assembled that it was their responsibility as progressives to suppress facts that hurt the cause and to print only those facts that helped it—a practice in which the *Nation* editors are well versed.[32] How, in the light of this reality, was Jessica Mitford one of Christopher's heroines?

Or how, for that matter, is Trotsky? The unsentimental Peter Hitchens observes that the Trotskyist left to which his brother and he belonged was in the habit of attacking Communists in power as tyrants but supporting Communists, when they were out of power, as liberators. As examples, he cites the lionization of Rosa Luxemburg and Leon Trotsky, who, as it happens, were two of his brother's "favorite characters in history." (The other three were Socrates, Spinoza and Thomas Paine.)[33]

Rosa Luxemburg was a revolutionary who was murdered while she was still young and therefore, as Peter comments, "never lived to touch power." Trotsky, on the other hand, became a revolutionary in power and was deeply implicated in the creation of the totalitarian state. He was the commander of the Red Army forces sent to crush the revolt of the Kronstadt sailors, who were Bolsheviks protesting the sinister turn the revolution had already taken in its first years. He was a promoter of the forced labor policies that led to the *gulag* and author of the most articulate defense of the Red Terror, as well as one of its enforcers. He was a champion of the principle that the ends justify the means. How, then, did Trotsky become one of Christopher's historical favorites?

One way was to put on political blinders and focus on the figure of Trotsky out of power—to view him as the author of *The Revolution Betrayed* and the leader of the sect of former Communists seeking to overthrow the totalitarian regime that Trotsky had done so much to

---

[32]Horowitz, *Radical Son*, op. cit., pp. 320–321.
[33]Christopher Hitchens, "The Life of Johnson," op. cit., p. 333. This was an answer Christopher gave to the "Proust questionnaire.".

create. This, in fact, was how Christopher did see and admire him, although he framed the picture a little more indulgently, portraying Trotsky as the hero of an "epic struggle to mount an international resistance" to Stalin and the totalitarian state.[34] It was as an avatar of the anti-Stalinist left, a movement Christopher romanticizes in his memoir, that Trotsky inspired his adulation. Trotskyism evidently meant to Christopher that he could regard himself as a Marxist and a revolutionary without having to say he's sorry.[35]

There is another way that Trotsky can appear a worthy paladin, which is if one believes that the engine of "history" is still running, and that the epic oppressions of Stalinism were merely an unpleasant prelude to an authentic Communist future. This is, in fact, the way Trotsky's biographer and Christopher's hero (and, as it happens, my own one-time mentor) Isaac Deutscher actually did portray and justify Trotsky in his three-volume hagiography—*The Prophet Armed, The Prophet Unarmed* and *The Prophet Outcast*. This trilogy was the object of Christopher's intemperate praise in a review he wrote for *The Atlantic Monthly* in 2009. The reason for Christopher's enthusiasm was that Deutscher was a Marxist, and the framework of his trilogy is the assumption that the engine of history is still running.

According to Deutscher, who wrote his trilogy while the Berlin Wall was still in place and the Cold War still raging, the socialist foundations of Soviet society would assert themselves at some point in the future and give birth to an authentic socialist state. This would be the ultimate vindication of Trotsky's ideas.[36]

---

[34]Ibid., p. 87.

[35]"Christopher Hitchens Called Trotskyist" (video), June 4, 2010, http://sciencestage.com/v/32455/why-christopher-hitchens-called-himself-a-trotskyist.

[36]I have written about Deutscher's misreading of the Russian Revolution in an essay titled "The Road to Nowhere" which can be found in *The Politics of Bad Faith*, 1998, as well as in the present volume of *The Black Book of the American Left*. My commentary on Christopher's review of the Deutscher trilogy can be found here: David Horowitz, "David Horowitz Versus Christopher Hitchens," *History News Network*, July 31, 2002, http://historynewsnetwork.org/article/893.

Without such an outcome, there could be no justification for what Trotsky and the Bolsheviks did; for what they did was horrible, and without a liberating outcome would rank among history's greatest crimes. Hence Deutscher's wager on the future.

But, as events were to show, Deutscher was wrong: the socialist foundations of the Soviet Union were in fact the engines of its bankruptcy, not the prelude to a democratic future, and caused the system's collapse. Deutscher died in 1967 and did not live to see this result or evaluate his own theories in light of the facts. But there was no such excuse for Christopher, whose memoir displays no recognition of the failure of Marx's theories, or of Deutscher's hypotheses, or of Trotsky's crimes.

Instead there is the suggestion in Christopher's memoir that "a faint, saintly penumbra still emanates from the Old Man" since the spirit of his "revolution within the revolution" can still be detected in the magical moment of 1968 or the presence of a handful of Trotskyists in the Solidarity movement, which brought down the Communist regime in Poland.[37] But this is sentimental trash. The "magic" of 1968 was in Christopher's imagination while an historical force against Communism, immeasurably greater than the handful of Christopher's favored Trotskyists was the Catholic Church— an institution the author loathes so much he doesn't deign to mention it.

A better understanding of Christopher's attitudes comes with the realization that he was really more about sensibility than politics, or perhaps that politics was a matter of sensibility for him. Deutscher, a writer of considerable literary talent, made Trotsky into an existential hero, a Prometheus daring the gods. This is why Christopher was enamored of him—because Trotsky was the archromantic, the incarnation of the lost Yvonne.[38]

---

[37]Christopher Hitchens, "The Old Man," *The* Atlantic, July-August 2004, http://www.theatlantic.com/magazine/archive/2004/07/the-old-man/302984/.
[38]I am indebted to Peter Collier for this observation.

The same sensibility underlies his otherwise inexplicable attachment to the tattered figure of Marx. In a conversation with Martin Amis, he said: "For most of my life I thought the only principle worth upholding, worth defending, worth advocating, worth witnessing for, was socialist internationalism"—then added, "I am no longer a socialist, but I am still a Marxist."[39]

But how? The stab Christopher makes in his memoir at resurrecting the Old Mole to explain the financial collapse of 2008 is embarrassing: "My old Marxism came back to me as I contemplated the 'dead labor' that had been hoarded ... saw it being squandered in a victory for finance capital over industrial capital, noticed the ancient dichotomy between use value and exchange value, and saw again the victory of those monopolists who 'make' money over those who only have the power to earn it."[40]

This explication can only be tolerated as a literary trope. As economic analysis it is archaic and absurd. *The triumph of finance capital over industrial capital! The dichotomy between use value and exchange value! The suggestion that capitalists are monopolists who make money rather than earn it!* These are themes of a political romance of Tertullian dimensions—belief in an age where God is dead. *Credo quia impossibile est.* I believe *because* it is impossible.[41]

Christopher's comments to Amis seemed to imply that he no longer regarded socialism as a future that could actually work. In an interview with *Reason Magazine* conducted just prior to 9/11, he virtually conceded as much. "There is no longer a general socialist critique of capitalism—certainly not the sort of critique that proposes an alternative or a replacement."[42] But why then

---

[39]Martin Amis and Christopher Hitchens, "A Conversation about Anti-Semitism and Saul Bellow, Part 3," https://www.youtube.com/v/K6rRA64f9ug%26hl=en%26fs=1.

[40]Christopher Hitchens, "The Life of Johnson," op. cit., p. 5.

[41]Again, I am indebted to Peter Collier for this observation.

[42]"An Interview with Christopher Hitchens" in Simon Cottee and Thomas Cushman, eds. *Christopher Hitchens and His Critics*, NYU Press, 2008, p. 169.

describe oneself as a Marxist, since Marx's entire critique of capitalism was based on the assumption that socialism was a practical alternative? More importantly, why would Christopher fail to understand that in seeking to achieve an impossible future revolutionaries become merely destroyers—*nihilists?* If a socialist future is impossible, the effort to achieve one by putting a wrecking ball to existing institutions can only be regarded as malignant and evil.

Notwithstanding Christopher's express doubts about a socialist future, his memoir is laced with unrepentant utopianism. A notable example is his paean to the labor movement, of which he says, "For me, this 'movement' is everything." He then makes a remarkable statement: "Official Britain may have its Valhalla of heroes and statesmen and conquerors and empire builders, but *we* know that the highest point ever reached in the history of civilization was in the city of Basel in 1912 when the leaders of the socialist parties of all countries met to coordinate an opposition to the coming World War."[43]

For those who remember the Basel declaration Christopher's remark is a particularly ludicrous triumph of sentiment over history. The opposition to war that the socialist parties coordinated in Basel in 1912 was quickly and notoriously repudiated—by socialists. They had resolved to vote against the war credits in their respective national parliaments and thus prevent the impending conflict. For Marx had written—and "socialist internationalists" professed to believe—that the working classes had no country, and "nothing to lose but their chains." But this was a Marxist fantasy, unanchored in reality, and two years after "the highest point ever reached in human civilization" the same socialist leaders turned their backs on this pledge and voted to go to war. Marx was proved wrong: the workers did have a country, and socialism was exposed as an empty and dangerous illusion. The "highest point ever reached in the history of civilization" was thus little more than a memorable hypocrisy.

---

[43]Christopher Hitchens, "The Life of Johnson," op. cit., p. 139.

Although he danced away from his "internationalist" faith and even abandoned his anti-war stance with regard to America's conflict in Iraq, the romantic Christopher still clung to the old fantasy and continued the impossible dream in which the engine of history is still running: "The names of real heroes like [the socialists] Jean Jaurès and Karl Liebknecht make the figures of Asquith and Churchill seem like pygmies." And why would this be so? Because, in Christopher's mind, had an international socialist revolution taken place in 1919, it would have precluded all the nightmares of the 20th century, including the ones that *faux* socialists like Stalin created: "The violence and disruption of a socialist transformation in those years would have been infinitely less than the insane sacrifice of culture to barbarism, and the Nazism and Stalinism that ensued from it."[44]

In other words, the alternatives mankind faced in 1919 were bloody socialism or bloodier barbarism. Christopher is here paying tacit tribute to the German Marxist, Rosa Luxemburg, who used exactly that slogan—"Socialism or barbarism"—to inspire her fellow revolutionaries in 1919. There can hardly be doubt that Christopher would still have liked to count himself among them when he wrote these words. Rather than posing actual historical alternatives, Luxemburg's challenge was little more than a secularized version of the religious choice between heaven or eternal damnation to keep the faithful in line. It was one of the oddities of Christopher's compartmentalized life that the author of *God Is Not Great* and of its brazen subtitle—*religion poisons everything*—was so passionately attached to this political version of an earthly redemption.

In his back pocket, the author of *Hitch-22* kept his own escape clause to provide an exit from the *cul-de-sac* he had worked himself into. The "movement, which for me is everything," he wrote, is "all gone now, gone to pieces." Consequently, in his mind there were no real-world consequences for believing and promoting the

---

[44]Ibid.

revolutionary myth.[45] It was just an idea. But—and here was the hitch—an idea that for him contained the ever- present possibility that one day it might spring back to life. It was another case of Christopher wanting to eat his cake and have it too.

In the 1970s Christopher adopted a second identity, making more and more frequent trips to America, eventually migrating across the Atlantic and setting up shop at *The Nation* magazine. It was another two-track engagement. On the one hand there was the America that functioned as the left's symbol of capitalist hell—a racist, imperialist bastion of oppression. Exposing the evils of his new homeland was the way Christopher earned his keep at *The Nation*, a flagship publication of the pro-Soviet, pro-Castro, pro-Vietcong, anti-American left. On the other hand he was deeply attracted to another America, a land of expansive contradictions and bracing freedoms—which distinguished him markedly from his comrades. The other America was entirely seductive to the distaff side of Christopher's personality: "Here was a country that could engage in a frightening and debilitating and unjust war, and undergo a simultaneous convulsion of its cities on the question of justice for its oldest and largest minority, *and* start a conversation on the rights of women ... *and* have a show trial of confessed saboteurs in Chicago where the incredibly guilty defendants actually got off...."[46]

Would that Christopher had allowed the generous, free-spirited dimension of America, which resonated with the better angels of his own nature, to temper the scorn he poured on his adopted country during his *Nation* years. But the guilty pleasures he experienced in enemy territory had to be paid for by the pact he had made with the socialist devil, and that precluded a just accounting. "My personal way of becoming Americanized," as he explains, "was to remain a blood brother of the American left."[47]

---

[45]Ibid., p. 138.
[46]Ibid., p. 215.
[47]Ibid., p. 236.

Unfortunately, the left that had emerged from the campaign against the Vietnam War was characterized by a corrosive anti-Americanism, which was incompatible with Christopher's otherwise keen sense of America's virtues.

As Christopher became more familiar with his new environment, the increasing irrationality of the *Nation* hostiles started to take its toll. It began with the warm attitudes they showed towards the totalitarian enemy, which did not sit well with a Trotskyist familiar with the depraved nature of the Soviet regime. "I was often made aware in *Nation* circles that there really were people who did think that Joseph McCarthy had been far, far worse than Joseph Stalin."[48] At one point, progressive icon Noam Chomsky unnerved him by saying that America's democracy was morally worse than the Soviet police state. His "much-admired" friend Gore Vidal also jolted him by describing the FBI as "our KGB,"[49] and then by writing an anti-Semitic diatribe, which Christopher protested to his *Nation* editors. Victor Navasky, the editor-in-chief and best man at Christopher's wedding, decided to publish it anyway, saying, "Well, Gore is Gore."[50]

These conflicts intensified when Christopher trained his sights on Bill Clinton, a veteran of the anti-Vietnam war movement, and the first Sixties alumnus to reach the White House. Christopher, who had met Clinton when they were both students at Oxford, took a strong disliking to the candidate when he ordered the execution of a mentally retarded black prisoner, Ricky Ray Rector, to prove that he was tough enough on crime. The dislike increased with Clinton's continuing duplicity in office and led to a sharp tract Christopher wrote about the Clintons called *No One Left to Lie To: The Values of the Worst Family*. The bad blood created by his attacks on Clinton accumulated to the point where he felt he might have to give up his *Nation* column. "The determination of

---

[48]Ibid., p. 237.
[49]Ibid.
[50]Ibid., p. 238.

the editors to defend Clinton's indefensible actions," he writes in his memoir, "completely squandered the claim of a magazine like *The Nation* to be a journal of opposition."[51] But of course the *Nation* wasn't just a "journal of opposition;" it was a journal of the anti-American opposition, and, as Christopher well knew, its audience inevitably gave such hypocrisies a political pass.

Tensions between Christopher and the left came to a head in the spring of 1999 when he appeared before a congressional committee to testify against Clinton adviser, fellow progressive and close personal friend, Sidney Blumenthal. His testimony ended their fifteen-year friendship and inspired attacks from the comrades. It is another telling lacuna in Christopher's memoir that there is no mention of Blumenthal or this matter, which became a minor *cause célèbre*. Hence the reader is provided with no insight into Christopher's complex personal and political relationships, or into the compass that provided his guide through these uncharted waters.

The White House had given Blumenthal the task of neutralizing potential female witnesses to Clinton's abusive sexual advances by spreading defamatory stories about them to Washington reporters. Blumenthal made the mistake of turning to his friend Christopher as a reporter he could trust to pass on the slanders. Christopher chose instead to expose Blumenthal. In the eyes of the comrades, this betrayal—bad enough in itself—was compounded by the fact that Christopher gave his testimony to a congressional committee chaired by Republican Henry Hyde, a pro-life conservative who was a target of their hate.

This hatred now descended on Christopher's head. Radicals like longtime friend and *Nation* colleague Alex Cockburn began reviling him as "Snitchens" and worse. (Cockburn, with whom Christopher was once joined at the hip, is yet another figure

---

[51]Cottee and Cushman, eds. *Christopher Hitchens and His Critics*, op. cit., p. 173.

inexplicably missing from his memoir.) In a purification ritual reminiscent of religious witch-hunts, prominent leftists like Todd Gitlin stepped forward to piously declare that Christopher Hitchens would never be allowed to darken their doors again. While Christopher fails to mention his broken friendship with Blumenthal or the internal wrenching it undoubtedly caused him, as well as the general reactions and the long-term impact they may have had on his relations with the left, he does reproduce one telling message he received on his telephone answering machine. It was left by Dorothy Healy, a well-known Communist and long-time friend, in an archaic argot: "You stinking little rat. I always knew you were no good. You are a stool pigeon and a fink. I hope you rot in scab and blackleg hell...."[52] So much for the warm fraternity in the party of the workers.

While failing to mention the Blumenthal episode in his book, Christopher referred to it in the *Reason* interview, where he recalled how his progressive friends were now attacking him as a "McCarthyite" in the pages of *The Nation*. This reaction, he comments, "showed the amazing persistence of antediluvian categories and thoughts on the Left ... [which were] applied to me in a very mendacious and I thought thuggish way." He concluded: "There is no such thing as a radical Left anymore. The world of Gloria Steinem and Jesse Jackson, let's say, has all been, though it does not realize it, hopelessly compromised by selling out to Clintonism. It became, under no pressure at all, and with no excuse and in no danger, a voluntary apologist for abuse of power."[53] But in light of the left's long service to the thugs of Stalinism and Maoism and Castroism, was it really any different before?

Witnessing the way Christopher's comrades turned on him, I could not help thinking of my own experience as an apostate radical. I was writing a guest column for the left-wing magazine *Salon*

---

[52]Christopher Hitchens, "The Life of Johnson," op. cit., p. 410.
[53]Cottee and Cushman, eds. *Christopher Hitchens and His Critics*, op. cit. p. 173.

and decided to post an article defending him.[54] "This tainting and ostracism of sinners," I wrote, "is, in fact, the secret power of the leftist faith.... The spectacle of what happens to a heretic like Hitchens when he challenges the party code is a warning to others not to try it."[55] The attempt to purge him I explained this way: "The community of the left is a community of meaning and is bound by ties that are fundamentally religious. For the non-religious, politics is the art of managing the possible. For the left it is the path to social redemption ... it is about *us* being on the side of the angels, and *them* as the party of the damned."[56]

Like every secret agent, Christopher still possessed his packet of false passports and was able to reach a *modus vivendi* with *The Nation*'s editors, who agreed not to print any more defamatory attacks on him in exchange for what readers were not told.[57] This rendered the purge incomplete, and enabled him to retain a foothold in the left. When a year passed and he hadn't contacted me about my defense of him, I thought he was probably resentful that a political enemy had spoken in his behalf and worsened his case. But then we chanced on each other at a *Los Angeles Times* book festival. Quite unexpectedly he thanked me, warmly and graciously, for the article, and we agreed to make a date for a longer talk. It was the beginning of our friendship. In that moment I also knew Christopher was in a state of motion in regard to his allegiances on the left and therefore in regard to his loyalties to his new country, which he was clear-eyed enough to see was responsible for defending the very freedoms he cherished.

---

[54]David Horowitz, "Hats Off to a Condemned Man," *Salon*, March 1, 1999, http://www.salon.com/1999/03/01/nc_01horo/.

[55]David Horowitz, "The Secret Power of the Leftist Faith" in Volume 2 of this series, *Progressives*. The article first appeared in *Salon* under the title "Defending Christopher." My *Salon* column was terminated when it became a paid subscription magazine because, its editors explained, their readership wouldn't pay to read the views of a conservative.

[56]Horowitz, *Hating Whitey*, op. cit. pp. 246–247.

[57]Cottee and Cushman, eds. *Christopher Hitchens and His Critics*, op. cit.

The turn in Christopher's political life would culminate on 9/11 when the United States was attacked by a new totalitarian foe. The threat posed by Islamic jihadists had been brought home to Christopher much earlier. "The realization that we were in a cultural and political war with Islamic theocracy came to me with force and certainty not on September 11, 2001 but on February 14, 1989," he observed in an interview, "when the Ayatollah Khomeini offered money in his own name to suborn the murder of my friend Salman Rushdie."[58]

Soon afterwards there was another revelation. This time it was about the leviathan that the left regarded as the command center of global oppression but that Christopher now saw as the guardian of religious freedom. The United States military had intervened to stop the genocide of Bosnian Muslims in the heart of Europe when no European or Muslim nation would. "The realization that American power could and should be used for the defense of pluralism and as a punishment for fascism came to me in Sarajevo a year or two later," Christopher writes. "It was the first time I found myself in the same trench as people like Paul Wolfowitz and Jeane Kirkpatrick: a shock I had to learn to get over."[59]

There were shocks to come. On September 11, 2001, Christopher was lecturing in the Northwest about one of his personal *bêtes-noires*, Henry Kissinger, when his wife called from their Washington home to tell him Islamic jihadists had attacked the World Trade Center and the Pentagon. It was the same enemy that had attempted to kill Rushdie, and thus an episode in the same war of "everything I hated versus everything I loved." As Christopher reflected on what had happened, he was immediately torn by two thoughts: the first a fear of being swept up in an unthinking "totalitarian" patriotism, and the second his revulsion at a

---

[58]Interview in Frontpagemag.com, December 10, 2003. Reprinted in Cottee and Cushman, eds. *Christopher Hitchens and His Critics*, op. cit., p. 173.
[59]Ibid., p. 174.

comment made by one of the left-wing students who had attended his lecture: "You know what my friends are saying? They are saying it is the chickens coming home to roost."[60]

The remark infuriated him, provoking a response which "came welling up in me with an almost tidal force: What bloody chickens? Come to think of it, whose bloody 'home?'" This last was a telling comment about the loyalties of his *Nation* comrades. When the most prominent among them, Noam Chomsky, regurgitated the same anti-American sentiments, a seismic fissure opened in the ground underneath them: "[Chomsky regarded] almost everything since Columbus as having been one big succession of genocides and land-thefts, [and] did not really believe that America was a good idea to begin with. Whereas I had come to appreciate that it most certainly was."[61]

Christopher began speaking and writing publicly to the same effect, and the more he did so the more vicious were the attacks directed against him from the left. Troubling thoughts began to percolate in Christopher's head: "I could not bear the idea that anything I had written or said myself had contributed to this mood of cynicism and defeatism, not to mention moral imbecility on the left."[62]

Christopher had found a new cause that was not radical and no longer a fantasy about an imagined future, but a cause that involved the defense of a flesh-and-blood reality: "Shall I take out papers of citizenship?" he asked at the end of a poignant post-9/11 article he wrote for *Vanity Fair*. "Wrong question. In every essential way, I already have."[63]

Once he had allowed himself to acknowledge that capitalist America, with its passion for liberty and openness to change, could be a force for good, other realizations followed. Christopher

---

[60]Christopher Hitchens, "The Life of Johnson," op. cit., p. 243.
[61]Ibid., p. 244.
[62]Ibid., p. 245.
[63]Ibid., p. 247.

became, in his own words, "part of [the] public opinion" that supported America's campaigns to remove the perpetrators from Afghanistan and to unseat the despot and mass murderer, Saddam Hussein, in Iraq. "The idea of 'Reds for Bush' might be incongruous," he observed wryly of his support for the president, "but it was a great deal more wholesome than 'pacifists for Saddam,'" which is what the anti-Iraq war movement supported by most of Christopher's friends had become.[64]

Six months after the beginning of war in Iraq, Christopher reviewed a book of my political writings called *Left Illusions.* "With the Cold War so to speak behind us," he wrote, "I suspected that Horowitz would find life without the old enemy a little dull. How much of an audience would there be for his twice-told tale about growing up in a doggedly loyal Communist family and his agonizing over the series of wrenches and shocks that had detached him from Marxism all together? But then, I didn't anticipate that in the fall of 2001, I would be reading solemn polemics by leading intellectualoids proposing a strict moral equivalence—moral equivalence at best in some cases—between America and the Taliban. Nor did I expect to see street theater anti-war demonstrations, organized by open admirers of Fidel Castro, Slobodan Milosevic, and Kim Jong-Il, united in the sinister line of, in effect, 'hands off Saddam Hussein.' So I admit that I now find the sardonic, experienced pessimism in Horowitz's book a bit more serviceable than I once did."[65]

While gratifying for the concession it offered, this was less than the full-throated endorsement of second thoughts I had hoped for. It was one more Hitch-22. If the totalitarian enemies of the American experiment were real, why imply that they were something conservatives like myself had invented to prevent life from

[64]Ibid., p. 295.

[65]Christopher's review appeared in the November 16, 2003 *Los Angeles Times* and is reprinted in Cottee and Cushman, eds. *Christopher Hitchens and His Critics,* op. cit. The citation appears on p. 191.

becoming dull? The suggestion that these threats were a figment of conservative imaginations was, in fact, a standard trope of leftists to deflect attention from the fact that they were sympathetic to America's enemies. To see Christopher's ambivalent reassessment of my second thoughts was less than reassuring.

Only in the final chapter of his memoir did Christopher even begin to address the task of calibrating his own political revisions. He framed these reflections as a question about the arc of his career: "Decline, Mutation or Metamorphosis?" By this point in his narrative, there was no mystery that the middle term was going to be the preferred one, and the ends excluded. One of the unkinder cuts delivered in his *envoi* is aimed at those of us who did not regard our second thoughts as shedding a once-serviceable skin, but as an occasion to reassess what we had done and undertake an accounting of the damage we had inflicted—to make a painful but necessary break from our past. To distance himself from us and avoid the perdition to which his comrades would have assigned him, Christopher wrote: "I didn't so much repudiate a former loyalty, like some attention-grabbing defector, as feel it falling away from me."[66]

Christopher should have known better than to ascribe attention-getting to others, particularly those of us who—because of our opposition to the left—were cut off from the same cultural platforms that had made him such an intellectual celebrity. I can't help wondering whether it was fear of losing these audiences that prevented Christopher from repudiating loyalties which had helped to seal the fates of so many innocents. At one point in his memoir, he quotes Wilde's famous comment that a map of the world that did not have utopia on it would not be worth consulting, and makes this acid observation: "I used to adore that phrase, but now reflect more upon the shipwrecks and prison islands to which the quest has led." Just so. But how, then, could he also

---

[66]Christopher Hitchens, "The Life of Johnson," op. cit., p. 411.

speak of a loyalty "falling away" as though it were a matter of discarding some old school tie, rather than discovering he had once served a cause that destroyed the lives of millions?

Christopher's unsatisfying attempt to answer these questions begins with the unexpected appearance of his brother, Peter, who had just completed a memoir pointedly titled *The Broken Compass*. In this passage Christopher singles out a specific chapter of his brother's book as "unsettling." The chapter, called "A Comfortable Hotel on the Road to Damascus," is about the dissent of some leftists—Christopher pointedly among them—over the Iraq War and more broadly over the "War on Terror." As a paleo-conservative, Peter opposed both wars as crusades to change the world, and therefore as endeavors appropriate to the utopian left. "For the habitual leftist," Peter wrote of his brother, the War on Terror "has the virtue of making him look as if he can change his mind, even when he has not really done so."[67]

It is a shrewd perception. In Christopher's perspective the war against terror is first of all the crusade of reason against religion and its fanatical believers, which is why he can embrace it without repudiating his progressive roots. The conflict between reason and religion was the theme of his defense of Rushdie. Following the attacks of 9/11 and the publication of his best-selling *God Is Not Great: How Religion Poisons Everything*, it became a personal obsession and the central mission of his life and work. "The defense of science and reason is the great imperative of our time," he announces in oracular fashion on the final page of his memoir.[68]

But is it? The *jihad* against the West is certainly the product of totalitarian Islam; but it is opposed by believing Christians, Jews, Hindus and members of other religious faiths. Is it really the case that science and reason are in great jeopardy in the West, as Christopher claimed? It is difficult to see how. Science and reason

---

[67]Ibid., pp. 405–6; Peter Hitchens, *The Broken Compass*, op. cit., pp. 173, et seq.
[68]Christopher Hitchens, "The Life of Johnson," op. cit., p. 422.

are hardly the targets of scorched-earth attacks such as those mounted against all religions by Christopher and his new utopian allies. There are no best-selling broadsides called "Reason Is Not Great" or "The Science Delusion." Nor are scientific institutions being blown up and desecrated, the way synagogues and churches routinely are at the hands of Muslim jihadists.

An insight into the religious nature of some leftist convictions that Christopher offers in his text turns out to be self-reflective: "Rather like our then friend Chomsky, Edward [Said] in the final instance believed that if the United States was doing something, then that thing could not *by definition* be a moral or ethical action."[69] Said and Chomsky took this view because, in the Manichaean world that radicals inhabited, the United States was the center of global oppression, personifying the rule of evil which no good deed could mitigate. But is not Christopher's view of religion, as an institution that "poisons everything," identical? Did he not view religion as an institution that *by definition* could do no right?

Christopher's war against religion thrust him up against his own origins. He had not become aware that his mother, Yvonne, was a Jew until he was forty-five years old, and she was long gone. The discovery launched him on a pursuit of the past and forced him into reflections on Judaism, which he recorded in his memoir. "As a convinced atheist, I ought to agree with Voltaire that Judaism is not just one more religion, but in its way the root of religious evil," he writes in a disturbing passage. "Without the stern, joyless rabbis and their 613 dour prohibitions, we might have avoided the whole nightmare of the Old Testament, and the brutal, crude wrenching of that into prophecy-derived Christianity, and the later plagiarism of Judaism and Christianity into the various forms of Islam."[70] This uncharacteristically leaden—one might say totalitarian—prose is alarmingly present in Christopher's

---

[69]Ibid., p. 394. Emphasis in original.
[70]Ibid., p. 376.

writings about religion; the very opposite of the supple textures and multivalent cadences that normally seduce and reward his readers. "Leaden prose," he warns us in another context, "always tends to be a symptom of other problems."[71] And so it is.

The problem here is that Christopher views religion generally, and Judaism in particular, through Marxist lenses. He sees religion reductively as the "opium of the people, a sigh of the oppressed," and posits a future world liberation in the elimination of the oppressor. Pursuing the cliché, Christopher casts the Biblical rabbis as a ruling class imposing their yoke on a passive flock. This is the kind of misreading of history that ideological formulas inevitably invite. The 613 commandments are not simply prohibitions, and are not merely dour. Among many to which one could point, two of the commandments enjoin the flock *not* to oppress the weak and to honor one's father and mother. Those are commandments that a less ideologically blinkered Christopher might embrace. But even if this were not the case, the rabbis could hardly impose prohibitions lasting thousands of years on congregations that did not ultimately seek or need them, or regard them as useful for their earthly survival.

Did Christopher ever consider how it was that a tiny, dispersed people like the Jews could have survived for several millennia—outlasting all their conquerors—without the beliefs and prohibitions that inspired and held them together? Unaccountably for someone whose mind is at other times so attentive, Christopher is blind to the way religion speaks to needs that are timeless and provides comforts that are beneficial, and has contributed to the most spectacular achievements of human culture, including those that are scientific. The very concepts of individual rights and democracy so dear to Christopher are contributions of religious thought.

After the discovery of Yvonne's secret, Christopher embarked on a quest for his own origins. But the search was destined to end

---

[71]Ibid., p. 282.

in ambivalence because he regarded Israel, the home of the Jews and the cultural center of Judaism, as an imperial oppressor, and the hostile Arabs of the Jordan as merely passive and oppressed victims. Christopher's dilemma was poignant. In a conversation he had had with Yvonne just before she took her life, she expressed her desire "to move to Israel" without revealing to her son the reason why. It was a desire, Christopher believed, that—had she actually gone through with it—would not have meant a personal liberation for her as a Jew, because she would have been "taking part in the perpetuation of an injustice."[72]

For Christopher the injustice was Israel itself. He regarded the Jewish inhabitants of Israel as "land-thieves" inspired by a religious myth to establish a "divine claim" and therefore a people who "wanted the land without the people."[73] According to Christopher, in stealing Arab land the Jews became oppressors who "made" the Arabs victims, "with infinite cause of complaint and indefinite justification for violent retaliation."[74] Was Christopher referring here to the creation of a death cult that promises sainthood and paradise to suicide bombers who blow up women and children because they are Jews?

But the premise itself is fallacious, and the passion misplaced. Israel was created out of the ruins of the Turkish Empire, not from an Arab—let alone a Palestinian—land. There would long ago have been a Palestinian state on the West Bank and Gaza (as there already is a majority Palestinian state in Jordan) but for the fact that the Arab Muslim goal is not to create a Palestinian homeland; it is to obliterate the Jewish homeland and replace it with a Muslim umma "from the river to the sea."

Even disregarding the fact of Israel's origins, consider the war in the Middle East as it is prosecuted today and as it was when

---

[72]Ibid., p. 380.
[73]Ibid., p. 382.
[74]Ibid., p. 381.

Christopher wrote those words: On the one side Israel, a thriving, modern, democracy containing a million Arab citizens who enjoy more individual rights in the Jewish state than do Arabs in any Arab country. On the other side, a religious theocracy in Gaza and a fascist regime on the West Bank, both lacking individual rights, both prosecuting a holy war against the Jews *as Jews*. "Islamo-fascism" is a term that Christopher was rightly proud to have coined. Is there a single Palestinian faction on the West Bank or in Gaza that does *not* align itself with the Islamo-fascists and their war against the West? Is not Israel's war in the Middle East a war of everything that Christopher professes to love against everything he hates? What was it that bound him to the Arab cause, if not his unexamined and un-repudiated loyalties to a Marxist past and a utopian future?

Christopher's blind hate towards the home of the Jews was the most troubling of the confusions to which his uncompleted second thoughts had led him. The fact that my friend should have been so morally deficient and intellectually incoherent in matters so important—and so important to him—is a personal tragedy and public misfortune.

How to understand Christopher finally? He described one side of his family root as "stern and flinty and martial and continent and pessimistic; the other exotic and beseeching and hopeful and tentative ..." This heritage left him "with a strong sense of fight or flight" on family occasions."[75] More accurately, it left him with a sense of flight *and* fight on all occasions, which is as good a summation of him as we are likely to get. The utopian romance he never gave up was the perfect prescription for continual fight in the present, and a never-ending flight into the future.

---

[75]Ibid., p. 46.

Epilogue

I had just completed the above reflections on Christopher's life and work and was preparing them for publication when he collapsed during his book tour. Rushed to the hospital, he was diagnosed with the carcinoma that had killed his father before him. Esophageal cancer is a particularly virulent disease, bearing a short sentence with little room for sanguine outcomes.

Barely a month later he resumed his writing and speaking, leaving no doubt that the sense of irony that had served as such a notable element of his verbal armory would accompany him in his final skirmishes. He had been a life-long, aggressive abuser of alcohol and tobacco even though, genetics aside, these were the principal risk factors for the adversary that now confronted him. In his first article for *Vanity Fair* after his collapse, he acknowledged that he had recklessly baited the Reaper, and consequently would look foolish if he were to be seen "smiting my brow with shock or ... whining about how it is all so unfair." But, characteristically, he also proclaimed a romantic defiance of his fate, in a phrase lifted from the poet Edna St. Vincent Millay, in which he described himself as one "knowingly burning the candle at both ends and finding that it often gives a lovely light."[76]

At the time of his collapse Christopher was the most famous atheist alive, raucously engaged in a crusade to persuade his publics to dispense with irrational creeds and live by reason alone. He had recently taken on the believers in a mammoth bestseller, *God Is Not Great*, which was spiked with acid wit and verbal malice, accusing religionists of poisoning everything. But when his misfortune became known, the targets of these bilious attacks failed generally to rise to his occasion and look on his misery as their revenge. On the contrary, many announced their intention to pray for his soul and the restoration of his health. In a televised

---

[76]Christopher Hitchens, "Topic of Cancer," *Vanity Fair*, August 2010, http://www.vanityfair.com/culture/2010/09/hitchens-201009.

interview, Christopher paid these sentiments a genteel respect but also assured such well-wishers that their interventions were useless. He then turned their sympathy into an extension of the conflict he had started, warning them not to expect a deathbed conversion.

When my stricken friend appeared in a video interview a little over a month later, it felt like a personal wound. The chemotherapy he had undergone had taken a distressing toll, rendering him wan and hairless except for unkempt wisps that trailed distractedly from his skull. An unfamiliar slouch tilted his frame, beginning at the right clavicle, which seemed hollowed where the cancer had entered his lymph nodes. His facial skin was sallow and his upper lip pursed as he summoned the effort to push out his words, gulping at intervals for air. I winced at the damage, but Christopher had already turned it into a literary prop, complaining in heroic mode that he had succumbed to something "so predictable and banal that it bores even me."[77]

Who could believe such bravado? Can one's own extinction be boring? Similar rhetorical effects peppered the texts of an article series he had begun about his illness for *Vanity Fair*. In the first, smartly titled "Topic of Cancer," he observed himself clinically, before resuming his crusade against the believers. Reading it, I was struck by how these gestures that now absorbed his waning time and energy were those of a man staging his exit as the terminal chapter in a public narrative begun long ago. The only introspective look he seemed to allow himself in the interviews he now gave about his impending disappearance was when he got around to mentioning his children. The thought of their lives without him, he admitted, made him "moist." When his closest friend, the novelist Martin Amis, was asked how Christopher managed the brave display, he replied, "Not all of you will die is what you think if you're a writer. Because of what you leave. Hitch believes that."

---

[77]Ibid.

But how could he believe that? Was not Simone de Beauvoir's observation about her mother's death more credible? "Whether you think of it as heavenly or as earthly, if you cling to living, immortality is no consolation for death." And Christopher did seem to cling to living in regard to what he thought of as his unfinished work. Of his diminishing future he wrote: "I am badly oppressed by a gnawing sense of waste. I had real plans for my next decade and felt I'd worked hard enough to earn it."[78] And so he had. But to whom could he appeal this sentence? And to what end, given that he and his potential readers were all bound for extinction?

Judging by the public speeches and interviews he continued to give in his ravaged state and the commentaries he continued to publish, a good part of the work Christopher feared he would not live to finish was his continuing assault on the faith of others—his desire to strip them of their illusions and apparently of the comforts they might derive from them. Christopher and I had discussed these matters in the past, and it struck me as odd that he would not now consider rethinking the hard edge he had brought to the subject. "Pascal is a fraud!" he bellowed at me over a lunch we shared in Beverly Hills. This was his reaction to one of the most poignant souls ever to walk the earth, all because he had hoped for a God to rescue him from the cold night of oblivion. Now Christopher was once again mocking believers for seeking solace in a future beyond the grave. I considered confronting him over this but quickly relented. I could hardly persuade him of the folly of the illusion that he *knew* that God didn't exist and that his knowledge mattered. And even if I could, how would it serve my friend for me to return his favor?

In the audiences Christopher gave after the diagnosis, his mother's suicide surfaced as a recurrent theme. Although the events had taken place when Christopher was in his twenties,

[78]Ibid.

they still gnawed at him nearly forty years later. At the very last, Yvonne had placed several calls from her Athens hotel to England but he was not at home to receive them, and so they went unanswered. "I could never lose the feeling," he told the TV anchor Anderson Cooper, "that she was probably calling in the hope of finding a handhold of some sort to cling to, and that if she'd heard my voice—because I could always make her laugh no matter how blue she was—that I could have saved her. So, as a result I've never had what people like to call 'closure.'"[79]

Cooper, whose brother had taken his own life, was uncomfortable with the word "closure," which he thought meaningless; there was no end to such a grief. Christopher assented, observing that if there were such an end, "it would only be saying that some quite important part of you had gone numb." As one who has lost a daughter, I can affirm that there is a recession of heartbreak until grief no longer gathers like a thundercloud. But does this reflect a diminution of feeling, as Christopher suggests, or is it simply a resignation to the fact of who we are? Our initial distress is a frantic desire to reverse the event. But the march of ordinary days soon forces us to acknowledge the inevitable and submit to it, realizing that it is not just the one we loved who is lost, but we all are. And there is no escape and no turning back.

"We approach truth," Aristotle remarked, "only inasmuch as we depart from life." He may have had other meanings in mind, but my reading is this: The closer we get to understanding our end, the more we are able to see through the stories that shield us from who and what we are—to see face to face. It was disconcerting to note how little this seemed to be true of Christopher in his final journey.

After the terminal call, Christopher's prodigious workdays became shorter and more arduous. From his own account he was not out of bed before eleven, and he awoke nauseated from the

---

[79]"Christopher Hitchens Interviewed by Anderson Cooper," August 5, 2010, https://www.youtube.com/watch?v=LgCq2T-v-Mo.

chemicals his doctors poured into his veins in an effort to kill the cells that had run amok. He was thirty pounds lighter and anemic, his skin ashen and riddled with sores; he faced endless battles against exhaustion in order to pursue his tasks.

These images of a life brutally mugged triggered memories of times past, when I had witnessed Christopher's abusive indulgences and thought, *My friend is killing himself,* knowing full well that it was futile to try to stop him. Even after his collapse, he insisted to the interviewers who appeared for his deathwatch that he was without regrets and, even more implausibly, that his addictions were choices whose rewards were so positive that he would make them again: "I can't imagine what it would have been like otherwise ... because so much of life to me has been about prolonging the moment, keeping the argument going for another stage, keeping the dinner party alive for another hour."[80]

Braving his way along the last mile, he was still forced to concede that there were moments in which he thought of his children and their futures without him, and it was more than he could bear. Of his youngest, Antonia, who was seventeen, he said, "I cracked up almost exactly the day when I was going to take her on her first college trip. I felt ashamed, depressed and miserable." But when asked whether this did not lead to second thoughts about the reckless course he had pursued, he would not hear of it: "I'd have to say, not to be a hypocrite, that my life is my writing before it is anything. Because that's who I am and my children come later and that's what they've had to put up with."[81]

Harsh words from a dying father, although they were not intended to be an unnecessary wound to hearts most vulnerable, but rather offered in the way of excusing the life he had lived and

[80]Sonia Verma, "Christopher Hitchens: 'My life is my writing ... my children come later'" *The Globe and Mail*, October 22, 2010, http://www.theglobeandmail.com/news/world/christopher-hitchens-my-life-is-my-writing-my-children-come-later/article1769836/singlepage/.
[81]Ibid.

was planning to continue. Determined to be undaunted by death, Christopher was busily taking up the thread of the story he had started long ago. Instead of reflecting on final things—and on himself—he had resumed his mission to change the world. It was his bread of life, providing him the promise of immortality.

Why else would Christopher think that writing was any different from the occupations of other mortals that did not save them? In the house of mortality, what do the scraps left behind add up to? And why should their production come before those we love, especially our children, whom we have summoned unbidden to a thankless fate and who look to us for comfort along the way?

Christopher's crusade would have been arduous in any circumstance, but it had become particularly grueling in his new existence. Shuffling between chemotherapy sessions and oncology visits, pressing his crippled voice and failing organs into service, he soldiered on. On more occasions than one might imagine possible, he dragged himself onto trains and airplanes, crossing the country to slay the dragons of ignorance and superstition. Lungs rasping, he debated one day the existence of God in Atlanta and denied it the next in Montana; then it was on to Toronto for a theological skirmish with Tony Blair, the former prime minister of Great Britain. On one day Christopher could be observed warning the public about the sinister revival of the Christian religion in Russia; the next on a radio show sharing his last wishes with strangers, and regretting that he wouldn't live to write the obituaries of evildoers whom he proceeded to name—an African dictator, a former American Secretary of State and the current Catholic Pope: "It does gash me to think that people like that would outlive me, I have to say. It really does."[82]

Nor did Christopher hesitate to rub his truth in the noses of the well-wishers who wrote to say they would pray for him, telling

---

[82]NPR Staff, "Christopher Hitchens On Suffering, Beliefs and Dying," NPR, October 29, 2010, http://www.npr.org/templates/story/story.php?storyId=130917506.

them to never mind. "I wrote back to some of the people—some of them in holy orders who are running registered organizations— "When you say, 'Oh pray for me,' do you mind if I ask, 'What for?'"[83] (Clever, Christopher, but cold.) Instead of connecting with other condemned souls, Christopher was running through the pages of the last drama he had scripted for himself, whose *catharsis* was a thumb in the eye of death, a martyrdom for the life of reason.

"One of my occasionally silly thoughts is: I wish I was suffering in a good Cause—a cause larger than myself. Or, larger than just the mere survival. If you're in pain and being tortured, and you felt it was helping the liberation of humanity, then you can bear it better, I think."[84] The liberation of humanity, no less. The banner of Yvonne's romantic spirit borne aloft by the loyal son. "Until you have done something for humanity you should be ashamed to die."[85] It was another Hitchens flourish.

In the fall of 2011, Christopher published a thick collection of book reviews and other journalistic ephemera under the title *Arguably*, referring to it as "probably my last." In a brief introduction he explained that he had dedicated his final production to three martyrs of the "Arab spring." This referred to a series of eruptions in the Arab world that had begun the previous February with high hopes for a democratic outcome but had already turned into an Islamist winter, rendering his enthusiasm even more quixotic. After identifying his three Arab heroes, Christopher linked them to a fourth—a Czech who, during the final stages of the Cold War, had immolated himself as a symbol of the Prague Spring. He concluded these thoughts by recalling a visit he made to Beirut two years before to speak to a left-wing audience on "Who Are The Real Revolutionaries in the Middle East?" It was

---

[83]Ibid.
[84]Ibid.
[85]Christopher Hitchens, "Tumortown," *Vanity Fair*, November 2010, http://www.vanityfair.com/culture/2010/11/hitchens-201011.

Christopher's attempt to fan the fires of an Arab revolution within the revolution, a telling tribute to the path he had pursued with such steadfast loyalty since joining the International Socialists forty years before.

In the speech he praised an anti-Syrian dissident in Lebanon, a political prisoner in Egypt and a Palestinian critic of "the baroque corruption of the Palestinian Authority"—all dissenters within the revolution, like himself. But the gathering of fellow leftists who came to hear his words in person remained singularly unmoved: "It was clear that a good number of the audience (including, I regret to say, most of the Americans) regarded me as some kind of stooge. For them, revolutionary authority belonged to groups like Hamas or Hezbollah, resolute opponents of the global colossus and tireless fighters against Zionism. For me this was yet another round in a long historic dispute. Briefly stated, this ongoing polemic takes place between the anti-imperialist left and the anti-totalitarian Left. In one shape or another, I have been involved—on both sides of it—all my life."[86]

It was a telling admission. For all his life Christopher had misconstrued this polemic and dispute. The side of Hezbollah and Hamas was not that of an "anti-imperialist" left but of a fascist, genocidal left. Hezbollah and Hamas were parties of Islamic imperialism and Jew-hatred—as Christopher certainly understood but somehow denied. Why would he even seek an audience among their Western supporters if not for the fact that he was unable to relinquish the utopian dream that connected them—perversely—to him? It was the glare of the imaginary future that obscured (and had always obscured) Christopher's political vision.

A week or so after learning of Christopher's condition, I decided to publish the profile I had written, calling it "The Two

---

[86]Christopher Hitchens, "From 9/11 to the Arab Spring," *The Guardian*, September 9, 2011, http://www.theguardian.com/books/2011/sep/09/christopher-hitchens-911-arab-spring.

Christophers" after the unruly life he had chosen. Despite the harshness of some of its judgments, I decided to go ahead with its publication for two reasons. First, because my contentions with Christopher over his incomplete "second thoughts" went to the heart of my own political identity and work; and then because I had not given up hope that he might yet complete his own second thoughts or at least extend them. I sent him the article with the following explanation:

> July 7, 2010
> Dear Christopher,
>   I hope that by now your doctors have managed to make you feel more comfortable and have alleviated some of the pain you are experiencing. I am told that chemotherapy is an unpleasant matter and I hope that every effort has been made to make this passage easier on you. As you may or may not know, I have written a fairly long piece engaging some of the issues raised by your memoir.... Some of it is critical, as you would expect. When all is said and done, however, my heart is with you. I am grieved that this misfortune has befallen you, and I look to you to pull yourself through it and get on with your journey.
> David
> July 7, 2010
> Dear David,
>   Sorry that I can't read everything on myself these days (I haven't really even tried Buruma's piece in the *NY Review*) and sorry to tell you that I stopped here with "the Rosenbergs, Hamas and Alger Hiss." I can't quite think what made you do that.
>   Thanks for your kind words on other matters.
> As always
> Christopher

The sentence he had stopped at was on page 2 of the article. When I located it, I realized he had misconstrued the text, thinking that I had referred to him as an apologist for "the Rosenbergs, Hamas and Alger Hiss"—which he most assuredly was not. What I had actually written about was his irreconcilable contradictions—

that he was "a friend both to neo-conservative hawk Paul Wolfowitz and to Victor Navasky, apologist for the Rosenbergs, Hamas, and Hiss." Navasky, of course, was not only his editor at *The Nation* but the best man at his wedding, and one to whom he had given the manuscript of his memoir for advice. I wrote him an email to clarify the point and he promptly conceded his mistake:

> Ah, ok—it was *Navasky* you meant. See, I am not reading well enough to distinguish commas from semi-colons.... No idea what V's views on Hamas might be and don't see *The Nation* anymore. Still and all, I think a careless reader might have thought you meant me.

I never heard any more from him on the essay and I don't know whether he ever actually read it or what his thoughts were if he did. Important as they may have seemed to me, they were evidently not as important to him. Despite my disappointment over this rejection, it was no more than I should have expected. In the memoir he had written of his political life he had revealed how deeply committed he was to the illusions that, in our conversations, he had given me the impression he had abandoned—his double-entry bookkeeping.

Much as it distressed me to accept this, the path he had resumed after receiving his death sentence confirmed it. He had lived as a crusader and would die as one. Three weeks after receiving his email, I sent him this note:

Jul 29, 2010
Dear Christopher,
    I hope you're progressing with your therapy and that its downsides are not too burdensome. I will be in DC Monday evening through Wednesday and would like to drop by and pay you a call if that is something you would like to do .... I have been thinking about you a lot lately and regretting that the timing of my article was so inopportune. I am not proposing this as an occasion to discuss those issues, just a visit from a friend.
David

July 29, 2010

Dear David,

   I'd like that very much. Can you try me nearer the time? I have a rather fluctuating condition.

   Hope to coincide.

Christopher

We never did coincide. When I arrived in Washington he was too ill to see me, and then the cancer took his voice from him, which would have made any discourse problematic; and even though it was later partially restored he was by then too sick or too busy. I had to come to terms with his choice to be silent in regard to the issues that had connected us in the first place.

   A little over a year after his collapse, Christopher's life came to an end in a state-of-the-art cancer ward in Houston. During that interval I thought about Christopher often, and I thought about him fondly; even though, as I must now accept, Christopher never abandoned the dream of a future redeemed, and of his place in "history" as one who gave a life to achieve it.

PART TWO

The Life and Work
of David Horowitz
By Jamie Glazov, Ph.D.

D avid Horowitz was born in Forest Hills, New York, on January 10, 1939, the year of the Nazi-Soviet non-aggression pact which shattered the illusions of many Communists and other members of the progressive left. But Horowitz's schoolteacher parents, Blanche and Phil, remained steadfast in their commitment to the Party. They had met in Communist meetings in the early 1930s and engaged in what turned out to be a lifelong "political romance," as David later described it in his autobiography *Radical Son*, thinking of themselves as "secret agents" of the Soviet future.[1]

Horowitz grew up in a Communist enclave in Queens called Sunnyside Gardens. As a child he attended the Sunnyside Progressive School, a pre-kindergarten program the Party had set up; as an adolescent he spent summers at a Party-run children's camp called "Wo-Chi-Ca," short for "Workers' Children's Camp."

In 1956, when Horowitz was seventeen, the Soviet leader Nikita Khrushchev delivered a secret speech in the Kremlin about the crimes of Stalin. The "Khrushchev Report," as it was subsequently called, was leaked by Israeli intelligence agents to the public, causing a crisis among the faithful. Party members, who had previously dismissed as "slander" claims by their opponents that Stalin was responsible for the deaths of millions, now had no choice but to admit that the charges were true. They left the Party

---

[1] David Horowitz, *Radical Son: A Generational Odyssey*, Free Press, 1997.

in a mass exodus that killed the Communist Party as a force in U.S. political life, although for many like Blanche and Phil Horowitz it was impossible to give up the socialist faith.

Horowitz was a college freshman at Columbia University when the fallout from the Khrushchev revelations was causing a crisis in his parents' circle. Opposed to Stalin but not to the socialist cause, he focused on his literary studies, taking courses with Lionel Trilling and other of Columbia's distinguished faculty members. When he graduated in 1959 he married his college sweetheart, and moved to California where he began graduate studies in English literature at the University of California at Berkeley. There he met other "red diaper" babies who were determined to create a radical politics that would not bear the totalitarian baggage he believed had weighed his parents' generation down and corrupted their political dreams.

Horowitz became an editor of *Root and Branch*, a new magazine in which his circle of activists published essays embodying the political vision of a New Left two years before the Students for Democratic Society published the Port Huron Statement, which is generally regarded as the birth announcement of that movement. In 1962, he became an organizer of the first campus demonstration against the Vietnam War (then being prosecuted by a few hundred advisors JFK had sent to support the Saigon regime). Also in that year, while still a graduate student, he published *Student*, the first book to express the aspirations and worldview of the new radical generation.

Student portrays the university as the symbol of an oppressive corporate culture, foreshadowing the New Left critiques and campus eruptions to come. Mario Savio, leader of the Berkeley student revolt, later told Horowitz that reading *Student* was what had convinced him to go to Berkeley. In dedicating the book to Supreme Court Justice Hugo Black and stressing his commitment to democratic politics, Horowitz also crystallized a difference between the fledgling New Left and the old Communist vanguard. Horowitz criticized the Soviet invasion of Hungary and equated it with

America's intervention in Cuba; he broke with economic determinism and the idea that socialism had to follow a centralized plan.[2] He knew how far he had strayed from the political world he had grown up in when the book was attacked by a reviewer in the *People's World*, the Party's West Coast organ.

Horowitz saw himself as a dedicated socialist, but some of his intellectual work in the early sixties strayed from dogma in a preview of the second thoughts that would shape his perspective two decades later. His literary studies led him to publish *Shakespeare: An Existential View* in 1965, a book that follows the Hegelian idea that human existence is defined not just by what actually *is*, but also by what might be. He mined the work of Shakespeare to explore the tension between this romance of the possible and the skeptical outlook, which constantly reminds us of the brute facts of an existence from which we cannot escape.

In an article for *Root and Branch* called "The Question About Meaning" Horowitz rejected Marxist determinism and endorsed the view that values are created by human will, and therefore that consciousness also determines being: "Everywhere, value attends commitment. Where men do not address their condition in the fullness of its claim, their experience fails to cross the threshold of significance; for value can exist effectively only where there are men committed to it. It is the commitment of men to the possible, to what is loftier than their attainment, beyond what the present has achieved, that permits the realization of the potential whose seed is already there."[3]

The idea of a spiritual dimension in which consciousness determines being, not the other way around, was a trope from existentialism that contradicted Marxist materialism—even though at the time, and in the flush of enthusiasm created by the notion of a "new" left, Horowitz did not pursue the implications of his ideas.

---

[2] See "New Politics," chapter 5 in David Horowitz, *Left Illusions: An Intellectual Odyssey*, Spence, 2003.
[3] See Chapter 4 in *Left Illusions*.

After publishing *Student,* Horowitz left California, taking his young family—his wife Elissa and a son born in 1961—to Sweden, in part because he admired the work of the great Swedish film director Ingmar Bergman. During the year he spent there, he wrote *The Free World Colossus,* a "revisionist" history of the Cold War. It was one of the first expressions of the New Left's fixation with the repressive workings of an American "empire," and was ultimately translated into several languages.[4] In the U.S., *The Free World Colossus* became a handbook for the growing anti-Vietnam War movement, providing a litany of America's "misdeeds" abroad—the coups in Iran and Guatemala, the Bay of Pigs and Vietnam—that became a staple of left-wing indictments of America.[5]

Needing a publisher for his manuscript, Horowitz wrote the Bertrand Russell Peace Foundation and was somewhat surprised to receive a job offer. He spent the years 1964–1967 in London, working for the British philosopher and for the man some saw as Russell's Rasputin, Ralph Schoenman, but balked at the International War Crimes Tribunal, which Schoenman organized. The Tribunal was headed by Russell, Jean-Paul Sartre and other left-wing intellectuals who condemned America's "war crimes" in Vietnam but ignored those committed by the Communists. It was a small but potent sign of the New Left's ongoing reversion to Old Left politics, which would lead to Horowitz's eventual exit from the movement.

Horowitz had only a casual relationship with Russell, but while in London he became close to and profoundly influenced by two European Marxists—Ralph Miliband, whose two sons eventually

---

[4] David Horowitz, *The Free World Colossus: A Critique of American Foreign Policy in the Cold War,* Hill and Wang, 1965. Under the title *From Yalta to Vietnam: American Foreign Policy in the Cold War,* Penguin Books, 1967, it was translated into French, German, Dutch, Swedish, Norwegian, Spanish, Japanese and Hebrew.

[5] "[Horowitz was] the author of some of [the Left's] best thumbed pages." Paul Berman, "The Intellectual Life and the Renegade Horowitz," *Village Voice,* August 1986.

became leaders of the British Labor Party, and the Polish Trotsky-ist Isaac Deutscher, the famed biographer of Stalin and Trotsky. Under the tutelage of Deutscher, Horowitz's writing career as a New Left intellectual flourished. He edited two books, *Containment and Revolution* and *Corporations and the Cold War*, and wrote *Empire and Revolution: A Radical Interpretation of Contemporary History*.[6]

Empire and Revolution was a reinterpretation of Marxism that offered a New Left perspective on imperialism, communism and the Cold War. Heavily influenced by Deutscher and Trotsky, it represented Horowitz's effort to rescue socialism from its Stalinist past and to reformulate a Marxist theory that would account for the horrors of Stalinism while keeping the prospect of a revolutionary future alive.

Horowitz returned to the U.S. in 1968 to become an editor at *Ramparts* magazine, the New Left's largest and most successful publication, with a circulation of a quarter million readers. A liberal Catholic quarterly when it began in 1962, *Ramparts* revived the muckraking journalism of the Progressive era, becoming the voice of the antiwar movement. A few months before Horowitz was added to the staff (to provide "more theory," in the words of then-editor Warren Hinckle), *Ramparts* had caused a national furor with its revelation that the CIA had infiltrated the National Student Association and used it as a "front," the first of several such exposés.

In 1969 Horowitz and his friend Peter Collier took over *Ramparts* in a palace coup against its editor Robert Scheer, whose peremptory style of leadership was creating major problems for its overworked staff. In 1973 Horowitz published *The Fate of Midas and Other Essays*, a collection of essays, which summarized his intellectual development including his attempt to integrate

---

[6]David Horowitz, *Empire and Revolution: A Radical Interpretation of Contemporary History*, Random House, 1969. Published in England under its original title, *Imperialism and Revolution*, Allen Lane, 1969.

Keynesian economic theory with traditional Marxist analysis, part of his continuing project to provide the theoretical foundation for an authentically *new* left. The collection also featured personal appreciations of both Deutscher and Russell, and critiques of the violent Weather Underground and SDS.

By 1969, when he and Collier assumed the reins at *Ramparts*, the New Left was disintegrating into futile acts of "revolutionary" violence and rhetorical narcissism. Disturbed at the direction the movement was taking, but not yet able to contemplate a future as an outsider, Horowitz later said of his predicament: "I pretty well realized even at that time that you couldn't really remake the world as the left intended without totalitarian coercion. But it was much more difficult to accept the consequences of that realization. For a long time, I simply could not face the possibility that there was no socialist future, that I was not going to be a social redeemer, and that we didn't have the answers to humanity's problems—in short, that I wasn't part of an historic movement that would change the world."[7]

He thought that he had found an answer to the political paralysis of the early 1970s when he became close to Huey Newton, the leader of the Black Panther Party for Self-Defense, a group of black radicals that had jumped into the public view by making a point of carrying weapons in public and had been anointed the "vanguard of the revolution" by SDS leaders like Tom Hayden. Horowitz had avoided contacts with the Panthers in their overtly violent phase, but in 1970 Newton announced that it was "time to put away the gun" and turn to community activities.

Seeing this as a constructive leftism, Horowitz found himself raising funds to purchase a Baptist church in Oakland's inner city for the Panthers, which he turned into a "learning center" for 150 Panther children. He bought Newton's view of incremental, community-based radical change, which seemed particularly salutary

---

[7]Interview with the author, June 28, 2002.

when juxtaposed to the nihilism of the Weather Underground's bombing campaign that was reaching its height at the same time.

In September 1974 Horowitz recruited *Ramparts* bookkeeper Betty Van Patter to maintain the accounts of the tax-exempt foundation he had created to manage the Panther school. In December, Betty Van Patter's bludgeoned body was found adrift in San Francisco Bay. The police were convinced she had been murdered by members of the Panther Party, but local prosecutors were unable to bring an indictment, and the federal government, under siege from the left, also steered clear of this crime; as did the press, which had largely bought into the notion that the Panthers had been targeted for destruction by racist law enforcement.

Entering what would become a ten-year, slow-motion transformation from theorist of the left to its worst enemy, Horowitz undertook his own inquiry into the murder. As he collided with denial and threats of retribution if he continued to search, he was forced to confront three stark facts: his New Left outlook was unable to explain the events that had overtaken him; his lifelong friends and associates in the left were now a threat to his safety, since they would instinctively defend the Panther vanguard; and no one among them really cared about the murder of an innocent woman because the murderers were their political friends.[8]

In the mind of the left, even questioning the Panthers' role in Betty's fate reflected disloyalty to the cause, since such curiosity could lead to devastating criticism of the Panthers and by extension of the left itself, which had embraced the organization and turned its back on the truth that emerged from Van Patter's death: rather than a community service organization, Huey Newton had been running a black version of Murder, Inc. in the Oakland ghetto.

Forced to look at his own commitments in a way he had never allowed himself before, Horowitz realized it was the enemies of

---

[8] These events are described in the sections of *Radical* Son called "Panthers" and "Private Investigations." See also "Black Murder Inc.," in Volume 1 of this series, *My Life and Times.*

the left who had been correct in their assessment of the Panthers (just as they had been correct in their assessment of the Soviet Union), while the left had been disastrously wrong. The Panthers were not victims of police repression due to their political militancy. They were ghetto thugs running a con on credulous white supporters, and committing crimes against vulnerable black citizens. It was the left and its "revolution" that had conferred on them the aura of a political vanguard, protecting them from being held accountable for their deeds.

As Horowitz considered the cynicism of his comrades' reaction to Betty's death, he recognized a familiar historical reality being played out on this smaller scale. Lies were being told to cover up murder. A collusive silence followed. Horowitz couldn't help asking if there was something inherent in the socialist idea that led to the horrors committed in socialism's name. He had to face the possibility that his entire life until then had been based on a lie. He had to face the connection between what he had experienced with the Panthers and the crimes his parents' generation had defended—and thus to accept the fact that there was no "new" left, just a reiteration of the criminality that had been at the core of the left since Lenin (or the Jacobins and Babeuf). As he wrote: "It had been forty years since Stalin's purges. The victims were dead, their memories erased. They were un-persons without public defenders, expunged even from the consciousness of the living. Those who knew the truth had to keep their silence, even as I had to keep mine. If we actually succeeded in making a revolution in America, and if the Panthers or similar radical vanguards prevailed, how would our fate be different from theirs? Our injustice, albeit mercifully smaller in scale, was as brutal and final as Stalin's. As progressives we had no law to govern us, other than that of the gang."[9]

Everything Horowitz had previously believed, everything on which he had built his political life, now crumbled before him. In

---

[9] *Radical Son*, op. cit., p. 271.

a vignette that Horowitz wrote at the request of *The New York Times Magazine* (which the magazine predictably failed to print), he recounted the stages of his metamorphosis: "Being at the center of a heroic myth inspired passions that informed my youthful passage and guided me to the middle of my adult life. But then I was confronted by a reality so inescapable and harsh that it shattered the romance for good. A friend—the mother of three children—was brutally murdered by my political comrades, members of the very vanguard that had been appointed to redeem us all. Worse, since individuals may err, the deed was covered up by the vanguard itself who hoped, in so doing, to preserve the faith."[10]

"Like all radicals," he continued, "I lived in some fundamental way in a castle in the air. Now, I had hit the ground hard, and had no idea of how to get up or go on."[11] Just as his progressive friends were indifferent to Betty's death, so too had the left as a whole failed to reckon with the horrifying toll taken by Communist-led and New Left-backed revolutions in Cambodia, Vietnam, and elsewhere. Radicals still considered themselves socialists, while exonerating themselves from socialism's crimes.

In pursuing answers to Betty Van Patter's death, Horowitz discovered that the Panthers had murdered more than a dozen people in the course of running extortion, prostitution, and drug rackets in the Oakland ghetto. And yet, to his growing bewilderment, the Panthers continued to enjoy the support of the American left, the Democratic Party, Bay Area trade unions, and even the Oakland business establishment. They were praised by prominent writers such as Murray Kempton and Garry Wills in *The New York Times*

---

[10]"A Political Romance" included in Volume 1 of this series, *My Life and Times*. The piece was written on request for the "Life" feature of *The New York Times Sunday Magazine* and rejected by editor Eric Copage as not being suitable to the feature. Shortly thereafter, a similar "second-thoughts" piece by another author, but with the politics reversed, appeared in the "Life" section. Horowitz had written about leaving the left; the piece the Times chose to print was about remaining in the left despite its "mistakes.".

[11]*Radical Son*, op. cit., p. 308.

and by politicians like Governor Jerry Brown of California—a political confidant of Elaine Brown (no relation), the Panther leader who had ordered Betty's death.

Notwithstanding the media blackout and the silence of the Panthers' supporters, the details of their crimes have surfaced over the years, principally as a result of Horowitz's efforts. The first notice of what had happened was a courageous article in *The New Times Magazine* by a left-wing journalist named Kate Coleman, whom Horowitz had approached and provided with information.[12] In a 1986 piece in *The Village Voice*, Horowitz himself identified the Panthers as Betty's killers; in his 1997 book *Radical Son*, he gave a detailed account of his Panther experience and Betty's death.[13]

These efforts had an impact even on some of the Panther survivors. In his last televised interview on 60 *Minutes*, Eldridge Cleaver, the former Black Panther "minister of information," admitted the brutal ruthlessness of his comrades and himself: "If people had listened to Huey Newton and me in the 1960s, there would have been a holocaust in this country." Years later, former Panther chairman Bobby Seale also made a public confession about Panther criminality and specifically acknowledged that the Panthers had murdered Betty Van Patter.[14]

But for the most part, keepers of the progressive flame were silent. SDS leader (later California State Senator) Tom Hayden and *Los Angeles Times* journalist Robert Scheer, who worked with the Panthers and promoted their agendas, never wrote a word about Panther crimes in the forty-five years after Van Patter's murder.

---

[12] Kate Coleman, "The Party's Over," *New Times*, July 10, 1978, http://colemantruth.net/kate8.pdf.

[13] David Horowitz, "Better Ron Than Red," *The Village Voice*, September 30, 1986; reprinted under the title "Why I Am No Longer A Leftist," in Volume 1 of this series, *My Life and Times*.

[14] Dan Flynn, "Panther Leader Seale Confesses," FrontPageMag.com, April 23, 2002, http://archive.frontpagemag.com/readArticle.aspx?ARTID= 24216.

Former SDS president and later UC Berkeley professor Todd Gitlin, in his history of the 1960s, fails to acknowledge Panther criminality or mention Van Patter, or the murders of police officers for which the Panthers and other leftist groups were responsible.[15] Like other New Left historians, Gitlin presents the Panthers as abused victims who sometimes were driven to indefensible (but unspecified) acts because of their persecution. In Kenneth O'Reilly's *Racial Matters: The FBI's Secret File on Black America, 1960–1972*, the Panthers do no wrong and are the targets of legal genocide.[16]

In his essay "Still No Regrets," Horowitz wrote: "A library of memoirs by aging new leftists and 'progressive' academics recall the rebellions of the 1960s. But hardly a page in any of them has the basic honesty—or sheer decency—to say, 'Yes, we supported these murderers and those spies, and the agents of that evil empire,' or to say so without an alibi. I'd like to hear even one of these advocates of 'social justice' make this simple acknowledgement: 'We greatly exaggerated the sins of America and underestimated its decencies and virtues, and we're sorry.'"[17]

The political journey from left to right, of course, had been made before. But Horowitz's change of heart was of a somewhat different character than the conversions of the ex-Communists who had traveled to the right before him. Unlike the contributors to *The God That Failed*, for instance, most of whom remained men of the left, Horowitz made a comprehensive break with the radical worldview.[18] Horowitz's "conversion" was actually his second. The first was his break from communism after Khrushchev's

---

[15]Todd Gitlin, *The Sixties: Years of Hope, Days of Rage*, Bantam Books, 1987.

[16]Kenneth O'Reilly, *Racial Matters: The FBI's Secret File on Black America, 1960–1972*, Free Press, 1989.

[17]"Still No Regrets" in David Horowitz, *How To Beat the Democrats and Other Subversive Ideas*, Spence, 2002.

[18]Crossman, Richard, ed. *The God That Failed: Six Famous Men Tell How They Changed Their Minds About Communism*, Harper and Brothers, 1949.

revelations, while the second was from the socialist idea itself. For the writers of *The God That Failed*, Stalinism was a cruel socialist aberration. For Horowitz, the roots of Stalinism—and of totalitarianism—lay in socialism itself.

After Betty's murder, Horowitz ceased his radical activism and his political writing for most of the following decade.[19] Silence about politics became his refuge, as he painstakingly reassessed his life and outlook. He was already involved in a project with Peter Collier to complete a multi-generation biography of the Rockefeller family, and this became his cocoon. In 1975, *The Rockefellers: An American Dynasty* appeared to widespread acclaim, including a front-page rave in *The New York Times Book Review*. It became a bestseller and a nominee for a National Book Award. The success of *The Rockefellers* led to a series of other books—*The Kennedys: An American Drama* (1984), *The Fords: An American Epic* (1987), and *The Roosevelts: An American Saga* (1994).[20] These works earned Collier and Horowitz praise from the *Los Angeles Times* as "the premier chroniclers of American dynastic tragedy."

During this period, Horowitz also wrote *The First Frontier: The Indian Wars and America's Origins, 1607–1776* (1978), a book which remained somewhat within the parameters of the leftist outlook, while attempting to establish the idea that a nation's character, as defined in its early history, shaped its destiny.[21] While he was at work on this book, events in Southeast Asia were writing a final chapter to the narrative that had defined his own

---

[19]One of the exceptions is Horowitz's swansong to the past, an article for the *Nation* in 1979 that he called "Left Illusions," but which the *Nation* editors retitled "A Radical's Disenchantment." It is included in Volume I of this series, *My Life and Times*. The other exception, an article on foreign relations, appeared in *Mother Jones* in 1980.

[20]Despite the dual-authorship attribution, required for contractual reasons, Peter Collier was the sole author of *The Roosevelts*.

[21]David Horowitz, *The First Frontier: The Indian Wars & America's Origins: 1607–1776*, Simon & Schuster, 1978. The original title, *Promised Land*, was rejected by the publisher, even though it more accurately describes the subject of the book.

generation. After the Communist victory in Vietnam in 1975, the North Vietnamese began executing tens of thousands of South Vietnamese and setting up "re-education camps" where ideological offenders were held in "tiger cages." The general repression prompted an exodus of two million refugees, unprecedented in the history of Vietnam. Hundreds of thousands of South Vietnamese boat people perished in the Gulf of Thailand and in the South China Sea in their attempt to escape the new Communist order that the efforts of the New Left had helped to bring about.

In Cambodia, the victory of the Communists led to the slaughter of some three million Cambodian peasants.[22] More peasants were killed in Indochina in the first three years of Communist rule than had been killed on both sides during the thirteen years of the anti-Communist war. Horowitz later reflected on the cause of these events: "Every testimony by North Vietnamese generals in the postwar years has affirmed that they knew they could not defeat the United States on the battlefield, and that they counted on the division of our people at home to win the war for them. The Vietcong forces we were fighting in South Vietnam were destroyed in 1968. In other words, most of the war and most of the casualties in the war occurred because the dictatorship of North Vietnam counted on the fact Americans would give up the battle rather than pay the price necessary to win it. This is what happened. The blood of hundreds of thousands of Vietnamese, and tens of thousands of Americans, is on the hands of the anti-war activists who prolonged the struggle and gave victory to the Communists."[23]

As the Indochinese tragedy unfolded, Horowitz was struck by how the left refused to hold itself accountable for the result it had

---

[22]For an account of the bloodbath that occurred in Indochina after the Communist takeovers in Indochina, see Stéphane Courtois, Nicolas Werth, et al., eds., *The Black Book of Communism: Crimes, Terror, Repression*, Harvard University Press, 1999.

[23]"An Open Letter to the 'Anti-War' Demonstrators: Think Twice Before You Bring The War Home," in *How to Beat the Democrats and Other Subversive Ideas*, pp. 157–59.

fought so hard for—a Communist victory—and how it could not have cared less about the new suffering of the Vietnamese in whose name it had once purported to speak. He became increasingly convinced, as his friend and colleague Peter Collier had tried to persuade him, that "the element of malice played a larger role in the motives of the left than I had been willing to accept."[24] If the left really wanted a better world, why was it so indifferent to the terrible consequences of its own ideas and practices?

In 1979, Horowitz wrote a column for *The Nation* which its editors titled, "A Radical's Disenchantment."[25] It was the first public statement by a prominent New Leftist that the New Left had anything to answer for. "A Radical's Disenchantment" described his disillusion with the left, referring to many of the horrors that socialism had produced. Horowitz also confronted the silence with which the left had met these horrors, ending the piece with questions he had been asking himself: "Can the left take a really hard look at itself—the consequences of its failures, the credibility of its critiques, the viability of its goals? Can it begin to shed the arrogant cloak of self-righteousness that elevates it above its own history and makes it impervious to the lessons of experience?"[26] He already knew, however, what the answer was.

In November 1984, Horowitz turned another corner. He cast his first Republican ballot for Ronald Reagan. Shortly thereafter he learned that Peter Collier had done the same. On March 17, 1985, he and Collier wrote "Lefties for Reagan," a front-page story for the Sunday magazine of *The Washington Post*, in which they explained their vote by describing what they had seen and done while fighting against "Amerikkka" as part of the left.[27] As they expected, the article inspired vitriolic responses from their former

---

[24]Horowitz, *Radical Son*, op. cit., p. 337.

[25]It is included in Volume 1 in this series *My Life and Times*, under its original title, "Left Illusions.".

[26]David Horowitz, "A Radical's Disenchantment," *The Nation*, December 8, 1979, pp. 586–588.

[27]See Volume 1 of this series, *My Life and Times*.

comrades and forced them to re-enter the political arena to wage what became a two-person war against the Sixties left.

Dissecting the left's hypocrisy now became a Horowitz *métier*. As a former believer, Horowitz could attack the progressive myth with the familiarity of an insider. He and Collier delivered their first stunning blow in *Destructive Generation: Second Thoughts About the Sixties*, a 1989 book in which they analyzed the legacy of the New left and its corrosive effects on American culture.[28] *Destructive Generation* represented the first dissent from the celebration of the 1960s that had been issuing forth in volume after volume from publishing companies now edited by former New Leftists. For years *Destructive Generation* remained both the definitive and the only critical work on the radicalism of the decade. In a summary indictment, the authors charged that the left had steadfastly refused to make a balance sheet, let alone a profit-and-loss statement, of what it had done. Progressives who preened their "social conscience" showed no concern for the destructive consequences of their acts on ordinary people like the Vietnamese and Cambodian peasants who had been slaughtered in the wake of America's panicked withdrawal from Vietnam.

Before Collier and Horowitz turned on the left, they had enjoyed front-page reviews in the *New York Times* Book Review and bestseller status for their multi-generational biographies. *Destructive Generation* marked their eclipse in the literary culture. "Our books, once prominently reviewed everywhere, were now equally ignored. With a few notable exceptions, we became pariahs and un-persons in mainstream intellectual circles," Horowitz later recalled.[29] The last review of a Horowitz book in *The New York Review of Books* was in 1985, the very spring that Collier and Horowitz announced they had voted for Ronald Reagan.

---

[28]Peter Collier and David Horowitz, *Destructive Generation: Second Thoughts About the Sixties*, Summit Books, 1989. 2nd Ed., Encounter Books, 1995.
[29]Horowitz interview, June 7, 2002.

Horowitz's next work, *Radical Son*, published in 1997, was powerful enough that even his enemies had to admit that it called up comparisons to Whittaker Chambers's *Witness* and Arthur Koestler's *Darkness at Noon*. George Gilder called it "the first great American autobiography of his generation." In this memoir Horowitz provided an account of his life, the details of which were already being distorted by his political enemies, and described the intellectual process of his political change of heart.

Like Chambers's classic, *Radical Son* is an eloquent and riveting narrative, providing a cogent moral and intellectual basis for the changes it describes. It engages in a fearless examination of self—something almost unprecedented in political memoirs at the time Horowitz's book appeared. Going further than any previous narrative in demonstrating how deeply the Marxist fairy tale is entwined with the character and psychology of its believers, Horowitz reveals the seductive power of the progressive faith. He shows how the socialist lie reaches into every corner of a believer's soul, and why the break from radicalism can be a personally devastating decision.

Horowitz's next book, *The Politics of Bad Faith*, is a collection of six essays published in 1998 that provided what he called "an intellectual companion piece" to *Radical Son*—analysis counterpointing its narrative.[30] A central theme of the book is the refusal of radicals to accept the implications of communism's collapse for the future of socialism. "For radicals," Horowitz writes, "it is not socialism but only the language of socialism that is finally dead. To be reborn, the left had only to rename itself in terms that did not carry the memories of insurmountable defeat, to appropriate a past that could still be victorious."[31] Thus leftists now call themselves "progressives," even "liberals."

---

[30]David Horowitz, *The Politics of Bad Faith: The Radical Assault on America's Future*, Free Press, 1998.
[31]Ibid., p. 43.

The second chapter, "The Fate of the Marxist Idea," is one of the most powerful essays Horowitz has written.[32] An autobiographical segment, it takes the form of letters to two former radical friends. The first, called "Unnecessary Losses," is to Carol Pasternak Kaplan, a friend since childhood who refused to attend his father's memorial service because Horowitz had abandoned the socialist cause. "In the community of the left, it is perfectly normal to erase the intimacies of a lifetime over political differences," Horowitz notes.[33]

The second letter is to the English socialist Ralph Miliband. Titled "The Road to Nowhere," it examines the Soviet experience, the refuted positions of the New Left, and the bad faith arguments through which leftists propose to rescue their blighted dreams. "Wherever the revolutionary left has triumphed, its triumph has meant economic backwardness and social poverty, cultural deprivation and the loss of political freedom for all those unfortunate peoples under its yoke. This is the real legacy of the left of which you and I were a part. We called ourselves progressives; but we were the true reactionaries of the modern world."[34]

The fifth essay in the book, "A Radical Holocaust," examines how the post-Communist left has revived the Marxist paradigm by applying it to sexual orientation, gender, and race. Horowitz calls this maneuver "*kitsch* Marxism" and in this chapter reveals how the left has revived the destructive force of the original paradigm as well. In "A Radical Holocaust," Horowitz shows how the theory of "gay liberation" prompted leaders of the gay community to oppose and undermine proven public health methods for combating communicable diseases and in the process produced a public health disaster: "I think that the AIDS catastrophe is a metaphor for all the catastrophes that utopians have created. It's about the delusion that thinking can make it so, that an abstract idea can be

---

[32]Reprinted in the present volume.
[33]*The Politics of Bad Faith*, op. cit., p. 51.
[34]Ibid., p. 114.

imposed on reality, that the laws of nature can be defied with impunity. The story of the AIDS epidemic reveals how powerful the leftist idea remains and how far-reaching is its impact."[35]

Horowitz's next book, *Hating Whitey and Other Progressive Causes*, published in 1999, quickly became the most controversial work the author had written. It addressed the new cultural dimension of the radical cause, specifically the determination to make race function the way class had in the traditional Marxist paradigm. White males were demonized as an *ersatz* ruling class responsible for every social disparity between racial groups and genders.[36] In the absence of actual racists in university admissions offices, for instance, the left created a myth—"institutional racism"—that was alleged to explain all disparities in academic test scores and university admissions. The creation of this myth was essential to keep alive "the discredited Marxist idea that an alien power separates the citizens of democratic societies into rulers and ruled, the dominant race and the races that are oppressed."[37] Behind the idea that *all blacks are victims all the time*, according to Horowitz, lies the desire to perpetuate the failed Marxist vision and the social war it justifies.

In an article in *Hating Whitey* titled "Up From Multiculturalism," Horowitz analyzes another post-Communist radical doctrine.[38] Like socialism, "multiculturalism [is] an invention of well-fed intellectuals," he writes. "It did not well up from the immigrant communities and ethnic 'ghettoes' of America as an expression of cultural aspirations or communal needs. Instead it was manufactured by veterans of the Sixties left, who had established a new political base in the faculties of the universities." In

---

[35]Horowitz interview, June 10, 2002. For this and other Horowitz articles on AIDS and the left, see Volume 5 in this series, *Culture Wars*.

[36]The original title for the book was "Hating White People Is A Politically Correct Idea." The book was rejected by the editors of the Free Press on grounds of this title.

[37]*Hating Whitey*, Spence, 1999, p. 90.

[38]Included in Volume 5 of this series, *Culture Wars*.

the new multicultural version of the radical vision, racial and ethnic status replaces class status as a political trump card. Horowitz points out that emphasizing ethnic identity over class solidarity situates the multicultural left squarely in the tradition of classic European fascism. Intellectually, he observes, the multicultural left "owes more to Mussolini than to Marx."

In 1996, Horowitz, having gradually embraced the cause of conservatism, was approached by a disaffected Democratic strategist who wanted to put his talents at the service of Ward Connerly's campaign for a Civil Rights Initiative in California. The Initiative would ban racial preferences—the discriminatory laws and regulations functioning as a "progressive" version of Jim Crow, which had been reintroduced by the left into the American political framework as a slap against Martin Luther King's movement and its vision of a polity where people were judged not by the color of their skin but by the content of their character.

The strategist was appalled by what he saw as his party's defection from the principles of the movement he had supported as a young man, and he saw in Horowitz a kindred spirit. At their first meeting the strategist said to Horowitz: "Your side only wins when Democrats screw up big time. And that is because your position is always negative—*against* the policies of the left. You don't give people something to vote *for*."[39]

This began a relationship that resulted in a new theme of Horowitz's work—advice to conservatives on how to win the electoral battle and, more broadly, how to combat progressive ideas with a positive vision. Horowitz's first effort in this vein was a pamphlet that appeared in time for the 2000 election called "The Art of Political War," later expanded into a book called *The Art of Political War and Other Radical Pursuits* (2002). George Bush's campaign manager, Karl Rove, described the pamphlet as "the perfect guide to winning on the political battlefield."

---

[39]Interview with Horowitz, op. cit.

In *The Art of Political War* Horowitz observes that progressives have inverted Clausewitz's famous dictum and treat politics as "war continued by other means." By contrast, conservatives approach politics as a debate over policy. Conservatives generally, and Republicans in particular, either fail to understand that there is a political war taking place, or disapprove of the fact that there is. Conservatives approach politics as a series of management issues, and hope to impose limits on what government may do. Their paradigm is based on individualism, compromise, and partial solutions. This puts conservatives at a distinct disadvantage in political combats with the left, whose paradigm of oppression and liberation inspires missionary zeal and is perfectly suited to aggressive tactics and no-holds-barred combat.

At the center of America's imaginative life is what Horowitz calls "the romance of the underdog." America loves those who struggle against the odds. Consequently, a party that presents itself as a champion of the vulnerable and enemy of the powerful has an immediate edge in the political arena. Of course, when Democrats do so, it is an expression of rank hypocrisy. Democrats and political leftists control the governing councils and public schools of every major inner city in America and have for fifty years or more. They are thus responsible for everything that is wrong with inner-city America that policy can affect. Horowitz's political strategy is to turn the tables on the left, framing "liberals" and "progressives" as the actual oppressors of minorities and the poor.

In *How to Beat the Democrats and Other Subversive Ideas* (2000), Horowitz returned to these themes, attempting to reformulate and clarify the ideas laid out in "The Art of Political War," and offer them as advice to Republicans. He accompanied them with specific recommendations for Republicans on framing the issues. The new book collected a sampling of the 100 or so position papers that he was to write during the 2000 presidential campaign in a biweekly newsletter he called "The War Room," which House Majority Leader Tom DeLay posted on his congressional website.

But the campaign caused Horowitz to realize that while Republicans were generous with praise for his advice, they were temperamentally unsuited to act on it.

In the spring of 2001, Horowitz put his own advice to the test by launching an effort to oppose the left's campaign to secure reparations for slavery—137 years after the fact—as "bad for blacks and racist, too." Horowitz conducted his opposition by taking out ads in college newspapers across the country—or attempting to.[40] Forty college papers refused to print the ad, generating a furor by their denial of free speech. Donald Downs, a political scientist at the University of Wisconsin, summed up the reaction: "The Horowitz controversy has laid bare the cultural and intellectual splits that rivet the contemporary university."[41]

No Republicans and few conservatives—with the notable exceptions of Thomas Sowell and Walter Williams –stepped forward to support Horowitz, who was attacked by the left as a "racist" and whose speaking events were disrupted by protesters. At one appearance at the University of California Berkeley, university officials assigned 30 armed guards to protect Horowitz, who subsequently—and for the rest of his career—was unable to speak on campuses without a security complement.

Because the protests against the anti-reparations ads involved gross violations of free speech—at Brown University, leftists destroyed an entire issue of *The Brown Daily Herald* after its editors published the ad—Horowitz's campaign became the subject of 400 news stories. The attacks from the left made him a widely recognized conservative figure. In the fall, Horowitz published an account of these events, which he called *Uncivil Wars*.[42] In addition to providing a narrative of his campaign, the book made the

---

[40]The reparations campaign and the reactions to it are discussed in Volume 6 of this series, *Progressive Racism*.
[41]David Horowitz, *Uncivil Wars: The Controversy Over Reparations For Slavery*, Encounter, 2001 p. 7.
[42]Ibid.

case against reparations and provided a vivid portrait of the American campus under the reign of political correctness.

The reparations campaign exposed the hostility of American campuses to ideas that challenged the orthodoxies of the left. One consequence of this was the absence of any university interest in Horowitz's own work. To provide a guide to the growing corpus of his writings, he decided to publish a representative selection of his articles and excerpts from his books, along with a bibliography of his writings to date. An essay-length intellectual biography by this author served as its introduction. The book was titled *Left Illusions: An Intellectual Odyssey* and was published in 2003.

The reparations campaign had revealed how a small minority of activists were able to dominate the campus debate by calling "racist" anyone who stepped forward to challenge their views. The ads that Horowitz placed contained "10 Reasons" for the view that reparations were a bad idea at a time when American slavery was no more, and when most Americans were descendants of people who had opposed slavery or who had reached these shores after slavery had been abolished. But the spring term of the anti-reparations campaign went by without a single response by Horowitz's critics to the arguments and evidence presented in his ad. Only epithets and slanders were hurled in Horowitz's direction. Even though the claims of the ad were based firmly on historical grounds, not a single university professor with expertise in American slavery was willing to incur the risks associated with confirming those facts, because it would entail opposing the campus left and incurring similar insults. In the current environment of campus "political correctness," issues like reparations for slavery simply could not be rationally addressed.[43]

Horowitz viewed this as a troubling commentary on the state of the contemporary university and of university authorities who

---

[43]For an honest survey of this problem by a veteran liberal, see Kirsten Powers, *The Silencing: How the Left is Killing Free Speech*, Regnery, 2015.

were afraid to enforce an educational decorum allowing both sides of controversial issues to be addressed in a campus setting. Horowitz's encounters with students on more than 100 campuses in the previous decade had made him aware that the intimidation and suppression of conservative views extended to the classroom itself, where conservative ideas were ridiculed by faculty and fellow students and conservative texts were virtually absent from required reading lists.

As a result, in 2002 Horowitz launched a "Campaign for Fairness and Inclusion in Higher Education" to foster a pluralism of ideas and viewpoints; in the spring of 2003 he drafted an "Academic Bill of Rights" based on the classic 1915 statement on academic freedom by the American Association of University Professors. Over the next seven years, Horowitz urged universities to adopt a code to insure that students would have access to views on more than one side of controversial issues; and that faculty would conduct themselves professionally in the classroom, refraining from using their authority to indoctrinate students in partisan agendas. To advance these principles, Horowitz wrote four books analyzing the situation he encountered on the several hundred campuses he visited during the seven years of his campaign: *The Professors* (2006), *Indoctrination U* (2008), *One-Party Classroom* (2009), and *Reforming Our Universities* (2010).[44]

Of these texts, *The Professors* received the widest attention because it exposed a radical culture of academics who had corrupted the institutions of higher learning, using their faculty positions as platforms for political rather than scholarly agendas. Horowitz described this politicization of the classroom as the end of the ethos of the modern research university in liberal arts faculties. It represented, he wrote, a reversion to the doctrinal institutions of the 19th century when colleges were training centers for the clergy, and indoctrination was standard academic procedure.

---

[44]The campaign and these books are the subject of Volume 7 of this series, *The Left in the University.*

No previous work had taken on the radical subversion of the university as directly and forcefully as *The Professors*, which is why the book became such a target of attack by the academic left—with the president of the American Association of University Professors going so far as to urge others not to read the book.[45]

Indoctrination U unveiled the ferocity of the opposition to Horowitz's campaign; leftist critics smeared it as a "blacklist," "McCarthyism," and a "witch hunt." Notwithstanding the fierce opposition it encountered, Horowitz's campaign had some significant achievements. In June 2005 the American Council on Education, representing over 1,800 colleges and universities, issued a statement declaring that "academic freedom and intellectual pluralism [are] core principles of an American education." A Brookings Institution report made this comment: "Perhaps the peak of David Horowitz's national influence came in June 2005 when a coalition of twenty-eight mainstream national education associations, led by the American Council on Education, approved a statement on academic rights and responsibilities that blended traditional concepts of academic freedom with an endorsement of intellectual pluralism and student rights as championed by Horowitz."[46]

In Horowitz's view, however, the American Council's statement actually did nothing to change the academic curriculum or ensure that it reflected the pluralistic values that the statement endorsed. In 2009, as his campaign entered its final year, Horowitz co-authored *One-Party Classroom* with Jacob Laksin. The book examined more than 170 curricula from 12 major universities that

---

[45]"Please ignore this book. Don't buy it. Don't read it. Try not to mention it in idle conversation." Cary Nelson, "Ignore This Book," *Academe*, November–December 2006, Vol. 92, No. 6, pp. 81–82, 84, http://www.jstor.org/stable/40253534. Academe is the official publication of the American Association of University Professors.

[46]Bruce L.R. Smith, Jeremy D. Mayer and A. Lee Fritschler, *Closed Minds? Politics and Ideology in American Universities*, Brookings Institution, 2008, p. 98.

could only be described as courses designed to indoctrinate students in left-wing politics. The problem remained what it had been at the outset: how to get university authorities to require liberal arts faculties to behave professionally in the classroom, to teach their students *how* to think and not tell them *what* to think.

Horowitz concluded his campaign with a comprehensive account of his efforts, *Reforming Our Universities*, which was also a richly textured description of American institutions of higher learning and the forces within those institutions that had politicized the academic curriculum and were prepared to defend their "right" to indoctrinate students in political agendas.

Having been part of a progressive movement that identified with America's enemies, Horowitz was struck by the Democrats' reluctance to stop Saddam Hussein's aggression during the first Gulf War, when only 10 Democratic senators supported the coalition that George H.W. Bush had assembled to reverse Iraq's annexation of Kuwait. This was a sign of the commanding role the left had assumed in the Democratic Party. Since Saddam Hussein was one of the true monsters of the 20th century and did not justify his atrocities by appeals to "social justice," it also revealed the disturbing lengths to which the left would go to act on its hostility to America.

While he was writing his account of the reparations controversy in the summer of 2001, Horowitz was diagnosed with prostate cancer. In October, shortly after the 9/11 attacks, he underwent a radical prostatectomy and radiation treatments to remove the cancer. While recovering from the operation, Horowitz wrote a long essay titled, "How the Left Undermined America's Security Before and After 9/11," which traced the leftward march of the Democratic Party and its growing defection from the War on Terror.[47] This essay became the background to two important

---

[47]A version of this essay is reprinted in Volume 3 of this series, *The Great Betrayal.*

books on the war in Iraq and the continuing transformation of the Democratic Party into a party of the left.

The first of these volumes, *Unholy Alliance: Radical Islam and the American Left* (2004), described the events leading up to the invasion of Iraq and set out to explain how a secular left that championed Enlightenment values had aligned itself with the Islamist enemies of those values and the West. *Unholy Alliance* also described how the radical left, which organized massive demonstrations against the war, had dramatically influenced the course of Democratic policy and caused a break in the bipartisanship that had bound American foreign policy over the previous half century.

Unholy Alliance was the first book to trace the evolution of American radicalism from its support for the Soviet bloc to its opposition to the War on Terror; and to explain how the left and Islamist movements share a common mindset that creates a bond between them.[48] Both ideologies are utopian enterprises that require the suppression of dissent and/or the eradication of the opposition to achieve their vision of paradise on earth—the classless utopia for the left, and the sharia utopia for the Islamists. For the left, America is the hated seat of global capitalism and individualism. For Islamists, America is the hated seat of Western values, a bulwark against the global domination of Islam and a wellspring of spiritual iniquity. Consequently, both of these destructive movements have a shared conception of, and contempt for, the "Great Satan"—America—which they identify as the primary source of evil in the world and find common ground in their desire to annihilate or "fundamentally transform" it.

Five years later Horowitz followed *Unholy Alliance* with a second volume written with Ben Johnson, called *Party of Defeat: How Democrats and Radicals Undermined America's War on*

---

[48]A section of David Horowitz, *Unholy Alliance: Radical Islam And the American Left* (Regnery, 2006), describing "The Mind of the Left," is reprinted in Volume 2 of this series, *Progressives*.

Terror Before and After 9-11 (2008). Eighteen Republican senators and congressmen endorsed the book, including the ranking members of the committees on intelligence, foreign relations and military affairs in both houses. *Party of Defeat* examined in detail what Horowitz was later to call "the great betrayal"—the unprecedented defection of a major political party from a war-in-progress that it had voted to authorize and then proceeded to sabotage.[49]

The authors provided the historical background of the Democratic Party's defeatism, tracing its antipathy for America back to the Vietnam War and George McGovern's notorious 1972 "America Come Home" campaign which, like the Wallace progressives in 1948, identified America's resistance to Communism as the problem rather than the Communist aggression itself. The book is notable for its debunking of the major Democratic arguments against the war, and the detail it provides of the Democrats' treachery in destroying intelligence operations, undermining morale and conducting a psychological warfare campaign "worthy of the enemy" against America's war effort.

After the completion of *Unholy Alliance* in 2004, Horowitz turned his attention to an Internet project that would provide conservatives with a profile of the left, which he believed was effecting dramatic changes in the political landscape. <DiscovertheNetworks.org>, which went online in February 2005, was an encyclopedia of the left that provided a map of its networks, funding, personnel and agendas, both overt and covert.

The influence of "Discover the Networks" in shaping conservatives' understanding of the left, and making it possible for conservative journalists and authors to identify the thousands of organizations of the left, is difficult to calculate. But there is no question that it has been enormous, particularly in providing an indispensable resource for journalists and other writers in identifying the

---

[49]Volume 3 in this series, *The Great Betrayal*, contains Horowitz's writings on Iraq and the War on Terror from 9/11 to the death of Osama bin Laden.

constituents of the Islamist *jihad*, and describing the radical networks around Barack Obama and the Democratic Party leadership. Stanley Kurtz, whose *Radical-in-Chief* is a seminal book on the president's political career, has said that he "could not have written *Radical-in-Chief* without the information provided in Discover the Networks."[50] Aaron Klein's and Paul Kengor's works on Obama are similarly indebted. The rationale for this database and the uproar surrounding its publication are examined in Volume 2 of this series, *Progressives*.

In pursuing his efforts to document the left's infiltration and eventual control of the Democratic Party, Horowitz's attention was drawn to a recently formed network of funders and apparatchiks that *The Washington Post* had already described as a "shadow party," taking a term from the British political lexicon that denotes the government-in-waiting of the opposition party. In this case, however, the government-in-waiting was being formed inside the opposition party itself. With author Richard Poe, Horowitz published *The Shadow Party: How George Soros, Hillary Clinton, and Sixties Radicals Seized Control of the Democratic Party* (2006). Their book was an exposé of how billionaire George Soros had put together a coalition of wealthy funders, radical activists and political apparatchiks which quickly gained a lock on the Democratic Party's political apparatus and began a behind-the-scenes effort to exclude moderates and push party policies in a radical direction. Horowitz had already described the ideological influence the left exerted on the Democratic Party; now he unveiled the mechanism by which it was implemented.

Following the publication of *The Shadow Party*, Horowitz continued this work with another book, this time co-authored with Jacob Laksin: *The New Leviathan: How the Left-Wing Money Machine Shapes American Politics and Threatens America's Future* (2012). Drawing on the Discover the Networks database,

---

[50]Communication to the author.

the new book documented and analyzed what no other work of scholarship had noticed—that the left had successfully built the richest and most powerful political machine in American history. The authors' findings upended the conventional wisdom that conservatives and the Republican Party represent the rich and powerful, while progressives and the Democrats are "the party of the people." To the contrary, their research proved beyond a doubt that the financial assets of the left directed at policy formation actually exceed by a factor of ten or more those of the right and are being invested in "transforming" America—reorienting it in a socialist direction.

The New Leviathan reveals how a powerful network moves radical ideas like Obamacare from the margins of the political mainstream and makes them the priority agendas of the Democratic Party. In so doing, this network has shifted the national policy debate dramatically to the left and reconfigured the nation's own political agenda. One chapter of the book, "The Making of a President," documents how Barack Obama's entire political career was shaped, funded and made possible by the financial and political network they describe.

In 2014, Horowitz resumed his strategic lessons for Republicans and conservatives in *Take No Prisoners: The Battle Plan for Defeating the Left*, which is a summary statement of his twenty years of thinking about political warfare. According to Horowitz, conservatives fail to employ a political language that speaks to voters' emotions, and fail to highlight the *moral* imperative of opposing policies that are destructive to the poor, to the vulnerable, and ultimately to all Americans.

Picking up from where *The Art of Political War* left off, Horowitz analyzes the defeat Republicans suffered in the 2012 presidential election in which they were beaten by an incumbent who had only a failed record on which to run. Horowitz describes how this outcome is directly related to the fact that progressives and conservatives see the world differently. Progressives view themselves as social redeemers, as missionaries seeking to transform the world, which inspires their will to win. Conservatives are pragmatists whose goals are specific, practical and modest by comparison. But it is only by embracing their mission as defenders of freedom, and as champions of the victims of progressive policies, that conservatives can confront the fire of the left with a fire of their own.

In 2012 Horowitz published what with one large exception was to be a final episode in the work of the second half of his life—to understand the pathology of the left, its hatred of America, and its destructive agendas. He gave it the title *Radicals: Portraits of a Destructive Passion* (2012). Among its six chapters is a portrait of his friend Christopher Hitchens, whose incomplete second thoughts about his radical commitments becomes for Horowitz a measure of what it means to be of the left, and what it means to have left the left. This poignant rendering of both the man and his evolving ideology explores the seamless fabric joining radical ideas and lives, and the destructive consequences of both.[51]

The large exception alluded to is the series of nine volumes called *The Black Book of the American Left*, of which this is the final installment. It can be said with reasonable certitude that this is, and is likely to remain, the most complete first-hand portrait of the left as it evolved from the inception of the Cold War through the era of Barack Obama and the Islamic *jihad*.

Along with his political books, Horowitz began publishing in 2005 a series of four volumes of philosophical memoirs that reveal a different side of his personality and writing. Always known for his strong cerebral prose, in these volumes he shows a lyrical introspection that is unexpected. All four books engage issues of mortality and faith, and along the way show how the progressive quest for perfect justice, as Horowitz puts it, "is really an attempt to deny the permanence of injustice of which death is the exemplary case."[52]

The first of these volumes, *The End of Time* (2005), is all at once a meditation on the religious angst of the 17th-century

---

[51]"The Two Christophers," reprinted in the present volume.
[52]David Horowitz, *You're Going to Be Dead One Day: A Love Story*, Regnery, 2015, p. 5.

physicist and philosopher Blaise Pascal, a journal of his own battle with cancer, a look into the mind of 9/11 terrorist Mohammed Atta and the story of a romantic relationship that Horowitz never expected to have. Literary critic Stanley Fish wrote of the book: "Most memoirs only mime honesty. This one performs it. Beautifully written, unflinching in its contemplation of the abyss, and yet finally hopeful in its acceptance of human finitude. And as a bonus, it gives us a wonderful love story."

The second book in this series, *A Cracking of the Heart* (2009), is a moving tribute to his beloved daughter, Sarah, who died in her San Francisco apartment in 2008 at the young age of 44. Sarah was born with Turner Syndrome, a disability that often causes shortness of stature and progressive deafness, both of which afflicted Sarah. It also produced arthritis in one of her hips, which caused her pain, significantly limited her mobility and caused her to walk with a limp. At last it produced a heart condition associated with early death.

Yet *A Cracking of the Heart* is witness to an extraordinary human being who rejected self-pity and complaint, and who chose instead to live a life of perseverance, hard work and independence. A talented writer and Good Samaritan, Sarah refused to allow her obstacles to stifle her dreams. With exceptional bravery and magnanimity, she confronted the forces that were aiming to crush her. Horowitz reveals how, from an early age, while facing the cruel limitations imposed on her, she showed a tremendous compassion for the disadvantaged, became active in the Turner Syndrome Society, taught autistic youth, protested capital punishment, fed the homeless and sojourned to Israel, where she twice climbed Masada. She also traveled to El Salvador to build homes for poor Catholics, to Mumbai to help sexually abused Hindu girls, and to Uganda to teach English to the 3-to-5 year olds of the Abayudaya, a tribe of African Jews, with whom she lived in mud-floor huts with no electricity or running water.[53]

---

[53]David Horowitz, *A Cracking of the Heart*, Regnery, 2009, p. 150.

While celebrating Sarah's life, *A Cracking of the Heart* movingly examines the tensions between father and daughter arising from their political differences and also the conflicts that arose naturally from a parent's concern and a daughter's fierce quest for independence. We are privy to their ongoing dialogue and eventual reconciliation, and to a father's unassuageable grief in a brutal encounter with the finality of death.

Horowitz describes the next work in this meditative series as "a summa of my life's work." Subtitled "The Search for Redemption in this Life and the Next," *A Point in Time* (2011) is about the all-too-human fear that our existence will vanish into oblivion—and the consequences of coping with this fear by acting as gods and trying to remake the world. It begins with reflections on the meditations of Marcus Aurelius and moves on to the 19th-century novelist Fyodor Dostoevsky and his prescient vision of the totalitarian state.

In his fourth book of reflections on faith and mortality, *You're Going to Be Dead One Day: A Love Story,* Horowitz takes us on an inspirational journey inside his personal world, sharing his remarkable and unlikely love story with his wife April, his relationship with his children, his philosophical reflections about gratitude and perseverance in the face of adversity and illness and his evolving thoughts on death. This book is about the choice each of us faces: whether to embrace this world we are given and make the most of it, or to live a life of bitterness, as his own father did, because one can never reach the inexistent world of utopian fantasy.

In *You're Going to Be Dead One Day*, we see how far Horowitz has escaped from his father's shadow and from the destructive discontent that lies at the heart of the radical creed. While it looks unflinchingly at human limitations and the death that awaits us all, his story is nonetheless one of tenuous hope, even joy. His body may be failing him, but his spirit is strong. All his multiplicity of experience, belief and disillusion has left him with one ineradicable truth: that the here and now is to be treasured; that death, while a dark and formidable word, does not carry the day.

The last word is love—for his wife, his children, his friends and animals. This is a book in which Horowitz has fully followed Wordsworth's ideal of recollecting one's life in tranquility.

So how, finally, do we measure David Horowitz's life and work? This question is complicated by the fact that, in having second thoughts about the left and its catastrophic impact on American life, Horowitz alienated the literary and cultural establishment that had showered him with acclaim from the moment he burst onto the scene as one of the leaders of his radical generation. During the second half of his life he has worked against the grain as an outsider whose literary output, prodigious by any standard, has been largely ignored by the progressive cultural establishment, except when it was being condemned in an effort to place it beyond the pale of respectability.

Yet despite the effort to deprecate and diminish him, Horowitz has succeeded in his main task of exposing the left's agenda and decoding the way it seeks to control American culture and politics. He has never refused to do battle with his critics. But they have for the most part refused to do battle with him, launching hit-and-run attacks from the institutional heights of the mainstream culture, while Horowitz—denied access to their platforms—has answered those attacks with difficulty.

For example: when Garry Wills made an ignorant but damaging aside in a *Time* magazine cover story on the Sixties to the effect that Collier and Horowitz were merely "marginal" figures in the decade, the magazine refused to print a response. An irresponsible slander by *Time* columnist Jack White, who called Horowitz a "bigot," was allowed to stand, despite the embarrassment of *Time*'s editor, who was familiar with Horowitz's work and to whom Horowitz appealed.[54] No letter to the editor was allowed to

---

[54]The editor, Walter Isaacson, took the view that White had only expressed an "opinion," and that he was bound to defend his columnists' freedom of expression even if the opinion was wrong about the facts. This incident is described in detail in Volume 6 of this series, *Progressive Racism*, "Time Magazine's Attack" (p. 117).

answer a malicious insinuation by Slate editor-in-chief Jacob Weis-
berg in *The New York Times Magazine*. And so forth.[55]

Rather than entering a tough but reasonable dialogue,
Horowitz's critics have often chosen contemptuous hauteur.
When Horowitz dissected some writing by MIT professor Noam
Chomsky, the latter responded in an online venue, "I haven't read
Horowitz. I didn't . . . read him when he was a Stalinist and I don't
read him today."

Chomsky's claim was mendacious on all counts. First, he
knew that Horowitz's teenaged "Stalinism" was an accident of
birth, and that the mature Horowitz had been an outspoken, visi-
ble *anti*-Stalinist. Second, Chomsky had not only read Horowitz's
work as a leftist but had admiringly cited his *Ramparts* article,
"Sinews of Power," in his own book *Problems of Knowledge and
Freedom*.[56] Third, after Horowitz published "A Radical's Disenchantment," his farewell to the left, Chomsky sent him two nasty
letters, consisting of twelve single-spaced typewritten pages, and
never answered Horowitz's responses.[57]

Dismissive snark was not unique to Chomsky. Eric Alterman,
a commentator for MSNBC and a columnist for *The Nation*, wrote
a scathing review of *The Politics of Bad Faith* in which he failed to
discuss the ideas in the text, but instead passed on to readers Paul
Berman's unhinged claim that Horowitz was a "demented
lunatic"—a charge made in the course of a bitter attack in the
pages of the socialist magazine *Dissent*.[58] "When Horowitz finally

---

[55]Horowitz did reply via his own publication, in an article titled "Ordeal
by Slander," FrontPageMag.com, December 7, 1999, http://archive.front-
pagemag.com/readArticle.aspx?ARTID=24346. It is included in Volume
2 of this series, *Progressives*, p. 175.

[56]Noam Chomsky, *Problems of Knowledge and Freedom: The Russell
Lectures*, Pantheon Books, 1971, p. 71.

[57]Horowitz interview, June 28, 2002.

[58]Berman, *Dissent*, Winter 1998, p. 119; Horowitz reply, *Dissent*, Spring
1998, p. 112. Berman was irate because Horowitz, in an advertisement
for *Radical Son*, had used a passage from an earlier Berman article praising his work.

dies," Alterman wrote in the same review, "I suspect we will be confronted with a posthumous volume of memoirs titled 'The End of History.'"

The operative word here is the wishful *finally*. Leftists like Alterman now face a double bind: not only is Horowitz still with us, but in *The Black Book of the American Left* he has given them the living summary of his work that they have dreaded.

The tenured radicals of the university, perhaps because they have felt the sting of Horowitz's attack, have chosen to ignore his significant role in the events of the 1960s and 70s while composing their political and social histories and filling their archives with primary documents. Despite a virtual cottage industry involving that radical era, Horowitz has received no more than a handful of inquires about his views, recollections, expertise, or work from any of the thousands of left-wing scholars and their students writing theses, articles, and books, or logging oral histories about this swath of history. At the same time, numerous scholars devoted to these historical pursuits have boycotted his campus appearances.

Similarly, the journals that form an acropolis of our literary culture—*The New York Review of Books*, the *New Republic*, and *The New York Times*—have studiously ignored Horowitz's work since his move to the conservative camp. *The New York Review of Books* has not reviewed a Horowitz book since 1985, when *The Kennedys* was published; the *New Republic* stopped with *Destructive Generation* in 1989; and with the exception of one brief dismissive notice, *The New York Times* stopped with the publication of *Radical Son*.

Some sectors of intellectual conservatism have also kept a distance from Horowitz, reflecting a discomfort with his aggressive political and literary style. Norman Podhoretz, the former editor of *Commentary*, who published several pieces by Collier and Horowitz in the 1980s, observes: "Some conservatives think he goes too far, and my guess is that some also believe his relentless campaign against the left focuses too much on the 'pure' form of it that has become less influential than its adulterated versions traveling under the name of liberalism. Then there's his polemical style, which still resembles the one invented by the left. Even though it has made the left its target, there are conservatives, I think, who feel uncomfortable with it."[59]

The historian Richard Pipes is also puzzled by the failure of some conservative intellectuals to embrace Horowitz: "It may have to do with style and decorum. Conservatives do not like aggressive argumentation—they prefer to stand above the fray. For the same reason they ignore Rush Limbaugh for all his enormous success and influence. It is a weakness of the conservative movement, this fear of giving battle."[60]

Yet while some conservatives have kept him at arm's length, it cannot be denied that Horowitz has enjoyed substantial support in the conservative movement generally and even from the conservative media. While his later efforts may not always have received the attention they merit, *Radical Son* was a cover story in the *Weekly Standard;* Ramesh Ponnuru wrote an elegant and appreciative review in *First Things;* and the book received very favorable notices in *National Review* and other conservative publications.[61]

To overcome the many obstacles he has faced, Horowitz has been forced to create his own institutional base to carry on his work. He has done this with the help of a handful of conservative foundations and over 140,000 individual supporters who contribute to the David Horowitz Freedom Center. Its online journal, FrontPageMag.com, is devoted to "News of the War at Home and Abroad" and receives over one and a half million unique visitors a month. TruthRevolt.org, another daily site, "hits and unmasks" leftists in the media; and a campus campaign website, JewHatred.org., tracks

---

[59]Norman Podhoretz interview, June 17, 2002.

[60]Richard Pipes interview, June 21, 2002.

[61]Ramesh Ponnuru, "Radical Son: A Generational Odyssey," *First Things,* August/September 1997, pp. 61–66.

the growing anti-Semitism that has defaced the university and is creeping into mainstream politics.

The creation of the Freedom Center has enabled Horowitz to speak at over four hundred colleges and universities in the last twenty years—albeit in appearances that were ghettoized thanks to the protests and boycotts of the left—and to appear on well over a thousand radio talk shows and television programs. Through these efforts, Horowitz has been able to play a meaningful role in the battle of ideas. Paul Hollander, himself the author of notable books on radical politics, including *Political Pilgrims* and *Anti-Americanism*, has made the following comment on Horowitz's contribution: "He played a very important part in the culture wars, and has been exceptionally courageous and paid a price for it by becoming the most detested ex-radical among his former comrades. Especially valuable has been his willingness to 'dirty his hands' so to speak by debating and addressing often hostile debaters and audiences. I know that many people think that he has embraced another extreme, that he has been too confrontational, etc. He exemplifies to some degree the dilemma of how to avoid becoming like one's adversaries: how do you avoid the designation of 'ideologue' if you fight ideologues? Or avoid politicizing your own self as you fight the politicization of things which should not be political? Would he have been more effective if he had been perceived as more 'moderate?' Hard to know. I basically applaud virtually all the stands he has taken, including most recently on the reparations for slavery."[62]

The left's hatred for Horowitz's achievement in exposing and crystallizing the pathology of radicalism is his reward for a quarter century of writing and argumentation. It has drawn the following appreciation from Norman Podhoretz: "David Horowitz is hated by the left because he is not only an apostate but has been even more relentless and aggressive in attacking his former political allies than some of us who preceded him in what I once called

[62]Paul Hollander interview, May 13, 2002.

'breaking ranks' with that world. He has also taken the polemical and organizational techniques he learned in his days on the left, and figured out how to use them against the left, whose vulnerabilities he knows in his bones. (That he is such a good writer and speaker doesn't hurt, either.) In fact, he has done so much, and in so many different ways, that one might be justified in suspecting that 'David Horowitz' is actually more than one person."

Podhoretz's words explain why Horowitz continues to receive such tremendous praise from those who sense the left's pernicious threat to liberty and who respect and admire what he has contributed to its defense. Academic and social critic Camille Paglia, herself an independent leftist, calls Horowitz "one of America's most original and courageous political analysts," reflecting that "as a scholar who regularly surveys archival material, I think that, a century from now, cultural historians will find David Horowitz's spiritual and political odyssey paradigmatic for our time."[63] Roger Kimball, the editor and publisher of *The New Criterion* and the publisher of Encounter Books, refers to Horowitz as a "national treasure."[64] Emmy Award-winning writer, journalist, and political pundit Bernard Goldberg calls Horowitz "one of America's most important and interesting thinkers."[65] *Wall Street Journal* editorial board member Robert L. Pollock sees in Horowitz "one of America's foremost defenders of free speech and free thought."[66] *Publishers Weekly*, meanwhile, describes Horowitz as "one of the best political writers on either side of the aisle."[67]

---

[63]Camille Paglia, "Camille Paglia Defends David Horowitz," Salon.com, Thursday, Aug 26, 1999, http://www.salon.com/1999/08/26/paglia_6/.

[64]Excerpt from the back cover of David Horowitz, *Radicals: Portraits of a Destructive Passion*, Regnery, 2012.

[65]Ibid.

[66]Excerpt from the back cover of David Horowitz, *Indoctrination U. The Left's War Against Academic Freedom*, Encounter Books, 2007.

[67]See the "Editorial Reviews" section of the Amazon.com page for *Left Illusions: An Intellectual Odyssey*, http://www.amazon.com/Left-Illu-sions-Intellectual-David-Horowitz/dp/1890626511/ref=sr_1_1_twi_2_har?s=books&ie=UTF8&qid=1435447192&sr=1-1&keywords=left+illusions.

Horowitz exemplifies the irritating, threatening reminder to tyranny that human freedom and the triumph of the human spirit can ultimately never be suffocated or suppressed. Henry Mark Holzer, a libertarian lawyer who was Ayn Rand's attorney and has represented Soviet dissidents fleeing communism for freedom in the West, has given expression to sentiments shared by many of Horowitz's conservative supporters: "I don't say loosely that someone is a hero. But in my view, David Horowitz fits the definition of that term. He is a man who has stood up, and for a long time stood up alone, for his values. And his confessions are invaluable. We didn't have Alger Hiss providing us with a book about why he turned to treason. But Horowitz has expressed how and why many Americans betrayed their own country in the face of evil. In this sense, he has provided a great service. And this service is enhanced by the fact that he shows how this form of treason operated on the psychological level. I am not sure that this has ever been done before."[68]

Someone who has traced the arc of David Horowitz's life cannot help thinking that, despite all the efforts to silence him, he will ultimately be vindicated by history; and that the principles behind his work, to use William Faulkner's famous words, will not only endure but prevail.

---

[68]Hank Holzer interview, July 15, 2002

TWO

End Note

Because these volumes began as a collection of my mainly completed conservative writings, it was inevitable that there would be lacunae in its coverage of the left. At the outset of my conservative career, I had made a decision not to duplicate the work that conservatives were already doing well but rather to focus on dissecting those aspects of the radical agenda which either remained opaque to the conservative perspective, or whose malignancy was not fully appreciated by the conservative temperament. Consequently, I ceded certain areas to others who had been studying them longer than I and understood them better. Two of these were the constitutional framework of the American political system and the market economy. I did write a few essays on both, which are included in these volumes, but left the heavy lifting to conservative writers who had been contending with collectivists and statists far longer than I. A third area was the sacralizing of the environment and its exploitation in the service of collectivist agendas. I did write one essay on the subject for *National Review*, which I called "From Red to Green," in which I described how perfectly the environmental cause fit the Marxist paradigm.[5] It had the apocalyptic concerns, which could be used to justify a massive transfer of power to the state and a draconian assault on individual freedom. And it possessed an added advantage in that the oppressed class—inanimate objects like rocks and trees, and mute creatures like animals—could not speak for themselves the way proletarians had in rejecting the revolutionary role the left assigned to them.

Since others were ably engaged in these battles, I felt that expending my time and energy on them would be redundant, and would distract me from more pressing tasks. Perhaps this decision was a mistake, but it is too late to rectify.

David Horowitz
Los Angeles
December 2016

THREE

The Writings of David Horowitz,
1951–2017
A bibliography by Mike Bauer

(Another version of this listing can be found online at http://www.
frontpagemag.com/author/david-horowitz/bibliography)

I. Books by Horowitz, U.S. editions:

Student: The Political Activities of the Berkeley Students. Ballantine,
1962

The Free World Colossus. Hill & Wang, 1965

Shakespeare: An Existential View. Hill & Wang, 1965

Free World Colossus: From Yalta to Vietnam. American, 1967

Foreign Policy in the Cold War. Harmondsworth, Penguin, 1968

Empire and Revolution: A Radical Interpretation of Contemporary History. Random House, 1969

Empire and Revolution: A Radical Interpretation of Contemporary History. Vintage Books, 1970

Empire and Revolution: A Radical Interpretation of Contemporary History. Penguin, 1971

Free World Colossus. Hill and Wang, 1971

The Fate of Midas and Other Essays. Ramparts Press, 1973

The First Frontier: The Indian Wars and America's Origins, 1607–1776. Simon & Schuster, 1978

Radical Son: A Generational Odyssey. Free Press, 1997

The Politics of Bad Faith: The Radical Assault on America's Future. Free Press, 1998

Sex, Lies & Vast Conspiracies. Second Thoughts Books, 1998

Hating Whitey: And Other Progressive Causes. Spence, 1999

The Art of Political War and Other Radical Pursuits. Spence, 2000

How to Beat the Democrats and Other Subversive Ideas. Spence, 2002

Uncivil Wars: The Controversy Over Reparations for Slavery. Encounter, 2002

Left Illusions: An Intellectual Odyssey. Spence, 2003

Unholy Alliance: Radical Islam and the American Left. Regnery, 2004

The End of Time. Encounter, 2005

The Professors: 101 Most Dangerous Academics in America. Regnery, 2006

The Shadow Party: How George Soros, Hillary Clinton, and the Sixties Radicals Seized Control of the Democratic Party. Nelson Current, 2006

Indoctrination U.: The Left's War Against Academic Freedom. Encounter, 2007

One-Party Classroom: How Radical Professors at America's Top Colleges Indoctrinate Students and Undermine Our Democracy. Crown Forum, 2009

A Cracking of the Heart. Regnery, 2009

Reforming Our Universities: The Campaign For an Academic Bill of Rights. Regnery, 2010

A Point in Time. Regnery, 2011

The New Leviathan: How the Left-Wing Money Machine Shapes American Politics and Threatens America's Future. Crown Forum, 2012

Radicals: Portraits of a Destructive Passion. Regnery, 2012

The Black Book of the American Left, Volume I: My Life and Times. Encounter, 2013

The Black Book of the American Left, Volume II: Progressives. Second Thoughts, 2014

Take No Prisoners: The Battle Plan for Defeating the Left. Regnery, 2014

The Black Book of the American Left, Volume III: The Great Betrayal. Second Thoughts, 2014

The Black Book of the American Left, Volume IV: Islamo-Fascism and the War Against the Jews. Second Thoughts, 2015

You're Going to Be Dead One Day. Regnery, 2015

The Black Book of the American Left, Volume V: Culture Wars. Second Thoughts, 2015

The Black Book of the American Left, Volume VI: Progressive Racism. Encounter, 2016

The Black Book of the American Left, Volume VII: The Left in Power, Clinton to Obama. Second Thoughts, 2015

Big Agenda: President Trump's Plan to Save America. Humanix Books, 2017

The Black Book of the American Left, Volume VIII: The Left in the University. Second Thoughts, 2017

The Black Book of the American Left, Volume IX: Ruling Ideas. Second Thoughts, 2018

II. Books with Horowitz as co-author; U.S. editions:

The Rockefellers: An American Dynasty. Holt, Rinehart and Wilson, 1976 (with Peter Collier)

The Rockefellers: An American Dynasty. New American Library, 1977 (with Peter Collier)

The Year-Long Day: An American Dynasty (adaptation of *The Rockefellers: An American Dynasty*). Newsweek Books, 1977 (with Peter Collier)

The Kennedys: An American Drama. Summit Books, 1984 (with Peter Collier)

The Kennedys: An American Drama. Warner Books, 1985 (with Peter Collier)

The Fords: An American Epic. Summit Books, 1987 (with Peter Collier)

The Fords: An American Epic. Simon and Schuster, 1992 (with Peter Collier)

Destructive Generation: Second Thoughts About the Sixties. Summit Books, 1989 (with Peter Collier)

Destructive Generation: Second Thoughts About the Sixties. Free Press Paperbacks, 1989 (with Peter Collier)

The Rockefellers: An American Dynasty. Summit Books, 1989 (with Peter Collier)

Destructive Generation: Second Thoughts About the Sixties. Simon and Schuster, 1990 (with Peter Collier)

Deconstructing the Left: From Vietnam to the Persian Gulf. Second Thoughts Books, 1991

The Roosevelts: An American Saga. Simon and Schuster, 1994 (with Peter Collier)

Destructive Generation: Second Thoughts About the Sixties. Free Press Paperbacks, 1996 (with Peter Collier)

The Fords: An American Epic. Summit Books, 2002 (with Peter Collier)

The Kennedys: An American Drama. Summit Books, 2002 (with Peter Collier)

The Anti-Chomsky Reader. Encounter, 2004 (with Peter Collier)

Party of Defeat. Spence, 2008 (with Ben Johnson)

One-Party Classroom: How Radical Professors at America's Top Colleges Indoctrinate Students and Undermine Our Democracy. Crown Forum, 2009 (with Jacob Laksin)

Books with Horowitz as editor or co-editor, worldwide:
Containment and Revolution. Beacon Press, 1967
Marx and Modern Economics. Monthly Review Press, 1968
Marx and Modern Economics. Modern Reader Paperbacks, 1968
Corporations and the Cold War. Monthly Review Press, 1969
Corporations and the Cold War. New England Free Press, 1969
Isaac Deutscher: The Man and His Work. Macdonald & Co., U.K., 1971
Radical Sociology: An Introduction. Canfield Press, 1971
Counterculture and Revolution. Random House, 1972 (co-editor)
Second Thoughts: Former Radicals Look Back at the Sixties. Madison
    Books, 1989 (Peter Collier, co-editor)
Second Thoughts About Race in America. Madison Books, 1991 (Peter
    Collier, co-editor)
*Surviving the PC University: The Best of **Heterodoxy***. Second Thoughts
    Books, 1993 (Peter Collier, co-editor)
The Heterodoxy Handbook: How to Survive the PC Campus. Regnery,
    1994 (Peter Collier, co-editor)
Public Broadcasting and the Public Trust. Center for the Study of Popular
    Culture, 1995
Public Broadcasting and the Public Trust. Second Thoughts Books, 1995
*The Race Card: White Guilt, Black Resentment, and the Assault on
    Truth and Justice*. Prima Publications, U.K., 1997
Immigration & National Security Post-9/11. Center for the Study of Pop-
    ular Culture, 2002

Volumes with Horowitz as a contributor:
The Socialist Register. Monthly Review Press, 1964
Republic and Empire. Simon and Schuster, 1987
Call to Battle. Tom Doherty Associates, 1988

Other U.S. editions:
Today's Best Non-Fiction, The Reader's Digest Association Limited: con-
    densed version of "The Fords," 1992
Reader's Digest, Great biographies in large type: "The Fords," Reader's
    Digest Fund for the Blind, 1994

Foreign editions of Horowitz or Horowitz-coauthored books:
*The Free World Colossus: A Critique of American Foreign Policy in the
    Cold War*. London: Macgibbon & Kee, 1965
Shakespeare: An Existential View. London: Tavistock Publications, 1965

Fran Jalta till Vietnam; En Kritisk Granskning av USA's Utrikespolitik. ("The Free World Colossus") Sweden: Prisma, 1966

Containment and Revolution: Western Policy towards Social Revolution, 1917 to Vietnam. Blond Editorial U.K., 1967

From Yalta to Vietnam: American Foreign Policy in the Cold War. ("The Free World Colossus") Penguin U.K., 1967

Estados Unidos frente a la revolución mundial: de Yalta al Vietnam. ("The Free World Colossus") Barcelona: Ediciones de Cultura Popular, 1968

Marx and Modern Economics. London: Macgibbon & Kee, 1968

Shakespeare: An Existential View. U.K.: Social Science Paperbacks, 1968

Empire and Revolution: Imperialism and Revolution. London: Allen Lane, 1969

From Yalta to Vietnam: American Foreign Policy in the Cold War. ("The Free World Colossus") Penguin U.K., 1969

Kalter Krieg: Hintergründe der US-Aussenpolitik von Jalta bis Vietnam. ("The Free World Colossus") Berlin: Verlag Klaus Wagenbach, 1969

Imperialismus und Revolution: Neue Fakten zur Ggegenwärtigen Geschichte. ("Imperialism and Revolution") Berlin: Wagenbach, 1970

From Yalta to Vietnam: American Foreign Policy in the Cold War. ("The Free World Colossus") London: Macgibbon & Kee, 1971

De Yalta au Vietnam. ("The Free World Colossus") Paris: Union Générale d'Éditions, 1973-1974

Marx y la economía moderna: Cien años de la teoría económica marxista. ("Marx and Modern Economics") Barcelona: Editorial Laia, 1973

Gendai Keizaigaku to Marukusu. ("Marx and Modern Economics") Tokyo: Chikuma Shobo Ltd., 1974

Die Rockefellers: Eine amerikanische Dynastie. ("The Rockefellers") Berlin: Ullstein Verlag, 1976

Les Rockefeller: Une dynastie américaine. ("The Rockefellers") Paris: Éditions du Seuil, 1976

The Rockefellers: An American Dynasty. ("The Rockefellers") London: Jonathan Cape, 1976

Teikoku shugi to kakumei no jidai. ("Marx and Modern Economics") Tokyo: Tsuge Shobo, 1976

Rokp'ello ka. ("The Rockefellers") Korea: Samsung Publishing Ltd., 1977

Luokefeile wang chao. ("The Rockefellers") Shanghai, 1982

The Kennedys: An American Drama. London: Pan, 1984

The Kennedys: An American Drama. London: Secker & Warburg, 1984

Les Kennedy: une dynastie américaine. ("The Kennedys: An American Drama") Montréal: Éditions du Roseau, 1985

Les Kennedy: une dynastie américaine. ("The Kennedys: An American Drama") Paris: Éditions Payot, 1985

Los Kennedy: un drama americano. ("The Kennedys") Barcelona: Tusquets Editores, 1985

Los Rockefeller: una dinastía Americana. ("The Rockefellers") Barcelona: Tusquets Editores, 1987

The Fords: An American Epic. London: Collins Publishers, 1988

The Fords: An American Epic. ("The Fords") London: Futura Publications Ltd., 1988

Klan Kennedi: amerikanskaia drama. ("The Kennedys") Moscow: Progress Publishers, 1988

Fute zhuan: yi bu Meiguo ying xiong di shi shi. ("The Fords") People's Republic of China: Jilin, 1989

Klanen Kennedy: Ett amerikanskt drama. ("The Kennedys") Stockholm: Norstedts Förlag, 1989

Kenedi-ke no hitobito. ("The Kennedys,") Tokyo: Soshisha, 1990

Los Ford: una epopeya Americana. ("The Fords") Barcelona: Tusquets Editores, 1990

Fu te jia zu. ("The Fords") Beijing: Huaxia Press, 1991

Les Kennedy: une dynastie américaine. ("The Kennedys") Paris: Éditions Payot, 1992

Fordové: americký epos. (Czech edition of "The Fords,") Prague: J. Kanzelsberger, 1995

Meiguo kai mu: Fute shi shi. ("The Fords") Beijing: Hua xia chu ban she, 1999

Magazine/journal/scholarly articles by Horowitz (U.S. & foreign):

"Editorial," *Sunnyside Young Progressives Reporter,* 1951

"Economic Development and Democracy," *Journal of International Affairs,* 1962

"The Question About Meaning," *Root and Branch,* Winter 1962

"La Dolce Vita," *Root and Branch,* Winter 1962

"Correspondence: Reply to Mr. Kofsky," *Monthly Review,* December 1962

"The Roots of Alienation—A Critique of the Soviet Draft Program," *Root and Branch,* Spring 1963

"The Alliance for Progress," *Socialist Register,* Monthly Review Press, 1964

"Victims of Anomie," *The Nation*, June 15, 1964

"Pursuit of Victory," *Views*, Autumn 1964

"Review: The Technological Society," *Monthly Review*, June 1965

"Varför Fortsätter det Kalla Kriget?," *Tiden* [Sweden], December 1966

"Review: Monopoly Capital," *Monthly Review*, January 1967

"The Rise of [Conglomerate]Corporations," *New England Free Press* (1968; reprinted from *Ramparts*)

"Revisionist Tales of Negotiations With the Communists," *Ramparts*, June 29, 1968

"Big Brother as a Holding Company," (with David Kolodny), *Ramparts*, November 30, 1968

"Proving Poverty Pays," (with David Kolodny), *Ramparts*, December 14, 1968

"Foundations: Charity Begins at Home," *Ramparts*, April 1969

"Billion-Dollar Brains: How Wealth Puts Knowledge in Its Pocket," *Ramparts*, May 1969

"Behind the Sino/Soviet Dispute," *Ramparts*, June 1969

"Rocky Takes a Trip," *Ramparts*, August 1969

"Hand-Me-Down Marxism and the New Left," *Ramparts*, September 1969

"Sinews of Empire," *Ramparts*, October 1969

"Social Science or Ideology," *Berkeley Journal of Sociology*, 1970

"Sinews of Empire," New England Free Press, 1970 (reprinted from *Ramparts*)

"Bertrand Russell: The Final Passion," *Ramparts*, April 1970

"Social Science or Ideology?" *Social Policy*, September/October 1970

"Marxism and Its Place in Economic Science," *Berkeley Journal of Sociology*, 1971/1972

"Revolutionary Karma vs. Revolutionary Politics," *Ramparts*, March 1971

"Politics and Knowledge: an Unorthodox History of Modern China Studies," *Bulletin of Concerned Asian Scholars*, Summer-Fall 1971

"The Making of America's China Policy," *Ramparts*, October 1971

"The China Scholars and U.S. Intelligence," *Ramparts*, February 1972

"Asian Tragedy; Purge in China," *Ramparts*, March 1972

"The China Question and the American Left," *Ramparts*, July 1972

"Nixon's Vietnam Strategy," *Ramparts*, August 1972

"Cruel Reconciliation," *Ramparts*, November 1972

"U.S. Foreign Policy 1945–1970," *Encyclopedia Britannica*, 1972

"Historians and the Cold War: The Battle Over America's Image," *Ramparts*, August-September 1973

"Solzhenitsyn and the Radical Cause," *Ramparts*, June 1974

"Marx y la economía moderna," *Sistema* [Spain], July 1974

"Fascism and Other Nightmares," *Ramparts*, September 1974

"The Passion of the Jews," *Ramparts*, October 1974

"To Be Young, Rich and Unhappy in America," *Esquire*, February 1976

"A Radical's Disenchantment," *The Nation*, December 8, 1979

"Doing It: The Inside Story of the Rise and Fall of the Weather Underground" (with Peter Collier), *Rolling Stone*, September 30, 1982

"Whitewash," *California Magazine*, July 1983

"The First Hollywood President" (with Peter Collier), *California Magazine*, June 1984

"Why the Pain Hasn't Ended for Ethel's Family" (with Peter Collier), *Ladies' Home Journal*, September 1984

"Nicaragua: A Speech to My Former Comrades on the Left," *Commentary*, June 1986

"Another 'Low Dishonest Decade' on the Left," *Commentary*, January 1987

"Letters," *Commentary*, May 1987

"Letters," *Commentary*, July 1987

"Cristina" (with Peter Collier), *Good Housekeeping*, October 1987

"McCarthyism: The Last Refuge of the Left," *Commentary*, January 1988

"Letters," *Commentary*, April 1988

"Dartmouth Dignifies the Hate-Filled Angela Davis," *Human Events*, March 1989

"Panthers, Contras, and Other Wars: 'Destructive Generation': and Exchange," *The New Republic*, June 26, 1989

"Still Taking the Fifth," *Commentary*, July 1989

"Noam Chomsky's Paranoid Polemics Fuel Political Left," *Human Events*, July 1989

"Slouching Towards Berkeley: Socialism in One City" (with Peter Collier), *The Public Interest*, Winter 1989

"The Devastating Legacy of America's Liberal Left," *Human Events*, December 1989

"Making the Green One Red: Environmental Politics," *National Review*, March 19, 1990

"Environmentalists Are Simply Reds in Green Cloaks," *Utne Reader*, July-August 1990

"Responses," *Tikkun*, November-December 1990

"The Radical Paradigm and the New Racism," *First Things*, November 1990

"Socialism: Guilty as Charged," *Commentary*, December 1990

"Correspondence," *First Things*, February 1991

"Coalition Against the U.S.," *National Review*, February 25, 1991

"Review: Encyclopedia of the American Left," *First Things*, March 1991

"Conservative Questions," *National Review*, May 13, 1991

"Back to Our Roots," *National Review*, May 13, 1991

"The Politics of Public Television," *Commentary*, December 1991

"First Homo-Eroticism, Then Homo-Phobia, And Now... Homo-McCarthyism," *Heterodoxy*, April 1992

"Utopian Passions," *First Things*, April 1992

"Socialism by Any Other Name," *National Review*, April 13, 1992

"PC Riot," *Heterodoxy*, June 1992

"Anglophobia," *National Review*, July 20, 1992

"The Unforgiving," *Heterodoxy*, September 1992

"Shaping America's Values Debate," *Heritage Foundation Reports*, September 15, 1992

"Ms. America Goes to Battle," *National Review*, October 5, 1992

"Are We Conservatives? The Paradox of American Conservatism," *Heritage Foundation Reports*, December 15, 1992

"The Queer Fellows," *The American Spectator*, January 1993

"The Liberal Inheritance," *Heterodoxy*, January 1993

"Gays March on Pentagon," *Heterodoxy*, February 1993

"Black Murder, Inc.," *Heterodoxy*, March 1993

"Open Letter to John Dinges," *Comint*, Autumn 1993

"Tailhook Witch-Hunt," *Heterodoxy*, October 1993

"The Decline of Academic Discourse: The MLA Fiasco," *Heterodoxy*, January 1994

"The First Freedom Under the Gun," *The Defender*, March 1994

"Testimony of David Horowitz," *Comint*, Spring 1994

"Interview With Michael Moriarty," *The Defender*, July 1994

"Interview With Randall Kennedy," *The Defender*, July 1994

"Public Broadcasting: A Democratic Boondoggle," *Comint*, Fall 1994

"Interview With Marshall Whitman," *The Defender*, November 1994

"Panther Movie Glamorizes Violent Black Militants," *Human Events*, June 2, 1995

"The Race Card," *Heterodoxy*, October 1995

"Newton, Cleaver, Simpson," *The Weekly Standard*, October 16, 1995

"Hooked on Institutional Racism, " *Heterodoxy*, April 1996

"A Hero for Us All," *The Defender*, May/June 1996

"Clarence Page's Race Problem, And Mine, " *Heterodoxy*, May/June 1996

"Today's Culture Wars: A Message to Our Friends," *Center News*, Summer 1996

"Political Cross-Dresser," *Heterodoxy*, September 1996

"Queer Revolution," *The Material Queer: a LesBiGay Cultural Studies Reader*, Westview Press, 1996

"It's a War, Stupid!," *Heterodoxy*, November 1996

"Treason of the Heart, " *Heterodoxy*, January/February 1997

"Why I'm Not a Liberal," *Center News*, Spring 1997

"Scenes From the '60s: One Radical's Story," *American Enterprise*, May-June, 1997

"Many Thousands Gone, " *Heterodoxy*, June 1997

"The AIDS Epidemic Is Just Beginning," *Human Events*, June 27, 1997

"6-Martini Struggle," *Columbia Journalism Review*, July–August 1997

"Dealing With Those Who Wish You Were Dead," *The Jewish News of Northern California*, August 15, 1997

"Johnnie's Other O.J.," *Heterodoxy*, September 1997

"Up From Multiculturalism," *Heterodoxy*, January 1998

"Karl Marx at the *L.A. Times*," *Heterodoxy*, March 1998

"150 Years of Evil," *Heterodoxy*, April 1998

"The Clinton Scandal: A Feminist Titanic," *Center News*, Winter 1998

"An Intellectual *Omertà*: Marginalizing Conservative Ideas, " *Heterodoxy*, November 1998

"I, Rigoberta Menchú, Liar, " *Heterodoxy*, December 1998/January 1999

"Telling the Republican Story," *Rising Tide*, Spring 1999

"Correspondence," The American Prospect, May–June 1999

"The Last Survivor of Camelot," *Redbook*, October 1999

"What Would They Think of the '90s?," *American Enterprise*, November 1999

"Full-Contact Politics," *American Enterprise*, March 2000

"Hillary Rodham Clinton and The Third Way, " *American Enterprise*, July 2000

"The Bad Fight," *Heterodoxy*, November/December 2000

"A Controversial Newspaper Ad and Free Expression," *The Chronicle of Higher Education*, April 20, 2001

Newspaper articles by Horowitz (U.S. & foreign):

"Hiroshima—Shatterer of Worlds," *Oakland Tribune*, August 6, 1965

"Black Panther Position Paper," *Black Panther*, May 25, 1974

"Letters: 'First Frontier'," *The New York Times*, May 6, 1979

"'Journalism So Flawed'?" *The New York Times*, October 21, 1984

"Lefties for Reagan," *The Washington Post*, March 17, 1985

"We Aren't Marching Anymore," *San Francisco Chronicle*, May 19, 1985

"Saying Goodbye to the '60s," *Houston Chronicle*, May 19, 1985

"The Times, They Are A-Changin'," *The Seattle Times*, July 7, 1985

"Better Ron Than Red," *The Village Voice*, September 30, 1986

" 'Partial' Coverage of the Second-Thoughts Forum," *The Washington Post*, December 2, 1987

"'Destructive Generation'," *The New York Times*, May 28, 1989

"The Left Is Crying Wolf Over 'South Africa' Now," *Los Angeles Times*, November 19, 1990

"Peace Is Not the Real Agenda of the 'Anti-War' Movement," *The San Diego Union-Tribune*, March 3, 1991

"Public TV Must Let in the Voices of the World," *The New York Times*, August 23, 1991

"The Moyers Affair," *The New York Times*, August 23, 1991

"Does PBS Need Reforms, or New Subsidies?" *The San Diego Union-Tribune*, March 29, 1992

"Stop the Whining; This is War!," *Los Angeles Times*, August 26, 1992

"Stop the Whining, Democrats: This is War," *The Seattle Times*, August 27, 1992

"Stop the Democrat Whining—Politics is War," *Houston Chronicle*, August 27, 1992

"Stop the Whining—This is War," *Star Tribune*, August 30, 1992

"Democrats Dish Out Abuse But Whine About Taking It," *The Buffalo News*, September 6, 1992

"The Democrats Are a Legitimate Target," *The Philadelphia Inquirer*, September 8, 1992

"Cleverness, Cynicism and Character," *Los Angeles Times*, October 8, 1992

"Making Light of Murder," *The Washington Times*, October 19, 1992

"Thugs Or Heroes?" *The New York Times*, April 11, 1993

"Fine Print in the Line of March," *The Washington Times*, April 24, 1993

"Hollywood's 'Racism' Not So Black and White," *The San Francisco Examiner*, September 19, 1993

"'Balanced' Reporting," *The Washington Post*, May 24, 1994

"Perpetuating PBS With a Political Tilt," *The Washington Times*, June 14, 1994

"Are PBS and NPR Partisan to the DNC?," *Insight on the News*, July 18, 1994

"A '60s Revival We Don't Need: Black Panthers," *Los Angeles Times*, September 22, 1994

"Let the Panther Corpse Lie," *San Francisco Chronicle*, September 29, 1994

"Black Panthers: Don't Be Fooled," *The Columbian*, October 2, 1994

"Don't Be Fooled: Black Panthers Were Thugs," *Houston Chronicle*, October 3, 1994

"Vicious Criminals, Not Warm, Fuzzy Leftists," *San Jose Mercury News*, October 5, 1994

"When Strength in a Wife Isn't PC," *Los Angeles Times*, October 13, 1994

"Feminism Isn't Always 'Correct' Politics," *The Plain Dealer*, October 16, 1994

"Republican Landslide a Cultural Revolution," *Bridgeton Evening News*, December 28, 1994

"Republican Landslide a Cultural Revolution," *Millville News*, December 28, 1994

"Republican Landslide a Cultural Revolution," *Texas City Sun*, December 31, 1994

"Republican Landslide a Cultural Revolution," *The Daily Californian*, January 4, 1995

"Republican Landslide a Cultural Revolution," *Primos Sunday Times*, January 15, 1995

"Constitution Needs To Be Color-Blind, Not Color-Coded," *Big Rapids Pioneer*, February 7, 1995

"Constitution Needs To Be Color-Blind, Not Color-Coded," *Portsmouth Herald*, April 19, 1995

"Separating Panthers' Myth and Reality," *NY Daily News*, May 15, 1995

"Hollywood's Latest Outrage," *New York Post*, May 17, 1995

"Debunking Panther Myths," *The San Francisco Examiner*, June 4, 1995

"A Primer on Why We Lost Vietnam," *Los Angeles Times*, August 6, 1995

"Who Lost the War?," *San Jose Mercury News*, August 13, 1995

"Anti-War Left Cost U.S. a Win in Vietnam," *The Record*, August 16, 1995

"For Anti-War Movement; A Quick, Three-Step Primer on Why We Lost Vietnam," *The Record*, August 21, 1995

"Hanoi's McNamara," *New York Post*, August 21, 1995

"To Tell the Truth: 'Coming Out' an Act of Courage, Deserves Support," *The Arizona Republic*, October 11, 1995

"Identifying Black Racism: The Last Taboo," *Orange County Register*, December 10, 1995

"V is for Vacuous Censorship," *Los Angeles Times*, February 8, 1996

"Political Expediency, Not Violence, Behind V-Chip," *Houston Chronicle*, February 19, 1996

"V-Chip a Vote for Censorship," *The Seattle Times*, February 25, 1996

"Hollywood Isn't a Civil Rights Trophy," *Los Angeles Times*, March 24, 1996

"Socialism Never Dies," *The Weekly Standard*, April 1, 1996

"Brutality Charges Smear Police," *St. Louis Post-Dispatch*, April 30, 1996

"TV Control Is Met With Media Silence," *Los Angeles Times*, June 16, 1996

"What Happens to Free Speech If Feds Dictate Content for TV?," *The Sacramento Bee*, June 21, 1996

"President's Call for TV Content Control Met With Media Silence," *Bloomington Herald-Times*, June 21, 1996

"Denzel, Dennis and Shaq Belie the 'Color Bar'," *Los Angeles Times*, July 23, 1996

"What 'Color Bar'?" *Phoenix Gazette*, July 25, 1996

"Denzel, Dennis, Eddie and Shaq Belie a 'Color Bar'," *The Star Tribune*, July 26, 1996

"Denzel, Dennis, Shaq Belie the 'Color Bar'," *Tulsa World*, July 28, 1996

"Black Stars Hurdle 'Color Bar'," *The Denver Post*, July 28, 1996

"NBA Megabucks Add Up to End of the 'Color Bar'," *Houston Chronicle*, July 28, 1996

"Evidence Abounds That America's 'Color Bar' Is Finally Dead," *Milwaukee Journal Sentinel*, July 28, 1996

"Belying the 'Color Bar'," *The Tampa Tribune*, July 28, 1996

"When a White Kid Wants to 'Be Like Mike,'" The Sun, July 28, 1996

"Gang of Four Tackles TV and Constitution," *Los Angeles Times*, July 28, 1996

"Big Brother Goes Channel Surfing," *The Sacramento Bee*, August 4, 1996

"Clinton Proves GOP Right on Welfare," *San Francisco Chronicle*, August 9, 1996

"Suppose They Held a Convention and TV Never Came?" *The San Diego Union-Tribune*, August 18, 1996

"The Media's Arrogance in San Diego," *The Washington Times*, August 20, 1996

"'Non-Event'?," *The Winchester Star*, August 20, 1996

"A Test of Character for Bob Dole," *The Washington Times*, September 24, 1996

"Dole Can Win on the Coattails of CCRI," *Los Angeles Times*, September 27, 1996

"If You're Gay, Saying So Helps," *The Arizona Republic*, October 11, 1996

"Clinton is a Wolf in GOP Clothing," *Los Angeles Times*, October 17, 1996

"Fact Is, Clinton Already Proposing Medicare Cut," *Houston Chronicle*, October 24, 1996

"Dem Tactics Drive Republicans to Distraction," *The Arizona Republic*, November 3, 1996

"A Political Identity Crisis," *The Wall Street Journal*, November 22, 1996

"Left, Right Both Need to Face Realities If There Is to Be a Dialogue on Race," *The Buffalo News*, January 4, 1997

"Ability Is What Counts—On Any Playing Field," *San Francisco Chronicle*, February 28, 1997

"Black History Lesson," *San Francisco Chronicle*, February 28, 1997

"The Disaffection of Tammy Bruce," *Los Angeles Times*, March 11, 1997

"Hayden: A Revolutionary L.A. Can Skip," *Los Angeles Times*, March 11, 1997

"From Left to Right: A Political Switch," *Chicago Tribune*, April 9, 1997

"Jack Kemp's Strange Crusade to Bring Farrakhan into the Mainstream," Connecticut *Jewish Ledger*, April 11, 1997

"Liberating Oseola," *The Tampa Tribune*, April 13, 1997

"Liberals Should Rethink Race-Poverty Link," *Los Angeles Daily News*, April 18, 1997

"FDR Memorial Can't Change Sadness, Revulsion or History," *Los Angeles Daily News*, April 27, 1997

"Author Responds to Review," *The Press Democrat*, April 27, 1997

"Military Rape," *The San Diego Union-Tribune*, May 9, 1997

"A Dangerous Precedent at Aberdeen," *The San Diego Union-Tribune*, May 9, 1997

"Redistributing Wealth: Unfair and Useless," *Los Angeles Times*, May 27, 1997

"Forget 'Haves' and 'Have Nots'; What About 'Wills' and 'Will Nots'?" *Milwaukee Journal Sentinel*, June 1, 1997

"Lessons From a 'Radical Son'," *The San Diego Union-Tribune*, July 6, 1997

"Defining Race Adds to Racial Divisions," *The San Diego Union-Tribune*, August 3, 1997

"Bilingual Programs No Aid to Students," *Lebanon Daily News*, August 22, 1997

"Latinos Suffer From Bilingual System," *Primos Sunday Times*, August 24, 1997

"An Academic Lynching," *Austin American-Statesman*, September 26, 1997

"Latinos Must Be Set Free," *Pasadena Star-News*, October 22, 1997

"GOP Through the Looking Glass," *Los Angeles Daily News*, November 2, 1997

"Liberals Want a Racial Monologue," *Los Angeles Times*, December 18, 1997

"The Conversation: Liberals Want a Racial Monologue," *The Plain Dealer*, December 26, 1997

"All the President's Women," *Los Angeles Daily News*, January 25, 1998

"Why Read Marx?; Marx Reconsidered: A Symposium," *Los Angeles Times*, February 8, 1998

"Confessions of a Right-Wing Conspirator," *Los Angeles Times*, February 24, 1998

"Confessions of a Right-Wing Conspirator," *The Cincinnati Enquirer*, March 2, 1998

"Right-Wing Conspirator 'Fesses Up," *The Denver Post*, March 11, 1998

"Eldridge Cleaver's Last Gift: The Truth," *Los Angeles Times*, May 3, 1998

"From Black Panther to Republican," *The Cincinnati Enquirer*, May 7, 1998

"Cleaver's Radical Turnaround Took Courage," *The Detroit News*, May 7, 1998

"Give Radicals Some Respect for Honesty," *Milwaukee Journal Sentinel*, May 10, 1998

"Racial Face-Off," *Saint Paul Pioneer Press*, December 29, 1998

"Betty Friedan," *Ottawa Citizen*, April 11, 1999

"Mercy for a Terrorist?," *The Hamilton Spectator*, August 6, 1999

"Gore Declares Himself the Candidate of the Average-Sized Voter," *The Salt Lake Tribune*, November 17, 1999

"Using Labels as a Weapon," *The Washington Times*, November 22, 1999

"Even Standing Alone, the United States Can Still Be Right," *Los Angeles Times*, November 26, 1999

"V-Day," *The Washington Times*, February 9, 2001

"Racial McCarthyism," *The Wall Street Journal*, March 20, 2001

"Racial McCarthyism Jamming Dialogues on College Campuses," *The Arizona Republic*, March 22, 2001

"Provocative Message Fuels Conflict," *Chicago Tribune*, March 25, 2001

"The David Horowitz Controversy," *The Daily Tar Heel*, April 2, 2001

"David Horowitz: Reflections of a Campus Provocateur," *Yale Daily News*, April 2, 2001

"Horowitz Responds to Princetonian's 'Abuse'," *The Daily Princetonian*, April 9, 2001

"Ten Reasons Why Reparations For Slavery Is a Bad Idea—And Racist Too," *The Stanford Daily*, May 2, 2001

"UW Reply to Ad Is Nonsense," *The Capital Times*, May 16, 2001

"Slavery Reparations, College Papers, and Free Speech," *Columbia Daily Spectator*, June 6, 2001

"Open Letter to Future Anti-War Activists," *Rocky Mountain Collegian*, September 27, 2001

"Protesters Should Think Twice," *Columbia Daily Spectator*, September 27, 2001

"Students, Rethink How You Protest," *Los Angeles Times*, September 28, 2001

"Speaker Offers to Debate Advertisement Protesters," *The Chronicle* [Duke University], December 10, 2001

"David Horowitz: No," *Wisconsin State Journal*, December 16, 2001

"New Policy Hides Public School Failure," *Daily Bruin* [UCLA], January 7, 2002

"Coverage of Rally Shows Leftist Fear," *Daily Bruin* [UCLA], January 17, 2002

"Five Reasons Reparations Are Morally Wrong," Knight-Ridder [McClatchy] Tribune News Service, April 22, 2002

"Five Reasons Reparations Are Morally Wrong," *The Providence Journal*, April 23, 2002

"Views on the Middle East; Mideast Struggle Was Never About Land," *San Francisco Chronicle*, April 26, 2002

"The Washington Blame Game; Why Bush Is Innocent and the Democrats Are Guilty," *The Washington Times*, May 20, 2002

Pamphlets by Horowitz (and co-authors):

"The Universities and the Ruling Class: How Wealth Puts Knowledge in Its Pocket," Bay Area Radical Education Project, 1969

"Horowitz: A Reply to Slander," self-published, 1973

"My Vietnam Lessons," Accuracy in Media, 1985

"The 'Peace' Movement, Second Thoughts Project," 1991

"The Feminist Assault on the Military," Center for the Study of Popular Culture, 1992

"Queer Revolution: The Last Stage Of Radicalism," Center for the Study of Popular Culture, 1992

"Liberal Racism: The College Student's Common-Sense Guide to Radical Ideology and How to Fight It," Center for the Study of Popular Culture, 1994

"It's a War, Stupid!," Center for the Study of Popular Culture, 1996

"Why I'm Not a Liberal," Center for the Study of Popular Culture, 1997

"Marx's Manifesto: 150 Years of Evil," Center for the Study of Popular Culture, 1998

"The Art of Political War: How Republicans Can Fight to Win," Committee for a Non-Left Majority, 1999

"Who's Responsible for America's Security Crisis?," Center for the Study of Popular Culture, 1999

"The Death of the Civil Rights Movement," Center for the Study of Popular Culture, 2000

"Hillary Clinton And The Racial Left," Center for the Study of Popular Culture, 2000

"The War Room: A Pocket Guide to Victory," PoliticalWar.com 2000

"The Ayatollah of Anti-American Hate," Center for the Study of Popular Culture, 2001

"How to Beat the Democrats: A Primer for Republicans," PoliticalWar.com, 2001

"Noam Chomsky's *Jihad* Against America," Center for the Study of Popular Culture, 2001

"Progressive Crime Wave," Center for the Study of Popular Culture, 2001

"Think Twice … Before You Bring the War Home," Center for the Study of Popular Culture, 2001

"How the Left Undermined America's Security," Center for the Study of Popular Culture, 2002

"Know Your Enemy: America's War Against Radical Islam At Home And Abroad," Center for the Study of Popular Culture, 2002

"Political Bias in America's Universities," Center for the Study of Popular Culture, 2002

"Reparations and Racial Double Standards," Center for the Study of Popular Culture, 2002

"Immigration and National Security Post 9/11," David Horowitz Freedom Center, 2002

"Why Israel Is the Victim In the Middle East," Center for the Study of Popular Culture, 2002

"You Can't Get a Good Education ... If They're Only Telling You Half the Story," Center for the Study of Popular Culture, 2002

"The Hate-America Left," Center for the Study of Popular Culture, 2002

"Who Is the Peace Movement?" (with John Perazzo), Center for the Study of Popular Culture, 2003

"The Battle for Academic Freedom," Center for the Study of Popular Culture, 2003

"Campus Blacklist," Center for the Study of Popular Culture, 2003

"Indoctrination or Education," Center for the Study of Popular Culture, 2004

"Campus Support for Terrorism," Center for the Study of Popular Culture, 2004

"The Shadow Party" (with Richard Poe), Center for the Study of Popular Culture, 2004

"Why We Are in Iraq," Center for the Study of Popular Culture, 2005

"Know Your Enemy: America's War Against Radical Islam at Home and Abroad," Center for the Study of Popular Culture, 2005

"The Campaign for Academic Freedom," Center for the Study of Popular Culture, 2005

"Academic Freedom Hearings in Pennsylvania," David Horowitz Freedom Center, 2006

"Pennsylvania's Academic Freedom Reforms," David Horowitz Freedom Center, 2006

"Political Assault on America's Universities," David Horowitz Freedom Center, 2006

"The Islamic *Mein Kampf*," David Horowitz Freedom Center, 2007

"The Muslim Student Association and the Jihad Network," David Horowitz Freedom Center, 2008

"Why Israel Is the Victim and Why There Is No Peace In the Middle East" (with Steven Plaut), David Horowitz Freedom Center, 2009

"Barack Obama's Rules for Revolution: The Alinsky Model," David Horowitz Freedom Center, 2009

"Breaking the System: Obama's Strategy for Change" (with Liz Blaine), David Horowitz Freedom Center, 2010

"Obama and the War Against the Jews" (with Jacob Laksin), David Horowitz Freedom Center, 2010

"The Art of Political War for Tea Parties," David Horowitz Freedom Center, 2010

"Obama's Professor and America's Cultural Crisis," David Horowitz Freedom Center, 2010

"Obama and Islam" (with Robert Spencer), David Horowitz Freedom Center, 2010

"Campaign Against Israel Apartheid Week," David Horowitz Freedom Center, 2011

"Islamophobia (with Robert Spencer), David Horowitz Freedom Center, 2011

"From Shadow Party to Shadow Government" (with John Perazzo), David Horowitz Freedom Center, 2011

"Occupy Wall Street: The Communist Movement Reborn" (with John Perazzo), David Horowitz Freedom Center, 2012

"Government Versus the People" (with John Perazzo), David Horowitz Freedom Center, 2012

"Black Skin Privilege" (with John Perazzo), David Horowitz Freedom Center, 2013

"Obama and Islam—Updated and Revised" (with Robert Spencer), David Horowitz Freedom Center, 2013

"Why Israel Is the Victim," David Horowitz Freedom Center, 2013

"How Obama Betrayed America and No One Is Holding Him Accountable," David Horowitz Freedom Center, 2013

"Fight Fire With Fire," David Horowitz Freedom Center, 2013

"The Blood on Obama's Hands," David Horowitz Freedom Center, 2014

Online writings by Horowitz (current to October 2017):

"Mouth Control, Not More Gun Control, Is What We Need," www.frontpagemag.com, October 10, 2017

"The Left in the University," www.frontpagemag.com, September 29, 2017

"Stop the Blacklist," www.frontpagemag.com, September 6, 2017

"The Racist Attacks on America and Trump," www.frontpagemag.com, August 25, 2017

"Steve Bannon Leaves the White House," www.frontpagemag. com, August 21, 2017

"The Real Race War," www.frontpagemag.com, August 16, 2017

"Why Do Republicans Want to Kill Horses?," www.frontpagemag.com, August 4, 2017

"The Root Cause of the Disasters in the Middle East," www.frontpagemag.com, July 31, 2017

"Why the Jews Are Losing the War on College Campuses," www.frontpagemag.com, June 29, 2017

"Have You No Shame?," www.frontpagemag.com, June 20, 2017

"Reclaiming Our Schools: A Code of Ethics for K-12 Educators," www. frontpagemag.com, June 15, 2017

"The Democrats' Second Secession & America's New Civil War," www.frontpagemag.com, May 26, 2017

"I Wrote a Best-Seller on Donald Trump, and also on Democrats as a 'Party of Hate'... So Now the Left Is Coming After Me," www.front-pagemag.com, May 2, 2017

"My Free Speech at Berkeley, Not," www.frontpagemag.com, April 12, 2017

"Berkeley Hates Free Speech," www.frontpagemag.com, April 11, 2017

"A Game Changer For Syria—But Also For Trump," www.frontpagemag. com, April 10, 2017

"Prosecute the Sanctuary Secessionists," www.frontpagemag.com, March 18, 2017

"The War Against Trump," www.frontpagemag.com, March 8, 2017

"The Right Throws Milo to the Wolves," www.frontpagemag. com, February 21, 2017

"Stephen Miller: A Second-Thoughts Warrior," www.frontpagemag.com, February 8, 2017

"The Progressive Movement," FrontPageMag.com, January 20, 2017

"Trump's Message: Go on the Attack and Stay on It," www.front-pagemag.com, January 19, 2017

"The Inauguration War," www.frontpagemag.com, January 13, 2017

"David Horowitz Attacked During Senatorial Witch-Hunt of Jeff Sessions," www.frontpagemag.com, January 10, 2017

"Man of the Year: Chief Trump Strategist Stephen K. Bannon," www.frontpagemag.com, December 30, 2016

"Identity Politics Are Anti-American," www.frontpagemag.com, December 16, 2016

"Steve Bannon, Civil Rights Hero," www.frontpagemag.com, November 18, 2016

"Anti-Bannon Hysteria More Evidence the Left Has Lost Touch With American People," www.frontpagemag.com, November 14, 2016

"Is the University of Chicago a Safe Space?," www.frontpagemag. com, October 26, 2016

"Anatomy of a Lynching," www.frontpagemag.com, October 24, 2016

"A Champion for the Cause," www.frontpagemag.com, September 7, 2016

"Donald Trump's Lincoln-esque Moment," www.frontpagemag. com, August 19, 2016

"The Nature of the War Against Us," www.frontpagemag.com, August 12, 2016

"Why Trump Will Win in November," www.frontpagemag.com, July7, 2016

"The Most Frightening Political Fix," www.frontpagemag.com, July5, 2016

"Hamas on Campus," www.frontpagemag.com, July 2, 2016

"David Horowitz on 'Progressive Racism'," www.frontpagemag. com, June 24, 2016

"How the Democrats Are Disarming Us," www.frontpagemag. com, June 20, 2016

"The 'Never-Trump' Murder-Suicide Pact," www.frontpagemag. com, June 17, 2016

"Obama's Question: What's in a Name," www.frontpagemag.com, June 15, 2016

"Trump's Speech: A Game Changer," www.frontpagemag.com, June 14, 2016

"The Never-Trump Diehards," www.frontpagemag.com, June 2, 2016

"Horowitz Unplugged," www.frontpagemag.com, June 1, 2016

"Kristol's Betrayal Gets Serious," www.frontpagemag.com, May 30, 2016

"The Biggest Racial Lie," www.frontpagemag.com, May 26, 2016

"Renegade Jew Backlash," www.frontpagemag.com, May 19, 2016

"The Faith of Christopher," www.frontpagemag.com, May 18, 2016

"Bill Kristol: Republican Spoiler, Renegade Jew," www.frontpagemag. com, May 16, 2016

"Trump Derangement Syndrome," www.frontpagemag.com, May 12, 2016

"The 'Never-Trump' Pouters," www.frontpagemag.com, May 9, 2016

"David Horowitz Statement on San Diego State University Protests," www.frontpagemag.com, May 6, 2016

"The Biggest Election Deception," www.frontpagemag.com, April 29, 2016

"A Quick Reaction to Trump's Speech," www.frontpagemag.com, April 28, 2016

"Anti-White Racism," FrontPageMag.com, April 27, 2016

"Reflections on the Eve of Another Republican Primary," www.frontpagemag.com, April 25, 2016

"Reply to Slander," www.frontpagemag.com, April 20, 2016

"My Friend Eddie," www.frontpagemag.com, April 14, 2016

"Guilty Until Proven Innocent," www.frontpagemag.com, March 28, 2016

"How Not to Fight Our Enemies," www.frontpagemag.com, March 13, 2016

"Gang Rape," www.frontpagemag.com, March 4, 2016

"Election Fog," www.frontpagemag.com, February 15, 2016

"Treasons of the Democrats," www.frontpagemag.com, January 8, 2016

"Donald Trump and the American Future," www.frontpagemag. com, December 22, 2015

"Who's the Crazy One?," www.frontpagemag.com, December 10, 2015

"The President and Liberals Have a Lot to Answer For," www.frontpagemag.com, December 4, 2015

"Freedom Center Pressures Universities On Support for Pro-Terror Groups," www.frontpagemag.com, December 2, 2015

"The Terrorist Propaganda Campaign on Boston Campuses," www.frontpagemag.com, November 25, 2015

"An American Fascism," www.frontpagemag.com, November 12, 2015

"Culture Wars: Volume V of the Black Book of the American Left," www.frontpagemag.com, November 11, 2015

"When Students Cheer *Jihad*," www.frontpagemag.com, November 10, 2015

"A Time To Confront Our Enemies at Home," www.frontpagemag.com, July 20, 2015

"A Romance of Age," www.frontpagemag.com, June 15, 2015

"Jeb Bush Is Right About Iraq," www.frontpagemag.com, May 12, 2015

"Islamophobia: Thought Crime of the Totalitarian Future," www.frontpagemag.com, May 8, 2015

"A Malignant Cause," www.frontpagemag.com, May 1, 2015

"The Pro-Terrorist Front Groups On American Campuses," www.frontpagemag.com, April 29, 2015

"Islamo-Fascism and the War Against the Jews: Volume IV of the Black Book of the American Left," www.frontpagemag.com, April 24, 2015

"Islamic Jihad Comes to Campus," www.frontpagemag.com, April 17, 2015

"Muslim and Jewish Book-Burners," www.frontpagemag.com, April 4, 2015

"Reasons for Targeting Students for Justice in Palestine," www.frontpagemag.com, April 2, 2015

"SJP and the Anti-SJP Posters," www.frontpagemag.com, February 24, 2015

"Liar-in-Chief," www.frontpagemag.com, January 21, 2015

"Bush Was 100 Percent Right After 9/11," www.frontpagemag. com, January 9, 2015

"The Left's War Against Justice and Peace," www.frontpagemag. com, December 10, 2014

"How Many Lies Have Democrats Told to Sabotage the War on Terror?," www.frontpagemag.com, November 24, 2014

"The Great Betrayal: Vol. III of *The Black Book of the American Left*," www.frontpagemag.com, November 14, 2014

"The Democrats' Great Betrayal," www.frontpagemag.com, November 11, 2014

"The Election Was Fun But Don't Get Too Happy," www.frontpagemag. com, November 5, 2014

"Salon.com's Infantile Leftism," www.frontpagemag.com, November 3, 2014

"Why Are the Senate Races Close?," www.frontpagemag.com, October 31, 2014

"Democrats Join the Ferguson Lynch Mob Right As the Case Against Officer Wilson Collapses," www.frontpagemag.com, October 27, 2014

"The Blood on Obama's Hands," www.frontpagemag.com, October 21, 2014

"Thank You, ISIS," www.frontpagemag.com, October 10, 2014

"Hold Obama and the Democrats Accountable for the Terrorist Threat," www.frontpagemag.com, October 7, 2014

"Why Nice Guys Finish Last in Politics," www.frontpagemag. com, September 17, 2014

"The GOP's Missing Electoral Link," www.frontpagemag.com, September 15, 2014

"A Pound of White Flesh," www.frontpagemag.com, August 21, 2014

"The Hell That Is the Obama White House," www.frontpagemag. com, August 19, 2014

"Obama's Treachery and Republican Silence," www.frontpagemag.com, August 9, 2014

"Who Are Our Adversaries?," www.frontpagemag.com, April 29, 2014

"Glen Beck: America's Defender," www.frontpagemag.com, March 31, 2014

"War & Peace in the Age of Obama," www.frontpagemag.com, March 28, 2014

"Why Doesn't Obama Get to the Bottom of the IRS Scandal?," www.frontpagemag.com, March 6, 2014

"Atrocity," www.frontpagemag.com, January 31, 2014

"Latter-Day Marxist," www.frontpagemag.com, December 10, 2013

"Abetting the Holocaust: Arthur Hays Sulzberger and *The New York Times*," www.frontpagemag.com, December 9, 2013

"Nelson Mandela 1918-2013," www.frontpagemag.com, December 6, 2013

"Books About Rebel Lives," www.frontpagemag.com, December 2, 2013

"Uniting the Right," www.frontpagemag.com, November 5, 2013

"The Road to Nowhere," www.frontpagemag.com, October 12, 2013

"The Threat We Face," www.frontpagemag.com, October 10, 2013

"Another Personal Attack Inspired by West," www.frontpagemag.com, September 28, 2013

"Diana West Invents a New Conspiracy," www.frontpagemag. com, September 9, 2013

"Fight Fire With Fire," www.frontpagemag.com, September 2, 2013

"Our Controversy With Diana West," www.frontpagemag.com, August 8, 2013

"Our Articles on Trayvon Martin," www.frontpagemag.com, July 9, 2013

"Is the Zimmerman Case Really Open and Shut?," www.frontpagemag. com, July 5, 2013

"How Obama Betrayed America," www.frontpagemag.com, May 8, 2013

"My Thoughts on Boston," www.frontpagemag.com, April 19, 2013

"The Daily Beast's Disgraceful Interview With Bill Ayers," www.frontpagemag.com, April 4, 2013

"Thoughts on Learning That the Killer Kathy Boudin Is a Professor at Columbia," www.frontpagemag.com, April 3, 2013

"Why We Were In Iraq," www.frontpagemag.com, March 21, 2013

"Why Israel Is the Victim," www.frontpagemag.com, February 12, 2013

"Defending Our Country," www.frontpagemag.com, February 11, 2013

"Reading Horowitz," www.frontpagemag.com, February 4, 2013

"The Feminist Assault on the Military," www.frontpagemag.com, January 28, 2013

"It's the Message and, Yes, the Messengers — NOT the Voters," www.frontpagemag.com, January 21, 2013

"Neo-Communism Out of the Closet," www.frontpagemag.com, January 17, 2013

"Democrats Vote the Mentally Disabled," www.frontpagemag. com, November 23, 2012

"Oliver Stone's Unbelievable Crap," www.frontpagemag.com, October 31, 2012

"The Left After Communism," www.frontpagemag.com, October 15, 2012

"Obama Still Wants to Fundamentally Transform America," www.frontpagemag.com, October 2, 2012

"David Horowitz Discusses Persecution of Anti-Islam Filmmaker With Fox News' Megyn Kelly," www.frontpagemag.com, September 21, 2012

"Reflections of a Diaspora Jew on Zionism, America and the Fate of the Jews," www.frontpagemag.com, September 7, 2012

"Frontpage's New Blog," www.frontpagemag.com, August 28, 2012

"Palestinians: A Disgrace to the Human Race," www.frontpagemag.com, August 26, 2012

"Ryan's the One," www.frontpagemag.com, August 14, 2012

"An Olympic Heroine," www.frontpagemag.com, August 8, 2012

"The Root Cause of the Problem in the Middle East," www.frontpagemag.com, August 1, 2012

"Carl Bernstein's Communist Problem & Mine," www.frontpagemag.com, July 31, 2012

"Why Do Democrats Play Footsie With Islamic Nazis Like Farrakhan and the Muslim Brotherhood?," www.frontpagemag. com, July 26, 2012

"Alex Cockburn: A Bitter Life," www.frontpagemag.com, July 23, 2012

"Hillary's Muslim Adviser," www.frontpagemag.com, July 18, 2012

"Worse than Carter: Obama Nurtures Islamo-Nazis," www.frontpagemag.com, July 16, 2012

"Hiroshima and Detroit: The Damage Democrats Do to the Poor Lasts Longer Than a Nuclear Bomb," www.frontpagemag.com, July 9, 2012

"Politics—Liberal Logic 101," www.frontpagemag.com, July 5, 2012

"Supreme Decision: The Best Possible Result for 2012," www.frontpagemag.com, June 29, 2012

"Obama — A Bigger Liar Than Clinton. Much Bigger.," www.frontpagemag.com, June 21, 2012

"The Moral Sickness of the Palestinians and Their Supporters," www.frontpagemag.com, June 11, 2012

"Hitler Finds Out That Scott Walker Won the Wisconsin Recall Election," www.frontpagemag.com, June 7, 2012

"The Face of Islam: Kuffars Beware!," www.frontpagemag.com, May 21, 2012

"The Coming Muslim Reich," www.frontpagemag.com, May 14, 2012

"Who I Am," www.frontpagemag.com, May 9, 2012

"Another Leftist Failure to Either Respect or Understand Its Opponents: *Tablet* Magazine's Caricature of Yours Truly," www.frontpagemag.com, May 2, 2012

"The Barbarism That Is Muslim Egypt," www.frontpagemag.com, April 26, 2012

"Coalition of Leftist Groups to Disrupt 'Islamic Apartheid Conference'," www.frontpagemag.com, April 20, 2012

"Voices of Islam," www.frontpagemag.com, April 16, 2012

"Thank You 'Liberals' for All You've Done to Protect Us From Terrorists Like This One," www.frontpagemag.com, April 7, 2012

"African-American Lynch Mob," www.frontpagemag.com, March 25, 2012

"A Fistful of Truth If You Can Handle It," www.frontpagemag. com, March 23, 2012

"The Transcript of Horowitz's Speech at UNC," www.frontpagemag.com, March 23, 2012

"Jewish Students Who Stand With Israel's Enemies and Call Them 'Brothers'," www.frontpagemag.com, March 19, 2012

"How We Should Talk When We Talk About Islamists," www.frontpagemag.com, March 12, 2012

"Obama's Position on Israel," www.frontpagemag.com, March 6, 2012

"I Was Born in Kenya," www.frontpagemag.com, March 5, 2012

"The Day I Stopped Loving Steve Nash and the Suns," www.frontpagemag.com, February 24, 2012

"Communism Reborn," www.frontpagemag.com, January 30, 2012

"Dissent From the Majority: Obama's Tax Proposal a Good Idea," www.frontpagemag.com, January 26, 2012

"*The NYT* Shilling Again for Leftwing Murderers," www.frontpagemag. com, January 13, 2012

"My Friend Christopher," www.frontpagemag.com, December 16, 2011

"An Invented People Despite Some Doubters," www.frontpagemag.com, December 12, 2011

"Gingrich Gets It Right," www.frontpagemag.com, December 10, 2011

"Don't Pepper-spray Them: Expel Them," www.frontpagemag. com, November 23, 2011

"Jew-haters of Occupy Wall Street," www.frontpagemag.com, October 17, 2011

"The Destroyers," www.frontpagemag.com, October 15, 2011

"In Case You Didn't Think It Could Happen Here," www.frontpagemag.com, October 10, 2011

"Hatred Is Their Identity," www.frontpagemag.com, October 8, 2011

"Think Progress Witch-hunt," www.frontpagemag.com, August 26, 2011

"'Count Me a Jew'," www.frontpagemag.com, August 22, 2011

"The Consequences of Islamic Imperialism in Scandinavia," www.frontpagemag.com, July 27, 2011

"The Character Assassination of Robert Spencer," www.frontpagemag.com, July 25, 2011

"Why the UN Is the Problem and the US Should Leave It," www.frontpagemag.com, July 18, 2011

"Surveys Show Palestinians Far Worse than the Inhabitants of Nazi Germany," www.frontpagemag.com, July 15, 2011

"Obama Doctrine: Don't Imprison Suspects," www.frontpagemag.com, July 12, 2011

"Liberals (so-called) Are Racists, and Conservatives (who are not) Should Be Saying So," www.frontpagemag.com, July 6, 2011

"Demonic—Coulter's Valentine to the Left," www.frontpagemag.com, July 1, 2011

"The Totalitarians Within," www.frontpagemag.com, May 31, 2011

"Santa Barbara Update," www.frontpagemag.com, May 28, 2011

"Andrew Sullivan's Misguided Defense of the Regrettable Mr. Kushner," www.frontpagemag.com, May 7, 2011

"Bin Laden Is History. The Jihad Is Not.," www.frontpagemag. com, May 2, 2011

"How Not to Defend Yourself as a Jew at Yale," www.frontpagemag.com, April 29, 2011

"Muslim Liars: How the Muslim Students Association Deceives the Naive," www.frontpagemag.com, April 27, 2011

"Hillel's Coalition With the Enemies of Israel Becomes Increasingly Unseemly," www.frontpagemag.com, March 31, 2011

"The Vice Chancellor and the University of Michigan Dearborn Campus and the Arab Press Respond to the Wall of Lies Ad," www.frontpagemag.com, March 28, 2011

"Ominous Signals on Libya: A Response to Andrew Sullivan," www.frontpagemag.com, March 26, 2011

"Opposing the Palestinian War Against the Jews," www.frontpagemag.com, March 25, 2011

"Suicidal Jews and the Anti-Semites They Ignore (and Sometimes Embrace)," www.frontpagemag.com, March 24, 2011

"Why I Am Not a Neo-Conservative," www.frontpagemag.com, March 23, 2011

"Killing the Messenger: The Left Strikes Back," www.frontpagemag.com, March 13, 2011

"It's Time for the Jews to Stand Up for Themselves," www.frontpagemag.com, March 11, 2011

"A Misguided Petition Campaign to Ban the Muslim Students Association," www.frontpagemag.com, March 2, 2011

"Rhetoric vs. Reality," www.frontpagemag.com, February 17, 2011

"The Muslim Brotherhood and the Fellow-Traveling Left at *Slate*," www.frontpagemag.com, February 14, 2011

"The Muslim Brotherhood Inside the Conservative Movement," www.frontpagemag.com, February 13, 2011

"Glenn Beck and the Muslim Brotherhood," www.frontpagemag. com, February 2, 2011

"The American Left and the Crisis in Egypt," www.frontpagemag.com, January 31, 2011

"My Daughter Sarah and the Lack of Civil Dialogue in Our Culture," www.frontpagemag.com, January 14, 2011

"The Purging of Marty Peretz," www.frontpagemag.com, December 29, 2010

"A Historic Election, an Early Thanksgiving," www.frontpagemag.com, November 3, 2010

"The Politics of Public Television," www.frontpagemag.com, October 28, 2010

"Schrecker and Me at Brandeis," www.frontpagemag.com, October 25, 2010

"Something We Did," www.frontpagemag.com, October 4, 2010

"How the Left Undermined America's Security Before 9/11," www.frontpagemag.com, September 10, 2010

"Glen Beck's Rally," www.frontpagemag.com, August 31, 2010

"Adopt a Dissenting Book," www.frontpagemag.com, August 13, 2010

"Whitewashing Alinsky," www.frontpagemag.com, August 12, 2010

"The Two Christophers," www.frontpagemag.com, July 6, 2010

"What Makes Intelligent People Like Andrew Sullivan So Stupid? Gaza Again.," www.frontpagemag.com, June 2, 2010

"The War Against the Jews at UC San Diego," www.frontpagemag.com, May 28, 2010

"Obama's Professor and America's Cultural Crisis," www.frontpagemag. com, May 24, 2010

"Shall Not Perish," www.frontpagemag.com, May 17, 2010

The Greek Crisis and the Reactionary Left," www.frontpagemag. com, May 10, 2010

"Obama-style Socialism," www.frontpagemag.com, May 3, 2010

"A Disgraceful Evening at Cooper Union," www.frontpagemag. com, April 20, 2010

"Obamacare Bill: A Declaration of War," www.frontpagemag.com, March 22, 2010

"Keeping an Eye on the Domestic Threat," www.frontpagemag. com, March 16, 2010

"Oliver Stone and the Left Cannot See a Cup Half Full," www.front-pagemag.com, March 11, 2010

"Progressives and Conservatives," www.frontpagemag.com, March 5, 2010

"How Bad Is the Indoctrination in Our Colleges?," www.frontpagemag. com, March 2, 2010

"A Soundbite (on Howard Zinn) Heard 'Round the World," www.front-pagemag.com, February 12, 2010

"The Closing of the Liberal Mind," www.frontpagemag.com, February 11, 2010

"Spitting on Howard Zinn's Grave," www.frontpagemag.com, January 30, 2010

"St. Louis U's Inverted Values," www.frontpagemag.com, January 29, 2010

"Obama's Destructive Course," www.frontpagemag.com, January 28, 2010

"The Anti-Semitic Jihad on Campus: My Night at USC," www.front-pagemag.com, January 15, 2010

"Censorship and Libel at USC," www.frontpagemag.com, January 14, 2010

"Who Will Be Responsible for the American Dead?" www.frontpagemag. com, December 30, 2009

"What My Daughter Taught Me About Compassion," www.front-pagemag.com, December 29, 2009

"A Cracking of the Heart," www.frontpagemag.com, December 10, 2009

"Idiot Watch: Al Gore the Poet," www.frontpagemag.com, December 8, 2009

"Idiot Watch," www.frontpagemag.com, December 7, 2009

"The Art of Political War for Tea Parties," www.frontpagemag. com, December 1, 2009

"The Traitor Class," www.frontpagemag.com, November 26, 2009

"Barack Obama's Rules for Revolution: The Alinsky Model," www.front-pagemag.com, November 25, 2009

"The Worst Decision by a US President in History," www.frontpagemag.com, November 13, 2009

"Liberal Idiocy on Fort Hood," www.frontpagemag.com, November 11, 2009

"*The Nation* Magazine Pays Tribute to a Despot," www.frontpagemag.com, November 10, 2009

"Our Brain-Dead Country," www.frontpagemag.com, November 9, 2009

"A Candidate of the Left," www.frontpagemag.com, November 4, 2009

"The Totalitarians Among Us," www.frontpagemag.com, November 2, 2009

"The Hate Campaign at Temple," www.frontpagemag.com, October 19, 2009

"David Frum Careens Off the Deep End," www.frontpagemag. com, October 19, 2009

"Jihad at Temple," www.frontpagemag.com, October 16, 2009

"Marc Lamont Hill's Overrated Black People List: Michael Eric Dyson," www.frontpagemag.com, October 12, 2009

"Stop the Campus War Against Israel and the Jews," www.frontpagemag.com, October 9, 2009

"David Frum's Got It Wrong Again," www.frontpagemag.com, October 6, 2009

"The Worse the Better," www.frontpagemag.com, October 3, 2009

"Serious Fascist in America," www.frontpagemag.com, October 1, 2009

"Where Are the Body Bags," www.frontpagemag.com, October 1, 2009

"Creators Versus Destroyers," www.frontpagemag.com, September 29, 2009

"Whose Conspiracy," www.frontpagemag.com, September 28, 2009

"Fox's Affirmative Action Baby Whines," www.frontpagemag. com, September 27, 2009

"David Horowitz Challenges David Frum for Attack on Glenn Beck," www.frontpagemag.com, September 15, 2009

"The Manchurian Candidate," www.frontpagemag.com, September 11, 2009

"The ACLU and the Unholy Alliance," www.frontpagemag.com, September 9, 2009

"How to Defeat the Left," www.frontpagemag.com, September 4, 2009

"Defending Indoctrination," www.frontpagemag.com, June 12, 2009

"*Plus ça change,*" www.frontpagemag.com, June 9, 2009

"An American Leader Stands Up for His Country," www.frontpagemag. com, June 5, 2009

"Campus Leftist Don't Believe in Free Speech," www.frontpagemag.com, April 23, 2009

"Indoctrination U Revisited," www.frontpagemag.com, April 10, 2009

"Obama Derangement Syndrome," www.frontpagemag.com March 30, 2009

"Dialogue (Sort of) With a Bolshevik in Texas," www.frontpagemag.com, March 24, 2009

"The Great Betrayal," www.frontpagemag.com, March 19, 2009

"An Academic Tragedy," www.frontpagemag.com, March 13, 2009

"How Conservatives Should Celebrate the Inauguration," www.front-pagemag.com, January 20, 2009

"The War Against the Jews," www.frontpagemag.com, January 9, 2009

"More Evasions From the Left on the War," www.frontpagemag. com, November 21, 2008

"The Betrayal in Iraq," www.frontpagemag.com November 7, 2008

"Candidate of the Left," www.frontpagemag.com, October 30, 2008

"Did Critics of the War Go Too Far?," www.frontpagemag.com, October 21, 2008

"Kevin Mattson Can't Handle an Argument," www.frontpagemag.com, October 16, 2008

"How Liberals Get Conservatives Wrong," www.frontpagemag. com, October 15, 2008

"Orwell 101," www.frontpagemag.com, July 11, 2008

"The Party of Defeat, and Self-Defeat," www.frontpagemag.com, June 20, 2008

"Frontpage's $500 Challenge," www.frontpagemag.com, June 17, 2008

"Party of Defeat," www.frontpagemag.com, June 4, 2008

"My Encounter With the Enemy in Milwaukee," www.frontpagemag. com, May 2, 2008

"Remembering Sarah," www.frontpagemag.com, March 14, 2008

"William F. Buckley, Jr. Remembered," www.frontpagemag.com, February 28, 2008

"The Surreal World of the Progressive Left," www.frontpagemag. com, January 25, 2008

"A Response to Feminists on the Violent Oppression of Women in Islam," www.frontpagemag.com, January 24, 2008

"Have Academic Radicals Lost Their Minds?," www.frontpagemag.com, November 30, 2007

"It's Munich in America," www.frontpagemag.com, November 26, 2007

"The Problem for Our Country," www.frontpagemag.com, November 21, 2007

"The End of the University As We Know It," www.frontpagemag. com, November 9, 2007

"The New Campus Fascism," www.frontpagemag.com, November 2, 2007

"What I Said," www.frontpagemag.com, October 31, 2007

"What We Did Last Week," www.frontpagemag.com, October 29, 2007

"Vocabulary of War," www.frontpagemag.com, October 19, 2007

"Who's Afraid of Islamo-Fascism Awareness Week," www.frontpagemag. com, October 16, 2007

"Islamo-Fascism Awareness Week," www.frontpagemag.com, October 15, 2007

"A Forgery and a Hate Crime," www.frontpagemag.com, October 9, 2007

"Matthew Yglesias's Islamo-Fascism Petition," www.frontpagemag.com, October 2, 2007

"The Worst Person in the World," www.frontpagemag.com, October 1, 2007

"Jew Conspiracies at Huffington," www.frontpagemag.com, September 19, 2007

"Academic Freedom and the Chemerinsky Case," www.frontpagemag. com, September 14, 2007

"The Professors: New Preface," www.frontpagemag.com, September 12, 2007

"Does the Left Know Who the Enemy Is?," www.frontpagemag. com, August 17, 2007

"Why We Went to War in Iraq," www.frontpagemag.com, June 29, 2007

"A Student of Ward Churchill Complains," www.frontpagemag. com, June 4, 2007

"Emory U's Religious Left Can't Handle the Truth," www.frontpagemag. com, May 7, 2007

"Secular Creationism," www.frontpagemag.com, March 19, 2007

"Indoctrination Curriculum at the University of Missouri," www.frontpagemag.com, March 9, 2007

"Mad Max: An Inherited Genetic Disorder Bites Again," www.frontpagemag.com, March 8, 2007

"Indoctrination U: The Left's War Against Academic Freedom," www.frontpagemag.com, March 2, 2007

"A Misplaced Attack and an Apology to Frontpage Readers," www.frontpagemag.com, February 26, 2007

"The Two Universities of Texas," www.frontpagemag.com, February 20, 2007

"Intellectual Muggings," www.frontpagemag.com, February 16, 2007

"The Arizona Bill Is Half Wrong," www.frontpagemag.com, February 16, 2007

"The University of Pittsburgh," www.frontpagemag.com, January 26, 2007

"Breaking the Law at Penn State," www.frontpagemag.com, January 22, 2007

"Abusive Academics," www.frontpagemag.com, January 19, 2007

"The Lamest Excuse," www.frontpagemag.com, January 1, 2007

"Jimmy Carter: Jew-Hater, Genocide-Enabler, Liar," www.frontpagemag.com, December 14, 2006

"AAUP Prez Howls," www.frontpagemag.com, December 1, 2006

"We Have Changed the Face of Education in Pennsylvania," www.frontpagemag.com, November 22, 2006

"What We're Up Against—The Lying Pennsylvania Press," www.frontpagemag.com, November 21, 2006

"Restoration Weekend 2006: Storming the Universities," www.frontpagemag.com, November 20, 2006

"Miami U's Short-Course in Radical Politics," www.frontpagemag.com, November 16, 2006

"Pennsylvania Committee Finds Students Have No Rights," www.frontpagemag.com, November 15, 2006

"The Political Is Personal," www.frontpagemag.com, November 10, 2006

"The Professor Unions' Botched Battle," www.frontpagemag.com, November 7, 2006

"Intellectual Indoctrination and Academic Fraud at Temple University," www.frontpagemag.com, October 25, 2006

"What's Not Liberal About the Liberal Arts," www.frontpagemag.com, October 20, 2006

"Indoctrination U: Oregon," www.frontpagemag.com, September 21, 2006

"Indoctrination U: Arizona State," www.frontpagemag.com, September 20, 2006

"Indoctrination U: University of Texas," www.frontpagemag.com, September 18, 2006

"Indoctrination U: Colorado," www.frontpagemag.com, September 15, 2006

"How the Left Undermined National Security Before 9/11," www.frontpagemag.com, September 11, 2006

"Soros's Team Steps up to the Plate," www.frontpagemag.com, August 04, 2006

"Jaws of Defeat," www.frontpagemag.com, July 31, 2006

"Lebanon Is Not Innocent," www.frontpagemag.com, July 24, 2006

"Fellow Travelers," www.frontpagemag.com, July 18, 2006

"Moment of Truth," www.frontpagemag.com, July 14, 2006

"The Worst Defense," www.frontpagemag.com, July 10, 2006

"Hard Liberals vs. Conservatives," www.frontpagemag.com, July 05, 2006

"Is There an Academic Blacklist?," www.frontpagemag.com, June 30, 2006

"Steinberger vs. Horowitz, Part II," " www.frontpagemag.com, June 26, 2006

"Debating the Academic Bill of Rights," www.frontpagemag.com, June 23, 2006

"Cornel West's Favorite Communist," www.frontpagemag.com, June 12, 2006

"Joel Beinin: Apologist for Terrorists," www.frontpagemag.com, May 19, 2006

"Dangerous Academics at Duke," www.frontpagemag.com, April 27, 2006

"An Inherited Genetic Disorder," www.frontpagemag.com, April 19, 2006

"Intellectual Thuggery," www.frontpagemag.com, April 12, 2006

"'The Nation' Has a Little Lie...," www.frontpagemag.com, March 31, 2006

"Leading the Fight for Academic Freedom," www.frontpagemag. com, March 28, 2006

"Den of Thieves," www.frontpagemag.com, March 24, 2006

"Attack of an Academic Zero," www.frontpagemag.com, March 21, 2006

"Defending *The Professors*," www.frontpagemag.com, March 20, 2006

"The Political Attack on our Universities," www.frontpagemag.com, March 15, 2006

"The Pathetic Case Against the Academic Bill of Rights," www.frontpagemag.com, March 13, 2006

"Willful Misunderstanding," www.frontpagemag.com, March 06, 2006

"Academic Hanky Panky," www.frontpagemag.com, March 03, 2006

"Close, But No Cigar," www.frontpagemag.com, February 27, 2006

"Are You Now Or Have You Ever Been?," www.frontpagemag. com, February 21, 2006

"A Professor Who Wants to Be Dangerous," www.frontpagemag.com February 15, 2006

"An Academic Freedom Bill I Won't Support," www.frontpagemag.com, February 13, 2006

"The Professors: The 101 Most Dangerous Academics in America," www.frontpagemag.com, February 10, 2006

"Objectivity Begins at Home," www.frontpagemag.com, February 03, 2006

"The First Terrorist People," www.frontpagemag.com, January 26, 2006

"Ideologues at the Lectern," www.frontpagemag.com, January 23, 2006

"Betraying Academic Freedom," www.frontpagemag.com, January 20, 2006

"What I Told Pennsylvania's Academic Freedom Hearings," www.frontpagemag.com, January 11, 2006

"Enemy Press," www.frontpagemag.com, December 05, 2005

"Oriana Fallaci and the War Against Islamo-fascism," www.frontpagemag.com, November 29, 2005

"Happy Birthday, William F. Buckley, Jr.," www.frontpagemag. com, November 17, 2005

"Whose Side Are You On?," www.frontpagemag.com, October 27, 2005

"Remembering Susan," www.frontpagemag.com, October 21, 2005

"Not So Forgiving: The Reparations Argument Revisited," www.frontpagemag.com, October 17, 2005

"Victory In Ohio: The Universities Concede," www.frontpagemag.com, September 19, 2005

"How the Left Undermined America's Security Before 9/11," www.frontpagemag.com, September 09, 2005

"Traitor-Baiting?," www.frontpagemag.com, September 01, 2005

"Cindy, the War in Iraq, and Dissent in a Time of War," www.frontpagemag.com, August 19, 2005

"Gaza: Red-letter Day For Arab and Leftist Jew-haters," www. frontpagemag.com, August 18, 2005

"Academic Freedom: Horowitz v. Mattson," www.frontpagemag. com, August 05, 2005

"The Lies of the Destructive Generation," www.frontpagemag. com, August 03, 2005

"Academic Freedom: David Horowitz vs. Russell Jacoby," www.front-pagemag.com, July 29, 2005

"Why the Left (and Timothy Burke) Can't Handle the Truth," www.front-pagemag.com, July 22, 2005

"The London Bombings," www.frontpagemag.com, July 11, 2005

"Victory in Pennsylvania," www.frontpagemag.com, July 06, 2005

"A Major Victory in the Battle for Academic Freedom," www.front-pagemag.com, June 23, 2005

"Indoctrination in High School," www.frontpagemag.com, June 06, 2005

"Vindication: There Is an Unholy Alliance," www.frontpagemag. com, May 31, 2005

"The End of Time," www.frontpagemag.com, May 20, 2005

"The Multiple Lies of John Podesta and Friends," www.frontpagemag. com, May 13, 2005

"How to Get an 'A' at One Elite School," www.frontpagemag.com, May 11, 2005

"How Significant is the Left? What is Legitimate Dissent?," www.front-pagemag.com, May 10, 2005

"How Left is the Left, and How Important?," www.frontpagemag. com, May 09, 2005

"How Important is the Left's Influence on American Politics?," www.frontpagemag.com, May 06, 2005

"The Strange Dishonest Campaign Against Academic Freedom," www.frontpagemag.com, April 29, 2005

"An Ill-Bred Professor, and a Bad Situation," www.frontpagemag. com, April 25, 2005

"The Case of the Colorado Exam," www.frontpagemag.com, April 21, 2005

"How Credible Is David Corn?," www.frontpagemag.com, April 14, 2005

"Bowling Green Barbarians," www.frontpagemag.com, April 04, 2005

"Academic Freedom at Princeton," www.frontpagemag.com, March 25, 2005

"College Profs Should Teach, Not Preach," www.frontpagemag. com, March 24, 2005

"The Power of Pablum," www.frontpagemag.com, March 22, 2005

"The Orwellian Left," www.frontpagemag.com, March 21, 2005

"Colorado: The Student Speaks," www.frontpagemag.com, March 18, 2005

"Correction: We Were Right," www.frontpagemag.com, March 17, 2005

"Correction: Some Of Our Facts Were Wrong; Our Point Was Right," www.frontpagemag.com, March 15, 2005

"Why an Academic Bill of Rights Is Necessary," www.frontpagemag.com, March 15, 2005

"Why Michael Can't Read," www.frontpagemag.com, March 14, 2005

"Why We Are In Iraq," www.frontpagemag.com, March 11, 2005

"Defining the Left," www.frontpagemag.com, March 02, 2005

"In Denial: The Left Reacts to <discoverthenetworks.org>," www.frontpagemag.com, February 22, 2005

"Reforming Hamilton U. in the Wake of Ward Churchill," www.frontpagemag.com, February 14, 2005

"A Campaign of Lies," www.frontpagemag.com, February 10, 2005

"Ward Churchill Is Just the Beginning," www.frontpagemag.com, February 09, 2005

"State of the Democrats: Capitulation," www.frontpagemag.com, February 02, 2005

"Relatively Unbalanced: Reply to Larkin II," www.frontpagemag. com, February 01, 2005

"My Reply to Graham Larkin and the AAUP," www.frontpagemag.com, January 25, 2005

"The Torch of Freedom Has Passed to Conservatives," www.frontpagemag.com, January 24, 2005

"Lynne Stewart: The Left on Trial," www.frontpagemag.com, January 10, 2005

"The McGovern Syndrome," www.frontpagemag.com, December 27, 2004

"Restoration Weekend: Unholy Alliance," www.frontpagemag. com, December 17, 2004

"It's Time for Fairness and Inclusion in Our Universities," www.frontpagemag.com, December 14, 2004

"David Brudnoy: RIP," www.frontpagemag.com, December 13, 2004

"Liberals and Leftists in a Time of War," www.frontpagemag.com, December 10, 2004

"Franken-Style Smears From David Brock's Noise Machine," www.frontpagemag.com, December 01, 2004

"Al Franken: Racist," www.frontpagemag.com, November 30, 2004

"Why We Are in Iraq, Part II," www.frontpagemag.com, November 26, 2004

"Why We Are In Iraq," www.frontpagemag.com, November 26, 2004

"Editorial: Censoring the Message," www.frontpagemag.com, November 23, 2004

"Mission Accomplished," www.frontpagemag.com, November 15, 2004

"'One Man's Terrorist Is Another Man's Freedom Fighter," www.front-pagemag.com, November 08, 2004

"The Moral Factor in the Election," www.frontpagemag.com, November 05, 2004

"This is Not a Magazine About Republicans or Democrats But About a War We Have to Win," www.frontpagemag.com, November 01, 2004

"Softening Us Up for the Kill," www.frontpagemag.com, October 26, 2004

"Counsels of Cowardice and Defeat," www.frontpagemag.com, October 25, 2004

"The 'Liberal' Hate Campaign," www.frontpagemag.com, October 13, 2004

"On Iraq, It's Important to Ask the Right Questions," www.front-pagemag.com, October 08, 2004

"Unholy Alliance: How the Left Supports the Terrorists at Home," www.frontpagemag.com, September 24, 2004

"Unholy Alliance," www.frontpagemag.com, September 23, 2004

"Open Letter to Michael Adams," President, University of Georgia," www.frontpagemag.com, September 20, 2004

"California's Betrayal of Academic Freedom," www.frontpagemag.com, September 14, 2004

"Victory!," www.frontpagemag.com, September 13, 2004

"How the Left Undermined America's Security Before 9/11," www.front-pagemag.com, September 10, 2004

"Zell Miller: An American War Hero," www.frontpagemag.com, September 07, 2004

"The Biggest Liar of Them All," www.frontpagemag.com, July 30, 2004

"Where Have All the Democrats Gone?," www.frontpagemag. com, June 28, 2004

"How Unreliable Is David Brock?," www.frontpagemag.com, June 25, 2004

"The Big Lie Campaign," www.frontpagemag.com, June 18, 2004

"Liberals Hand Terrorists a Victory," www.frontpagemag.com, May 17, 2004

"Guided by God, or Guided by His Gonads?," www.frontpagemag. com, May 03, 2004

"Democratic Abuse of the Academy," www.frontpagemag.com, April 19, 2004

"How the Left Undermined America's Security Before 9/11," www.front-pagemag.com, March 24, 2004

"Marching Through Georgia," www.frontpagemag.com, February 27, 2004

"Personal Statement on Gay Marriage," www.frontpagemag.com, February 25, 2004

"Stab in the Back," www.frontpagemag.com, February 12, 2004

"In Defense of Intellectual Diversity," www.frontpagemag.com, February 10, 2004

"The Great Bloviator," www.frontpagemag.com, December 23, 2003

"Twenty Years Late, but Better Late Than Never," www.frontpagemag.com, December 08, 2003

"The Professors' Orwellian Case," www.frontpagemag.com, December 05, 2003

"Out of Many, One," www.frontpagemag.com, November 24, 2003

"My Visit to Brown," www.frontpagemag.com, November 18, 2003

"The Battle for the Bill of Rights," www.frontpagemag.com, October 15, 2003

"Editorial: California Crushes Liberals," www.frontpagemag.com, October 08, 2003

"My Secret Meeting With Governor Owens," www.frontpagemag.com, September 17, 2003

"Morris Dees's Hate Campaign," www.frontpagemag.com, September 16, 2003

"What Has Happened to American Liberals?," www.frontpagemag.com, September 15, 2003

"Harvard Lies," www.frontpagemag.com, September 12, 2003

"Colorado Frenzy," www.frontpagemag.com, September 12, 2003

"9/11 and the 'Anti-War' Left," www.frontpagemag.com, September 11, 2003

"Rodney King: Once a Bum, Always a Bum," www.frontpagemag.com, September 09, 2003

"How to Look at the War on Terror," www.frontpagemag.com, September 08, 2003

"An Open Letter To Morris Dees," www.frontpagemag.com, September 02, 2003

"How Arnold (and Pete Wilson) Will Do It," www.frontpagemag. com, August 13, 2003

"Total California Recall," www.frontpagemag.com, August 11, 2003

"The Party of Sabotage," www.frontpagemag.com, July 21, 2003

"The Trouble with 'Treason'," www.frontpagemag.com, July 08, 2003

"Norman Mailer's Burden," www.frontpagemag.com, July 07, 2003

"Guilt of the Son," www.frontpagemag.com, June 23, 2003

"Editorial: Hunt the Terrorists Down and Bring Them to Justice," www.frontpagemag.com, June 12, 2003

"Silent Slaughter," www.frontpagemag.com, June 10, 2003

"If You Would Rather Be Right Than President ... Find Something Else to Do," www.frontpagemag.com, June 03, 2003

"Sid Vicious," www.frontpagemag.com, May 30, 2003

"Render Unto Caesar," www.frontpagemag.com, May 27, 2003

"Pride Before a Fall," www.frontpagemag.com, May 20, 2003

"People Against the American Way," www.frontpagemag.com, May 13, 2003

"Taking on the Neo-Coms, Part II," www.frontpagemag.com, May 02, 2003

"Taking On The Neo-Coms, Part I," www.frontpagemag.com, May 01, 2003

"Everything the Left Said About the War Was Wrong," www.frontpagemag.com, April 29, 2003

"Neo-Communism," www.frontpagemag.com, April 22, 2003

"The Campus Blacklist," www.frontpagemag.com, April 18, 2003

"The Doctrine of Pre-Emption: A Strategy of Realism," www.frontpagemag.com, April 15, 2003

"Editorial: The Next Screwing," www.frontpagemag.com, April 14, 2003

"Editorial: Liberation," www.frontpagemag.com, April 09, 2003

"The Tip of a Dangerous Iceberg," www.frontpagemag.com, April 08, 2003

"The Peace Movement Isn't About Peace," www.frontpagemag. com, April 07, 2003

"Editorial: The War Has Refuted The Opposition," www.frontpagemag. com, April 03, 2003

"Moment of Truth (for the Anti-American Left)," www.frontpagemag. com, March 31, 2003

"Editorial: Black Muslim Traitors," www.frontpagemag.com, March 25, 2003

"The Second Front," www.frontpagemag.com, March 24, 2003

"Scheer vs. Hitchens on the War for Iraq," www.frontpagemag. com, March 18, 2003

"The Fifth Column Left Declares War," www.frontpagemag.com, March 17, 2003

"Editorial: Dealing With Secessionists," www.frontpagemag.com, March 14, 2003

"The Leftist Media," www.frontpagemag.com March 11, 2003

"The Terrorist Popular Front," www.frontpagemag.com, March 10, 2003

"Editorial: The March to Save Saddam," www.frontpagemag.com, February 17, 2003

"Editorial: Secessionists Against The War," www.frontpagemag. com, February 10, 2003

"Help Stop the Anti-Israeli Divestment Campaign," www.frontpagemag. com, February 10, 2003

"The 'Peace' Movement Isn't About Peace," www.frontpagemag. com, January 21, 2003

"Dr. King's Most Embarrassing Moment," www.frontpagemag. com, January 20, 2003

"America Under Siege," www.frontpagemag.com, January 20, 2003

"The Big Lie Before the Supreme Court," www.frontpagemag.com, January 15, 2003

"New Year's Message," www.frontpagemag.com, January 2, 2003

"A New Day for Republicans and America," www.frontpagemag. com, December 20, 2002

"Trent Lott Must Go," www.frontpagemag.com, December 16, 2002

"Anti-Americanism and the War on Terror," www.frontpagemag. com, December 9, 2002

"Campus Indoctrination," www.frontpagemag.com, December 6, 2002

"David Horowitz vs. Michael Bérubé," www.frontpagemag.com, November 27, 2002

"A Serious Problem for the Patriotic Left," www.frontpagemag. com, November 25, 2002

"America's Wars and the Progressive Left," www.frontpagemag. com, November 12, 2002

"Republican Surge," www.frontpagemag.com, November 6, 2002

"Defining the Opposition," www.frontpagemag.com, November 5, 2002

"100,000 Communists March On Washington To Give Aid and Comfort to Saddam Hussein," www.frontpagemag.com, October 28, 2002

"Message to Harry: Respect African-Americans Who Love Their Country or Leave It," www.frontpagemag.com, October 25, 2002

"Ad Censored By Emory Left," www.frontpagemag.com, October 22, 2002

"Grinding the Wheels of Censorship at Emory," www.frontpagemag.com, October 17, 2002

"Justin Raimondo Has His Say," www.frontpagemag.com, October 16, 2002

"An Open Letter to the Emory Community," www.frontpagemag.com, October 13, 2002

"Campus Ad Campaign," www.frontpagemag.com, October 9, 2002

"Evidence of the Politically Corrupt State of Academia," www.front-pagemag.com, September 21, 2002

"Today Is Pearl Harbor," www.frontpagemag.com, September 11, 2002

"Editorial: America Haters," www.frontpagemag.com, September 10, 2002

"The Dictatorship of the Professoriate," www.frontpagemag.com, September 6, 2002

"Harvard U: No Republicans or Conservatives and (Few) White Christians Need Apply," www.frontpagemag.com, September 5, 2002

"Wake Up America: My Visit to Vanderbilt," www.frontpagemag. com, September 4, 2002

"The Problem With America's Colleges and The Solution," www.front-pagemag.com, September 3, 2002

"My Argument With White Nationalists," www.salon.com, September 3, 2002

"Missing Diversity on America's Campuses," www.frontpagemag.com, September 3, 2002

"American Conservatism: an Argument With the Racial Right," www.frontpagemag.com, August 27, 2002

"Ted Koppel's Spin Zone: How Nightline Controls What You See," www.frontpagemag.com, August 23, 2002

"Reparations Buffoons on the Washington Mall," www.frontpagemag. com, August 19, 2002

"Sabotaging the War on Iraq," www.frontpagemag.com, August 19, 2002

"The Casual Racism of Phil Donahue," www.frontpagemag.com, August 12, 2002

"Alienation in a Time of War," www.frontpagemag.com, August 6, 2002

"The Destructive Romance of the Intellectuals," www.frontpagemag. com, July 29, 2002

"Port Huron and the War on Terror," www.frontpagemag.com, July 23, 2002

"Black Racism: The Hate Crime That Dares Not Speak Its Name," www.frontpagemag.com, July 16, 2002

"Postmodern Treacheries," www.frontpagemag.com, July 12, 2002

"Freedom From Race," www.frontpagemag.com, July 9, 2002

"Unnecessary Deaths," www.frontpagemag.com, July 8, 2002

"Disturbing Holiday Thoughts," www.frontpagemag.com, July 5, 2002

"Know The Enemy (and What He Believes)," www.frontpagemag. com, June 25, 2002

"Uncivil Wars: Alan Dershowitz's Capitulation to the Racial Left," www.frontpagemag.com, June 7, 2002

"Free the FBI," www.frontpagemag.com, June 3, 2002

"Why Bush Is Innocent and the Democrats Are Guilty," www.front-pagemag.com, May 20, 2000

"Netanyahu: No Terrorist State on the West Bank," www.frontpagemag. com, May 13, 2002

"On Campus, Nobody's Right," www.salon.com, May 6, 2002

"David Brock Is Still Wrong," www.salon.com, April 30, 2002

"Believe David Brock at Your Own Risk," www.salon.com, April 17, 2002

"The Palestinians' True Cause," www.salon.com, April 3, 2002

"Yes, Virginia, There Is a 'Decent Left'," www.salon.com, March 27, 2002

"The America-Hating Left Turns Up the Volume," www.salon. com, March 11, 2002

"Primary Reflections," www.frontpagemag.com, March 1, 2002

"The Latest Civil Rights Shakedown Scheme," www.salon.com, March 1, 2002

"A Bad Idea Whose Time Has Come," www.frontpagemag.com, February 27, 2002

"Campus Capers," www.frontpagemag.com, February 25, 2002

"Smart and Stupid Presidents," www.frontpagemag.com, February 15, 2002

"Axis of Snobbery," www.salon.com, February 15, 2002

"Bill Clinton in the Wake of 9/11," www.frontpagemag.com, February 11, 2002

"Why Israel Is the Victim and the Arabs Are the Indefensible Aggressors In the Middle East," www.frontpagemag.com, January 9, 2002

"Colleges Targeted by Anti-Reparations Campaign (and Censorship Scorecard)," www.frontpagemag.com, December 31, 2001

"Noam Chomsky's Jihad Against America," www.frontpagemag. com, December 19, 2001

"Horowitz v. Albert: The Rematch," www.frontpagemag.com, November 1, 2001

"Former 60's Radical David Horowitz Exposes Lies Spread by MIT Professor Noam Chomsky," www.frontpagemag.com, October 31, 2001

"The World's Most Shameless Liar Unloads Some More," FrontPageMag.com, October 22, 2001

"Refuting Chomsky," www.salon.com, October 8, 2001

"An Open Letter to the 'Anti-War' Demonstrators: Think Twice Before You Bring The War Home," www.frontpagemag.com, September 27, 2001

"The Sick Mind of Noam Chomsky," www.salon.com, September 26, 2001

"Enemies Within," www.frontpagemag.com, September 18, 2001

"Bin Laden's American Blood Brothers," www.salon.com, September 17, 2001

"Today is Pearl Harbor," www.frontpagemag.com, September 11, 2001

"Pardoned, But Unforgiving," www.salon.com, September 4, 2001

"Hate Crimes That Dare Not Speak Their Name," www.frontpagemag.com, August 30, 2001

"The AIDS Obstructionists," www.salon.com, August 21, 2001

"Social Security Shakedown," www.salon.com, August 7, 2001

"White, Blind, and Proud," www.frontpagemag.com, July 23, 2001

"Cops Are Not to Blame," www.salon.com, July 9, 2001

"Why Gays Shouldn't Serve," www.salon.com, June 25, 2001

"The Plague Abettors," www.salon.com, June 11, 2001

"The Triumph of 'Multicultural' Thugs," www.salon.com, May 21, 2001

"A Reply to Christopher Hitchens," www.frontpagemag.com, May 15, 2001

"Little Totalitarians," www.frontpagemag.com, May 14, 2001

"Bush's Political Lynching," www.salon.com, May 7, 2001

"A Slip of the Tongue," www.salon.com, April 25, 2001

"Why I Won't Pay the Daily Princetonian," www.salon.com, April 16, 2001

"No More Mr. Nice Guy," www.frontpagemag.com, April 9, 2001

"My 15 Minutes," www.salon.com, April 2, 2001

"Sour Gripes," www.frontpagemag.com, March 30, 2001

"A Lesson in Civil Discourse," www.frontpagemag.com, March 30, 2001

"Ten Reasons Why Reparations for Slavery Is a Bad Idea—The Advertisement," www.frontpagemag.com, March 30, 2001

"The Racial McCarthyism of Jonathan Alter," www.frontpagemag.com, March 29, 2001

"A Reply to John Doggett," www.frontpagemag.com, March 27, 2001

"The Debt," www.frontpagemag.com, March 26, 2001

"This Is Beyond Libel," www.salon.com, March 19, 2001

"Caricaturing Whitey," www.frontpagemag.com, March 16, 2001

"Horowitz: 'I'm Not a Racial Provocateur'," www.salon.com, March 13, 2001

"What Harvard Can't Read," www.frontpagemag.com, March 5, 2001

"Other People's Money," www.salon.com, March 5, 2001

"Lazy Daze," www.salon.com, February 20, 2001

"You Gotta Have Faith," www.salon.com, February 5, 2001

"The Democratic Inquisition," www.salon.com, January 22, 2001

"Politically Correct Hate Crimes," www.frontpagemag.com, January 17, 2001

"First Blood: The Fight Over Bush's Cabinet," www.salon.com, January 8, 2001

"Ten Reasons Why Reparations for Blacks is a Bad Idea for Blacks—and Racist Too," www.frontpagemag.com, January 3, 2001

"Now What?" (co-author), www.salon.com, December 15, 2000

"Party Without a Conscience," www.salon.com, December 11, 2000

"By Any Means Necessary," www.salon.com, November 22, 2000

"The Coup," www.salon.com, November 10, 2000

"Drink Tank (co-author)," www.salon.com, November 3, 2000

"The Politics of Hate," www.salon.com, October 30, 2000

"It's the Character, Stupid," www.salon.com, October 16, 2000

"Who Won the Debate? (co-author)," www.salon.com, October 4, 2000

"Wen Ho Lee's Reckless Defenders," www.salon.com, October 3, 2000

"A Miracle the Press Won't Report," www.salon.com, September 18, 2000

"Stop Being So Paranoid, GOP," www.salon.com, September 11, 2000

"Teacher From Hell," www.frontpagemag.com, September 11, 2000

"It's the Character, Stupid!," www.frontpagemag.com, September 9, 2000

"The Civil Rights Movement is Dead, RIP," www.salon.com, September 5, 2000

"I Need Your Help," www.frontpagemag.com, September 1, 2000

"Persuading People You Care," www.salon.com, August 28, 2000

"Hypocrisy Convention," www.salon.com, August 21, 2000

"Why Gore Can't Win," www.salon.com, August 17, 2000

"Why Bush Will Win," www.salon.com, August 7, 2000

"Bush Makes Sensible Choice," www.salon.com, July 26, 2000

"Bullies of the Left," www.salon.com, July 24, 2000

"The Anti-White, Anti-American Professor," www.frontpagemag. com, July 21, 2000

"License to Kill," www.frontpagemag.com, July 13, 2000

"The Smearing of 'The Patriot'," www.salon.com, July 10, 2000

"Excerpted From Hillary Clinton and the Racial Left: The Lynching of Clarence Thomas," www.frontpagemag.com, July 7, 2000

"Joe Conason vs. David Horowitz on the Gore Scandals," www.salon.com, June 30, 2000

"Al Gore's Missile-Defense Dodge," www.salon.com, June 26, 2000

"David Horowitz: Yes," www.salon.com, June 26, 2000

"Hillary's Solution: Screw the Children," www.frontpagemag. com, June 23, 2000

"Hillary Clinton and 'The Third Way'," www.frontpagemag.com, June 22, 2000

"Crimes of the Left," www.frontpagemag.com, June 14, 2000

"Battle of the Burnouts," www.frontpagemag.com, June 14, 2000

"Stuck on Oprah," www.salon.com, June 12, 2000

"Feminism's Dirtiest Secret," www.frontpagemag.com, June 9, 2000

"Black Stalinists Will Fail (Reply to Robert George)," www.frontpagemag.com, June 06, 2000

"Reparations Are Still A Bad Idea (Reply to Earl Ofari Hutchinson)," www.frontpagemag.com, June 5, 2000

"The Latest Civil Rights Disaster," www.salon.com, May 30, 2000

"March of the Racketeers," www.salon.com, May 15, 2000

"Where Cowards Have No Names," www.salon.com, May 10, 2000

"Quote From David Horowitz's Letter to *The Washington Post*," www.frontpagemag.com, May 1, 2000

"America's Totalitarian Shame," www.frontpagemag.com, April 25, 2000

"Shame on Janet Reno," www.salon.com, April 25, 2000

"Screw the Kids!," www.salon.com, April 17, 2000

"What Hillary Clinton Won't Say," www.salon.com, April 3, 2000

"No Reason to Glorify the Left's Legacy of Violence," www.frontpagemag.com, March 26, 2000

"Templegate," www.salon.com, March 20, 2000

"Deafening Silence," www.frontpagemag.com, March 15, 2000

"Smoke and Mirrors," www.salon.com, March 14, 2000

"License to Kill," www.frontpagemag.com, March 14, 2000

"Who the Hell Cares?," www.salon.com, March 13, 2000

"Post-Super Tuesday Poll: Now What?" (co-author), www.salon.com, March 8, 2000

"Shame on Liberal Hypocrites!," www.salon.com, March 6, 2000

"Racial Killings & Gun Control," www.frontpagemag.com, March 3, 2000

"Primary Reflections," www.frontpagemag.com, March 1, 2000

"Two for the Price of One," www.salon.com, February 28, 2000

"Follow the Money," www.salon.com, February 22, 2000

"Racial Shakedowns," www.frontpagemag.com, February 17, 2000

"Party Crashers," www.salon.com, February 7, 2000

"Exit Poll" (co-author), www.salon.com, February 2, 2000

"War of the Classes," www.salon.com, January 24, 2000

"A Question for the Millennium," www.salon.com, December 28, 1999

"Brain Dead Till the End," www.frontpagemag.com, December 21, 1999

"Letter to the Past," www.frontpagemag.com, December 14, 1999

"Black Murder, Inc.," www.frontpagemag.com, December 13, 1999

"Who Killed Betty Van Patter?," www.salon.com, December 13, 1999

"It Takes One to Know One," www.salon.com, December 6, 1999

"Why Republicans Lose," www.frontpagemag.com, November 29, 1999

"Even Alone, We Can Still Be Right," www.frontpagemag.com, November 26, 1999

"Throw Away the Key!," www.salon.com, November 22, 1999

"Together at Last," www.salon.com, November 8, 1999

"The Same Old Left," www.frontpagemag.com, October 26, 1999

"Don't Look Back," www.salon.com, October 25, 1999

"Reverse McCarthyism," www.frontpagemag.com, October 25, 1999

"No Light in His Attic," www.salon.com, October 11, 1999

"Hating Whitey: Memories in Memphis," www.frontpagemag. com, September 30, 1999

"The Myth Weavers," www.salon.com, September 27, 1999

"Lies of *The New Yorker*," www.frontpagemag.com, September 24, 1999

"National Review Fouls Its Own Nest, Again," www.frontpagemag.com, September 14, 1999

"NAACP Chairman Indulges in Racial Slurs," www.frontpagemag.com, September 14, 1999

"The American Way of Bigotry," www.salon.com, September 13, 1999

"A Message to Our Readers," www.frontpagemag.com, September 1, 1999

"Letter to Walter Isaacson," www.frontpagemag.com, September 1, 1999

"With Conservatives Like These, Who Needs Liberals?," www.salon.com, August 30, 1999

"My Response to Time's 'Slander'," www.salon.com, August 26, 1999

"Guns Don't Kill Black People, Other Blacks Do," www.salon. com, August 16, 1999

"Mercy For a Terrorist?," www.salon.com, August 2, 1999

"Why Gore Would Censor 'South Park'," www.salon.com, July 19, 1999

"The Last Kennedy," www.salon.com, July 17, 1999

"Hillary's Hypocrisy," www.salon.com, July 15, 1999

"What's Gun Control Got to Do With It?," www.salon.com, July 6, 1999

"The Manchurian Presidency," www.salon.com, June 21, 1999

"The Race Card," www.frontpagemag.com, June 14, 1999

"Disloyalty of Democrats," www.salon.com, June 7, 1999

"Traitor in Chief," www.salon.com, May 28, 1999

"Dialogue of the Deaf," www.salon.com, May 24, 1999

"The Reds and the Blacks," www.frontpagemag.com, May 20, 1999

"Stop This War," www.salon.com, May 10, 1999

"'W' in His Game," www.frontpagemag.com, May 6, 1999

"Don't Look Back," www.salon.com, May 6, 1999

"National Review Promotes a Rogue and Fouls Its Nest, Part II," www.frontpagemag.com, May 4, 1999

"National Review Promotes a Rogue and Fouls Its Nest, Part I," www.frontpagemag.com, May 3, 1999

"Enemy of the People," www.salon.com, April 26, 1999

"A Tribute to Henry Hyde," www.frontpagemag.com, April 22, 1999

"Kirkus Reviews—Shills for Stalin?," www.frontpagemag.com, April 14, 1999

"Prince of Deception," www.salon.com, April 12, 1999

"Kazan: Who Betrayed Whom?," www.salon.com, March 29, 1999

"Walking the Walk," www.salon.com, March 15, 1999

"Hats Off to a Condemned Man," www.salon.com, March 1, 1999

"Response to The Harvard Crimson," www.frontpagemag.com, February 25, 1999

"The Vast Left-Wing Conspiracy," www.salon.com, February 1, 1999

"Postmodern Professors and Partisan Politics," www.frontpagemag.com, January 31, 1999

"Betty Friedan's Secret Communist Past," www.salon.com, January 18, 1999

"I, Rigoberta Menchú, Liar," www.salon.com, January 11, 1999

"Telling It Like It Wasn't," www.frontpagemag.com, January 1, 1999

"How 'Low' Crimes and Misdemeanors Become 'High'," www.salon.com, December 21, 1998

"Fascism By Any Other Name," www.salon.com, December 7, 1998

"Why Dems Need Blacks Revisited," www.frontpagemag.com, December 3, 1998

"Marginalizing Conservative Ideas," www.frontpagemag.com, December 1, 1998

"Confessions of a Former Liberal," www.frontpagemag.com, December 1, 1998

"My Conversation With David Horowitz," www.frontpagemag. com, December 1, 1998

"Dictator of Choice," www.salon.com, November 23, 1998

"Stokely Carmichael (1941-1998): One Who Will Not Be Missed," www.frontpagemag.com, November 17, 1998

"Campaign '98 in Review," www.frontpagemag.com, November 14, 1998

"Baa Baa Black Sheep," www.salon.com, November 9, 1998

"Hate Crimes Go Both Ways," www.salon.com, October 26, 1998

"Clinton's Amen Chorus," www.salon.com, October 12, 1998

"Right Is Right," www.frontpagemag.com, October 6, 1998

"Why Clinton Should Not Be Impeached—Yet," www.salon.com, September 28, 1998

"The Beginning of the End," www.frontpagemag.com, September 14, 1998

"Repressed Memory Syndrome," www.salon.com, August 31, 1998

"Clarence Thomas: A Hero for Us All," www.frontpagemag.com, August 3, 1998

"Still Lying After All These Years," www.frontpagemag.com, July 30, 1998

"Upside-Down Politics," www.salon.com, July 27, 1998

"Mrs. Cosby's Racial Paranoia," www.salon.com, July 13, 1998

"Homosexuality and the Civic Responsibility of Politicians," www.salon.com, June 29, 1998

"Fight the Power!," www.salon.com, June 15, 1998

"Diversity at the *L.A. Times*," www.frontpagemag.com, June 3, 1998

"Bull****," www.salon.com, June 1, 1998

"Ethnic Studies or Racism?," www.frontpagemag.com, June 1, 1998

"Marx's Manifesto: 150 Years of Evil," www.frontpagemag.com, May 27, 1998

"A Modern Progressive Public School," www.frontpagemag.com, May 22, 1998

"Radical Son," www.frontpagemag.com, May 22, 1998

"Newt to the Rescue," www.salon.com, May 18, 1998

"Michael Lind Perpetrates a Hoax Political Cross-Dresser," www.frontpagemag.com, May 15, 1998

"The Party's Over," www.salon.com, May 4, 1998

"Eldridge Cleaver's Last Gift," www.frontpagemag.com, May 3, 1998

"Second Letter to Mark Willes," www.frontpagemag.com, April 22, 1998

"Salon's Conspiracy," www.salon.com, April 20, 1998

"Slick Victory," www.salon.com, April 6, 1998

"The David Brock Affair: Murder or Suicide?," www.frontpagemag.com, April 1, 1998

"First Letter to Mark Willes," www.frontpagemag.com, March 29, 1998

"It's 'Only Sex?'," www.salon.com, March 9, 1998

"David Brock's New Liberal Friends," www.salon.com, March 3, 1998

"Paging Joe McCarthy," www.salon.com, February 23, 1998

"Karl Marx and the *Los Angeles Times*," www.frontpagemag.com, February 16, 1998

"The Loafing Class," www.salon.com, February 9, 1998

"We Believe You, Scumbag," www.salon.com, January 26, 1998

"In Praise of William Jefferson Clinton," www.salon.com, January 12, 1998

"Op-ed: Reply to Paul Berman," www.frontpagemag.com, January 8, 1998

"It's Only Sex? Tell That to Commander Stumpf," www.frontpagemag.com, January 2, 1998

"The Drudge Affair and Its Ripple Effect," www.frontpagemag. com, January 1, 1998

"*The Communist Manifesto* After 150 Years," www.frontpagemag.com, January 1, 1998

"Ethnic Studies or Racism?," www.frontpagemag.com, January 1, 1998

"Elmer 'Geronimo' Pratt's Lawyer Faces Off With Salon Columnist David Horowitz Over Truth, the Pratt Case and American Justice," www.frontpagemag.com, January 1, 1998

"Johnnie Cochran Wins A Case," www.frontpagemag.com, January 1, 1998

"Liberals Want a Racial Monologue," www.frontpagemag.com, December 18, 1997

"Choke Your Coach, Become a Cause," www.salon.com, December 15, 1997

"Same-Sex Marriage is a Lost Cause Because Gays Are Not the 'Same'," www.frontpagemag.com, December 15, 1997

"'Progressive' Education," www.salon.com, December 10, 1997

"In Defense of Matt Drudge," www.salon.com, November 17, 1997

"The Boys in the Bathhouses," www.salon.com, November 3, 1997

"Spies Like Us," www.salon.com, October 10, 1997

"Conservatism Needs a Transplant," www.salon.com, October 6, 1997

"The Race Card," www.frontpagemag.com, October 1, 1997

"An Academic Lynching," www.salon.com, September 22, 1997

"When 'Civil Rights' Means Civil Wrongs," www.salon.com, September 15, 1997

"Johnnie's Other O.J.," www.frontpagemag.com, September 1, 1997

"Family Feud," www.salon.com, August 18, 1997

"The Bilingual Trap," www.salon.com, August 4, 1997

"Defining Race Adds to Racial Divisions," www.frontpagemag. com, August 3, 1997

"American Apartheid," www.salon.com, July 18, 1997

"Why Israel Shouldn't Trust Yasser Arafat," www.salon.com, July 4, 1997

"Alternative to Affirmative Action?," www.salon.com, June 23, 1997

"Respect, Yes; Equivalence, No," www.salon.com, June 9, 1997

"Robin Hood Lives," www.salon.com," May 24, 1997

"The Cochran-ization of American Justice," www.salon.com, May 12, 1997

"Reality and Dream," www.frontpagemag.com, May 5, 1997

"The AIDS Epidemic Is Just Beginning," www.salon.com, April 14, 1997

"An Old Black Washer Woman Shall Lead Them," www.salon. com, March 31, 1997

"Feminist Assault on the Military," www.salon.com, March 17, 1997

"Tom Hayden, Los Angeles and Me," www.salon.com, March 3, 1997

"Black History Lesson," www.salon.com, February 24, 1997

"Paging Joe McCarthy," www.frontpagemag.com, February 23, 1997

"It's the Teachers, Stupid," www.salon.com, February 17, 1997

"Hollywood's Longest Black List," www.salon.com, February 10, 1997

"The Loafing Class," www.frontpagemag.com, February 9, 1997

Front Page Magazine/

www.frontpagemag.com, articles by Horowitz under the rubric «Notepad»:

"Pointing the Finger," May 17, 2002

"Why The Left Is Not Ashamed," May 8, 2002

"Media Bias at Baylor," May 2, 2002

"Gray Davis Joins the Race-Baiting Left," April 26, 2002

"Baiting the Race-Baiters," April 15, 2002

"Five Reasons Why Reparations Are Morally Wrong, and Will Increase Racial Tensions," April 10, 2002

"Behind the Iron Curtain in Michigan," March 21, 2002

"Our Enemy Is One," March 20, 2002

"An Apology to Hussein Ibish," March 18, 2002

"Univ. of Wisconsin: Free to Speak," March 5, 2002

"Uncivil Discourse at Brown (Response to Victoria Harris) ," March 4, 2002

"Extremists at Michigan State University," February 25, 2002

"Horowitz's Notepad: How The Left Undermined America's Security," February 18, 2002

"A Troubling e-mail for Black History Month," February 11, 2002

"A Brilliant Performance by a Great Leader," January 30, 2002

"Reply to Ran HaCohen," January 23, 2002

"Amazon.com's Uncivil War," January 21, 2002

"An Open Letter to Amazon.com," January 18, 2002

"Israel and the Buchanan Conservatives," January 16, 2002

"UCLA: A One-Party School—A Letter to the Editor of the *Daily Bruin*," January 16, 2002

"How the Fascist Left Operates," January 14, 2002

"Why Israel Is the Victim and the Arabs Are the Indefensible Aggressors In the Middle East," January 11, 2002

"We Just Keep Growing," December 21, 2001

"The Intellectual Terror in Our Universities," December 10, 2001

"Beware Striking Airport Security Workers," December 7, 2001

"Academic Freedom Extends Even to Traitors," November 27, 2001

"Edward Said, Terrorist," November 19, 2001

"Black America at War," November 5, 2001

"Noam Chomsky Volunteers to Serve as Domestic Propaganda Chief for Taliban War Machine," October 29, 2001

"The World's Most Shameless Liar Unloads Some More," October 22, 2001

"Second Thoughts About *National Review*," October 10, 2001

"Introducing Ann Coulter—FrontPage Columnist," October 3, 2001

"An Open Letter to the 'Anti-War' Demonstrators: Think Twice Before You Bring The War Home," September 27, 2001

"In Defense of Bill Maher," September 21, 2001

"An Enemy Within," September 19, 2001

"Enemies Within," September 18, 2001

"This is War," September 11, 2001

"A Commie Network on the Brink," September 11, 2001

"Europe's Tradition of Appeasement," September 10, 2001

"Chomsky's Destructive Influence," August 23, 2001

"Black 'Leaders' and the Enemies of Israel," August 17, 2001

"Albert v. Horowitz, Part II," August 16, 2001

"Horowitz's Notepad: Albert v. Horowitz," August 15, 2001

"Why is Socialism Still on the Agenda?," August 13, 2001

"Institutional Racism at *The Washington Post*," July 31, 2001

"The 'Civil Rights' Phonies," July 16, 2001

"The Self-Righteous Will Never Learn (Part 2) ," July 13, 2001

"The Self-Righteous Will Never Learn," July 12, 2001

"Horowitz on Patriotism," July 4, 2001

"Socialist Books," July 3, 2001

"Gays in the Military Revisited," June 28, 2001

"Chicago Schools Succumb to Racial Intimidation," June 26, 2001

"A Response to Eric Alterman," June 25, 2001

"Crude White-Bashing on BET?," June 22, 2001

"Horowitz Challenges New York Times on Pro-AIDS Propaganda," June 19, 2001

"Does the American Flag Symbolize Freedom or Racism?," June 18, 2001

"Black Crime (In Your Face)," September 8, 2000

"Facing the Truth About AIDS," June 14, 2001

"Race Card Wins Again," June 8, 2001

"The Democrats' War Against Energy And Freedom," June 7, 2001

"Matters of Treason: Reply to Roger Clegg," June 6, 2001

"Open Letter to Stanley Crouch," May 21, 2001

"The War at Brown," May 17, 2001

"Selected Correspondence of Evan Gahr and David Horowitz," April 23, 2001

"The Patriot Restores Our National Legend," July 4, 2000

Salon

www.salon.com, articles by Horowitz under the rubric «In Your Face»:

"Black Crime," August 8, 2000

"Second Thoughts," September 6, 2000

"Turncoat," September 5, 2000

"Carry On!," September 1, 2000

"Scared to Death," August 29, 2000

"Liberal Lies," August 28, 2000

"Party Pooper," August 25, 2000

"Hillary: Pink Panther," August 24, 2000

"Brainwashed!," August 23, 2000

"Lieberman Moves Left," August 22, 2000

"Hair 'o the Dog," August 21, 2000

"Amazon Censors," August 18, 2000

FOUR

Index
for Volume IX

FIVE

Summary Index
The Black Book of the American Left

Note: Each of the nine volumes in this series has its own index of terms. The present summary index gathers the key terms that occur across the sequence of books.

This index does not try to be a comprehensive listing of all the terms in the nine volumes. It supplies quick, specific access to the key terms, listed by volume and page numbers. Almost all references are accompanied by brief descriptions.

Volume numbers are shown in boldface; more crucial terms are in boldface italic. For convenience, the nine volumes in the series with thumbnails of their subject matter are named at the top.

Chapter-lists at the beginning of each volume will be a further help in finding particular subjects. For deeper detail about the terms as they occur in each book, please consult the indexes in the relevant volumes.

Volumes

I   My Life and Times
    {the author in politics: embracing radicalism, then rejecting it}

II   Progressives
    {radical movements and how they function}

III   The Great Betrayal
    {the radical destruction of bipartisanship in U.S. politics}

IV   Islamo-Fascism and the War Against the Jews
    {Mideast conflict and global *jihad*}

V   Culture Wars
    {U.S. society in the age of political correctness}

VI   Progressive Racism
    {racial issues and how radicals utilize them}

Terms

334 VOLUME IX: RULING IDEAS

267; **V.** revelations about U.S. agents, including those in Hollywood, 48–49; Chambers vindicated while Hiss is shown guilty, 93

Speech codes, VIII. political correctness for the academy, 230

Stalin/Stalinism, I. compared with Black Panthers, 28; deformation of socialist ideal, says Deutscher, 32–33; alliance with Hitler, 161; Horowitz called "renegade," a Stalin epithet, 208; gangster in power, 212; neo-Stalinist rewriting of history, 220, 223; Stalinist writers taught to today's undergraduates, 267; Soviet rulers denounce Stalin in order to remain Stalinist, 299; **V.** Harold Bloom on today's academy, Stalinism without Stalin, 51; **VII.** Trotsky on Stalinism, 373; Stalin regime identiified with "imaginary progressive future," 374; **IX.** influence on Nazism, 55; relation to Marxism, 60

Stewart, Lynne, **II.** attorney charged with aiding in terrorist acts, 281 & ff.

Stone, I.F. "Izzy," **I.** view of communism as being on the better side of history, 256

Stone, Oliver, **II.** documentary on U.S. from extreme leftist perspective, 285 & ff.

Students for Academic Freedom, **VIII.** 122, 153

Students for a Democratic Society (SDS), **I.** proposes moral equivalence between U.S. and Soviet Union, 208; devolves into terrorist Weather Underground, 212; not a peace movement, it favors enemy victory in Vietnam, 244; made from traditional communism, 251–52; **II.** Hayden's plans for armed insurrection, 243; futile effort to rewrite that history, 246–47; **III.** three activists blown up while building a bomb, 86; **V.** Hayden's role in 1968 Chicago insurrection, 137–38

Students for Justice in Palestine, **IV.** pro-Hamas, pro-terror campus group, 40–41, 161; distributes "eviction notices" at Yale, 291–93

Syria, **VII.** Obama policy raises fortunes of al-Qaeda/ISIS, 335

Tablet magazine, **IV.** attack on anti-radical Muslim woman, Nonie Darwish, 301

Terror, movement pro, III. Democrats and U.S. security, 122; love of international institutions, 126; bringing the war home, 134; calls for U.S. citizens to protect enemies of U.S., 151; painting Bush policy as dictatorial, 157

Terror, War on, III. left in cahoots with Saddam, 150–51; Democrats opt out of Iraq War, 167; Bush's success in preventing further attacks, 169–71; interrogation by political correctness, 183; media efforts to lower U.S. threshold, 290–91; **IV.** Obama administration neuters policy with term "overseas contingency operations," 3; Islamic radical war against Judeo-Christian secular West, 201–203; false argument on Israel by paleo-